# Soul Mending

John Chryssavgis

# SOUL MENDING

## The Art of Spiritual Direction

Foreword
by
Bishop Kallistos Ware

HOLY CROSS ORTHODOX PRESS
Brookline, Massachusetts

Publication of this book was made possible
in part by a generous contribution from
Mary Dochios Kamberos, M.D.

© Copyright 2000 Holy Cross Orthodox Press
Published by Holy Cross Orthodox Press
50 Goddard Avenue
Brookline, MA 02445 USA

ISBN 1-885652-47-X

Cover photo by Melissa Lynch. Cover type design by Charlotte Smith.

The various chapters of this book were conceived and considered over a
number of years. Certain parts have appeared in earlier forms in journals
such as *Diakonia* (USA), *Tjurunga* (Australia), *Orthodoxes Forum* (Germany),
*Avaloka* (USA), *Sobornost/ Eastern Churches Review* (England), *Studia
Patristica* (Belgium), and *Synaxi* (Greece).

I am grateful to Dn. Markos Nickolas for making the editorial task a
commitment of love.

LIBRARY OF CONGRESS CATALOGING–IN–PUBLICATION DATA
Chryssavgis, John.
Soul mending: the art of spiritual direction/John Chryssavgis;
foreword by Kallistos Ware.
p.     cm.
Includes bibliographical references.
ISBN 1-885652-47-X (pbk.)
1. Spiritual direction. 2. Orthodox Eastern Church—Doctrines. I. Title.
BX 382.5.C47  2000
253.5'3—dc21                                      00-053989

in respectful memory of
a monk on Mount Athos

# *the Elder Paisios*

(1924-1994)

*in his discernment
a light shone through him*

*the light of Christ
overcoming all darkness*

# TABLE OF CONTENTS

# Foreword

As I came to the end of this new and very timely book by Deacon John Chryssavgis, my dominant feeling was a sense of joy and hope. In the first chapter, he reminds us that the words *Kyrie eleison*, "Lord have mercy" – so often repeated in Orthodox worship – are not only an expression of our helplessness and vulnerability, but are "always chanted in joyful notes." By joyfulness, however, Deacon John does not mean triumphalism or bland optimism. His approach is exactly that of Tito Colliander, who writes in *The Way of the Ascetics*: "True joy is quiet and constant;" it "does not need the bared teeth of laughter to express itself."

There are in fact many difficult and challenging statements in *Soul Mending: The Art of Spiritual Direction*. Deacon John does not evade the problems. He does not offer us an easy way out. The Cross is central to his understanding of the Christian life, but always he sees Gethsemane and Golgotha in the Light of Tabor and the empty tomb: "Through the Cross joy has come to all the world." When, for example, he speaks about repentance, he does not underestimate the pain and sacrifice which a genuine *metanoia* or "change of mind" demands from us. But he also emphasizes that repentance means resurrection; it is a new way of loving God, our neighbor – and our self.

A new way of loving: this is a central theme in *Soul Mending*. One of its most striking features is its personalism. When the author writes about the role of the spiritual father and mother, about obedience and freedom, about authority and service, he sees these things above all in personal terms. Obedience to a spiritual guide, to an *abba* or an *amma* – to the one whom Celtic Christianity called *amchara*, "soul friend" – means, not subjection to external rules, but the exploration of a personal relationship. The spiritual guide, as Deacon John says, is "a fellow-traveler, not a tour guide." Throughout this book, "personal" signifies "inter-personal," and in consequence the author has much to say about the Church, about its corporate worship and its mysteries. His approach is ecclesial and sacramental.

One of Deacon John's characteristic terms, expressing precisely this inter-personal perspective, is "responsibility." He quotes the Hasidic saying, "Human beings are God's language." As the Romanian theologian Archpriest Dumitru Staniloae has so often reminded us, each person is a word spoken to us by Christ the Divine Logos – a word to which we in our turn are invited to *respond*. This responsibility or responsiveness is to be shown especially, as Deacon John points out, towards the victims of abuse, outcasts, the handicapped, and also towards children. Our responsibility extends likewise to the material creation: "If you do not love trees, you do not love God." But we should not love trees more than children!

The present book combines Tradition and personal experience. Deacon John draws upon the Holy Fathers, and most notably upon St. Isaiah of Scetis and St. John Climacus, to both of whom he has devoted particular study. At the same time he has the gift of making the Fathers speak as our contemporaries. Although most of those whom he cites were monks, he himself is a married man, the father of a family, who in his pastoral ministry has worked with students and young people, and who knows well the pain and joy of serving the disabled. All of this enables him to speak to us with the clarity and humble authority that come only through direct experience.

Two chapters are devoted to clergy misconduct, sexual and otherwise, and to the abuse of children. These are thorny issues, about which we Orthodox usually choose to keep silent. Either we pretend that "these things don't happen in the Orthodox Church" (but they do!), or else we say that it is "not nice" to speak about such things in public (but if we say nothing, we are merely ensuring that the problems will continue). I admire Deacon John's courage in tackling these questions, and I also admire his non-judgmental stance, his avoidance of all censoriousness; as he puts it, "My purpose is not to blame." What he writes is, of course, exploratory in character; it is no more than a beginning, which he and others need to carry further. In this continuing exploration, as he rightly observes, we Orthodox need "to learn from the social sciences of psychology, sociology, and anthropology, each of which has its limitations but also much that is useful."

Not the least of Deacon John's hermeneutic talents is his ability to sum up his argument in a pithy and pregnant phrase.

Many of these I shall remember (and doubtless reuse). "Soul-mending for the disciple may become soul-rending for the spiritual director;" "One plus one equals infinity;" "Obedience is subversion, not subservience;" "My helplessness is itself part of God's grace;" "Saying 'no' may sometimes be the real way of love;" the priest at confession is "witness, not detective." I have been pondering in particular about his statement, "We become more whole when we recognize that we are incomplete... only when we confess the hole in our soul, can we be filled to overflowing." He likes to play with words, in a way that is illuminating as well as ingenious. Repentance is "re-membering;" *syn-choresis*, forgiveness means literally "in the same place with one another;" *exomologesis* denotes both "confession" and "thanksgiving;" *apatheia* is not apathy but empathy.

Summing up the teaching of St. Isaiah of Scetis, Deacon John calls it "an asceticism of sensitivity." The same words aptly describe the spirit of the present book. The author writes with both sensitivity and integrity. I have found my own spiritual imagination enlarged by reading these pages, and so (I am confident) will others as well. May Christ bless those who read this book, and may He bless the author and his family.

Bishop Kallistos (Ware) of Diokleia

# I

## Repentance as Resurrection

### the joy of pascha

### (i) Introduction

Perhaps most Christians intuitively understand a connection between the act of repentance and the joy of resurrection. Most, also, probably appreciate how repentance and forgiveness can lead to new life. What is in fact much harder to discern is the *equation* between repentance and resurrection, that repentance is resurrection begun.

Repentance (*metanoia*) not only prepares us for Pascha; repentance is itself the beginning of the Passover into life – the lifting up of the inner being in anticipation of the raising up of the total being. We have become so accustomed to thinking of repentance as an unpleasant, though necessary and obligatory rejection of the sin we "enjoy," that we have tended to lose sight of repentance as a fundamentally joyous, restorative return to life in its fullness. To repent is to awaken from the sleep of ignorance, to rediscover our soul, to gain the meaning and purpose of our lives by responding to the incomparable love of the One who is "not of this world," the One who "demonstrates His own love toward us, that while we were still sinners, Christ died for us" (Rom. 5:8).

At least four paradoxes lie at the heart of the mystery of repentance. Borrowing an expression from popular culture, we might call the first "back to the future." While taking critical stock of our own failure, and courageously assuming responsibility for it, the focal point of repentance is, nevertheless, not our imperfection but the perfect love of Christ who "is good and loves mankind."[1] In the mystery of Confession, for example, we confess not simply our sins but, even more fundamentally, our *faith* in the sinless One who is able to forgive sins. The primary orientation of repentance, in other words, is not toward our past but toward our future which has become much brighter in the light of the divine mercy, forgiveness and hope offered in Christ Jesus.

Second, this life-giving reconciliation in Jesus Christ occurs only, and paradoxically, by way of death – His death on the cross and our own acceptance and appropriation of this transfigurative death in ourselves. "For if we died with Him, we shall also live with Him" (2 Tim. 2:20).

Third, the deepening of self-knowledge which results from this process occurs, again paradoxically, through relationship with another person, specifically, with one's spiritual mentor. To find ourselves we must give ourselves away, and the spiritual father or mother helps us to do this.

Fourth, this healing relationship is set within the context of divine- human, ecclesial life. To be integrated into and "become" the body of Christ implies the healing and reconciliation not only of our selves individually and intrapsychically, but also interpersonally and communally, that is, in communion with all that belongs to God.

### (ii) The Beginning of Repentance: Baptism

Let us, then, begin by reflecting briefly on the moment of baptism, which marks our mystical death and rebirth into new life in Christ. Herein lies the first public moment of our repentance. It is by way of baptism that we mystically enter into the death of Christ as we are submerged into the water. It is here, as we are raised up by the strength of another as Christ was raised up by God, that we begin to experience the new birth of eternal life. No wonder, then, that the early Church saw a close connection between the illumination of baptism and the light of Pascha. In the Passion and Pascha of our Lord, we discern and celebrate the healing of all wounds and of all wounded relationships.

Through baptism we enter into this healing mystery. "You are complete in Him who is the head of all...," the Apostle tells us:

> In Him you were also...buried ... in baptism, in which you also were raised with Him through faith in the working of God, who raised Him from the dead. And you, being dead in your trespasses ... He has made alive together with Him, having forgiven

you all trespasses, having wiped out the handwriting of require-
ments that was against us... And He has taken it out of the way,
having nailed it to the cross" (Col. 2:14).

In his remarkable treatise, *On Repentance*, Mark the Monk (fl.
c. 430 CE) writes: "the person who knows reality does not repent for things done or wrongs remembered; rather he confesses
to God about things to come." The mystery of repentance is
not, in other words, a backward-looking reflection upon evils
committed in the past but a courageous forward movement into
life. It is an act of faith. "This one thing I do," writes St. Paul,
"forgetting what lies behind and straining forward to what lies
ahead" (Phil. 3:13). When the Baptist John cries "Repent, for
the Kingdom of heaven is coming" (Mt. 3:2), he is alerting our
attention forward, to the future.

Hesychius the Elder, who lived in the desert of Mt. Sinai during the ninth century, similarly envisions repentance not as a
return to something in the past but as the anticipation of a "reward from God." The world may turn backward, as did the
Jordan River at the baptism of its Creator, but in Christ, who
"has overcome the world," we are called to transcend the criteria of the world.

Repentance, accordingly, becomes not a repellent magnifica-
tion of our deformity but an attractive reflection of God's beauty.
It is an invitation not to hopeless guilt but to freedom and responsibility. The purpose is not that we be ashamed, as though
this were an end in itself. Demoralization is not the goal. The
aim, rather, is *true* life, a life characterized by honesty, integrity
and personal accountability to God, to all others and to oneself.
Only such a life can bring inner peace and happiness. We are
thus told by our Lord: "go and sin no more."

If repentance is a reward or gift of the age to come, then baptism is the beginning of this process; if the fruition of repentance
is eternal life, then baptism is its seed, or perhaps better, the
first watering of the seed which the word of God has planted.
Certainly, this is how it is viewed in the Orthodox patristic tradition. St. John (Climacus) of Sinai, whose *Ladder of Divine Ascent*
has for centuries challenged and nourished Orthodox believers, particularly during Lenten periods, defines repentance as
"the renewal of baptism." "Repentance," he writes, "is a con-

tract with God for a second life."[2] And in the words of the Orthodox rite of baptism, baptism "enables us to find life... and once again to rejoice in the world, that we may render praise to God."

The Church understands this baptismal renewal as a radical spiritual liberation. She speaks of a passover from death to life, from darkness into light, from hopelessness to joy. This is a complete reversal of the "normal" but fundamentally *unnatural* movement we ordinarily experience in the opposite direction. We pray: "Take away the death of the old Adam, and make this a child of your kingdom."

Much more than simply a social rite of communal initiation, baptism, in the Orthodox Christian tradition, is understood to inaugurate an ontological transformation. It is a spiritual transition from *"bios"* to *"zoe,"* form mere biological survival to "life in abundance" (Jn. 10:10). Baptism is our personal incarnation into the body of Christ. It is our point of entry into the passion and pascha of the Lord, and marks the beginning of our ascension to His kingdom of eternal life. Baptism thus signifies our turn toward the newness and fullness of life given to the world once and for all in Christ. It communicates a decision to shake off everything that is worn and dead in us, in order that we may live with all depth and intensity the life to which we are called. Baptism is not simply, then, an invitation to membership in the Church. It means, or ought to mean, our affirmative reply and response to that invitation.

All the mysteries of the life in Christ are synergistic, divine-human operations. They are cooperative endeavors of God and mortals together as co-workers. These sacramental mysteries symbolize our desire for God and His desire for us, our faith in Him and His in us. Baptism, then, is to be our personal acceptance of Christ's regenerative passion and resurrection; chrismation, our personal reception of the Holy Spirit's anointing; eucharist, our union with the life-giving, broken and poured-out body and blood of the crucified and risen Savior; confession, our personal, decisive act for continual renewal in Him. These sacred mysteries constitute our "ordination" into the kingdom of God. They mark our decision to seek our life in Him, so that our ordinary human life may become *divine liturgy* upon this earth.

Mark the Monk, whom we cited previously, sees the process of repentance as the progressive "revelation" and realization of the grace received originally at baptism:

> By the grace of Christ, you have become a new Adam... The Lord came for our sakes and died for us. He delivered us from inherited death. He cleansed us and renewed us through baptism. He now sets us in the paradise of the Church.[3]

The entire world – humanity and nature alike – is proclaimed to belong to Christ, from "the least of our brethren" (Mt. 18: 40, 45) to the last speck of dust.

The first prayer in the Service of Baptism reads:

> The sun sings to you, the moon glorifies you, the stars meet in your presence, the light obeys you, the deep is filled by you.... We confess your grace, we proclaim your mercy, we do not conceal your benefits.

Through baptism, St. Nicholas Cabasilas tells us, "God claims us for His own, and adopts us as divine children." We are God's own precious sons and daughters, and we know that "unless we become like little children we cannot enter the kingdom of heaven" (Mt. 18:3-4). We believe, as we chant in the Sunday vesperal *prokeimenon* of Great Lent, that God will "not turn His face away from His children." We remain secure that we can never fall beyond God's all-embracing, trinitarian love, that the arms of His unconditional care are forever open to us: "Our sins cannot surpass the multitude of God's mercy; our wounds are not greater than His healing power."[4]

### (iii) The End: Resurrection through Death

If baptism waters the seed of repentance which the word of God has planted within us, it remains for us to continually nurture this seed's growth. If the pledge of the kingdom is offered to us from the very outset of our life, such as in the case of infant baptism, nonetheless, the revelation of this promise demands a certain response on our part. The paradox, here, is that it is not self-assertion or self-justification that is called for but the simple surrender of our selves to the One who called us into being, the same One who "did not come to call the righteous, but sinners, to repentance" (Mt. 9:13).

The kingdom is already granted to little children, not, I think because of the subjective qualities that we tend to appreciate in them, such as their cuteness, their smallness, or their playfulness. The kingdom is theirs, I suspect, because objectively they are vulnerable, weak, lowly, and helpless. Left to themselves, they would die. This "leastness," I submit, is their title-deed to the highest place in the kingdom of God, the same God who once became an infant for us, who became "least" for us on the cross.

Just as repentance, then, does not begin with our determination to make changes in our life but with God's determination that we be saved, so also repentance is not a matter of doing or acquiring something, but of relinquishing our life into the loving hands of our Savior. Repentance, like baptism, is an act of faith and surrender, and this implies a kind of death. It requires unlearning all our self-centered behavior, undoing all our willfulness, and letting go of all our self-conceit. It is an act of trust, a risk. This is not a precondition for God to love us. God has already shown us the unconditional nature and extent of His love in Christ. Every day He shows us His love for us in multitudinous ways, not least of which is the simple fact that we "are." However, if we wish to love Him in return, if we wish to know life in its fullness, if we wish to become one with God, the source and giver of life, we must repent.

Repentance is described as a "death" because, having already turned away from life and sought our life outside the source of life, in repenting we turn away from pseudo-life. Light cannot but negate darkness. There is no other way. The grief of repentance can sometimes feel painful. Yet, such grief is creative and life-giving, unlike the agony which sin inflicts upon us and upon those whom it touches. The suffering associated with repentance is "unto life" while that associated with sin is a foretaste of death and utterly pointless unless it leads the sinner to repentance. "Most assuredly, I say to you," said our Lord, "the hour is coming and now is, when the dead will hear the voice of the Son of God, and those who hear will live" (Jn. 5:25).

This is precisely the reason why the baptismal service begins with exorcism.[5] In the past these marked the final act of the "catechumenate," while today they have become the prerequisite for those who desire the light and life of resurrection. Again the return is to origins, to the root of evil in the world and the renunciation of diabolical forces. I am not referring to evil here as merely the absence of good. I am referring to the actual experience of a power that is malevolent. Exorcism is not simply a matter of clearing the air of certain "negative" thoughts and feelings, such as anger, frustration, anxiety, depression, sadness, and grief. Evil is far worse than that and requires something even more powerful than positive thinking. Evil cannot, in the end, be reduced to manageable proportions which human reason can analyze and address with the normal therapeutic methods. Although the wider society generally prefers to think of it in this way, the "demonic" is not a myth, unfortunately. As with holiness, wickedness is a cooperative endeavor. Human beings do not act alone.

The reality of evil in our world seems impossible to deny when we consider the incalculable suffering which has occurred historically and occurs to this day in our midst. One need only draw upon recent historical memory: the horror wrought by the holocaust in Nazi Germany; the atrocities which occurred under communism, in Cambodia, in Rwanda, in the Sudan, in the Balkans, in Asia Minor and elsewhere; the misery inflicted upon victims of crime, abuse, torture, exploitation and all manner of injustice which have occurred and continue to occur and seem to increase daily – only a fraction of which we hear about in the news. Would that evil were nothing more than an outdated, medieval idea invented by clerics to frighten people into submission. Unfortunately, the situation is much worse than that.

It is fitting that the word "evil" in English is the reverse of "live." Evil opposes life and the source of life. We must learn to detect and recognize evil in order to avoid it, reject it and repent of it in our lives. We are called to "discern the spirits" which operate among us and upon us. It is true, Christ the Lord has shattered the gates of death and hell. Fundamentally, the war against evil has already been won; life has overcome death, good has triumphed over evil, Christ has risen. The final outcome is already known to us. Still, the enemy has not been annihilated and he continues to wreak as much havoc and inflict as much damage and suffering as he can while he is still able. Thus, until our Lord's mighty return upon the earth, the time for battle remains. All who wish to align themselves with Him must become warriors, taking up spiritual arms in this battle which is not "against flesh and blood, but against principalities, against powers, against the rulers of the darkness of this age, against spiritual hosts of wickedness in the heavenly places" (Eph. 6:12). The first step, then, is to confront evil at its source:

> The priest turns the person who is coming to baptism toward the west... and says: "Do you renounce Satan, and all his angels, and all his works, and all his services, and all his pride?" And the catechumen or sponsor answers, saying: "I do."

One cannot belong to Christ until one has recognized, confronted and renounced evil. We must make up our minds to renounce the spirit which opposes life, in order to avoid its bitter fruit. This initial step should be made by each of us as early as possible in life. Even toddlers know how to say "no." This innate ability to say "no" is given so that one may learn to reject evil. Being involved personally in the struggle against evil in the world is one of the most radical ways by which a Christian grows in likeness to God. Christianity is not simply a life of spiritual comfort; it is a path of spiritual combat (Eph. 6: 11). Christians must be spiritual warriors, in the manner of their Lord. By prayer, fasting and the word of God, Christ battled the demons in the desert and, finally, took up the cross of His voluntary suffering and death as the very weapon by which He defeated the killer.

It is this reality of evil that the Church feels and faces as it stands before a new human being who has just entered this life in Christ, and on whom evil lays a claim not only on the soul but on all of one's life. The first act in the Service of Baptism, then, is a challenge, a confrontation. Conversion is the next:

> The priest, turning [literally, "converting"] the catechumen to the east says: "Do you unite yourself to Christ? And do you believe in Him?"

Confrontation and conversion are the necessary conditions for the third step, which is confession. The confession of faith is the last act of preparation for baptism. It testifies to one's thoughtful acceptance and willing obedience to the faith of the Church and to its head, Christ the Lord: The priest then adds: "Bow down before Christ, and worship Him." And the catechumen replies: "I bow down before the Father, the Son, and the Holy Spirit."

It is only through death – death in Christ – that we come to life. "Unless a grain of wheat falls into the ground and dies, it remains alone, but if it dies, it produces much grain"(Jn. 12:24); "He who finds his life will lose it, and he who loses his life for my sake will find it" (Mt. 10:39); "I die every day... What you sow does not come to life unless it dies" (1 Cor. 15:30, 36). "I have been crucified with Christ; it is no longer I who live, but Christ lives in me..." (Gal. 2:20).

One of the most important truths I have learned is that the "light" which denies or avoids confronting darkness is the light of antichrist; the light which penetrates through darkness is the light of Christ. Death, or disease, or disability, or dysfunction is like "hitting rock bottom." It can become cause for a new and sincere beginning since it is the point at which there is nowhere to go but up, nowhere to move but forward. Then, deep down, one knows that it is no longer oneself who is making the decisions or calling the moves in one's life because one is enslaved. Then the heart knows that it is broken. Then one may pray in earnest, knowing that "a broken and contrite heart God will not despise" (Ps. 50:17). Thus, at every Great Compline Service in Lent, we pray: "Lord of the powers, be with us. For in times of distress, we have no other help but You. Lord of the powers, have mercy on us."

By some mysterious way, my weakness, my helplessness is itself part of God's grace, a shadow that reveals the light of His countenance, a mask that conceals His very intimacy. This is true even if I am partly responsible for creating it or aggravating it myself. Perhaps this is the reason for the wide variety of joyful expressions in which the words "Lord, have mercy" are chanted in all Orthodox services (once, thrice, twelve, and even forty times). These words are always chanted in joyful notes. By repeatedly singing "*Kyrie eleison*" we learn to be thankful instead of resentful, to express gratitude for who we are, to cease obsessing over ourselves and to begin glorifying God who alone can finally heal the wounds of sin and undo evil itself.

*(iv) Spiritual Direction: One Plus One Equals Infinity*

One does not, however, achieve resurrection through death on one's own; one can neither confront evil nor confess God's grace alone. In order to receive the healing grace of God, one needs to open up to at least one other person. This is not always easy in a world that teaches and encourages us from an early age to be self-sufficient and to assertively (if not aggressively) handle matters alone. Yet for the tradition of the Savior and the saints, individual self-sufficiency is not the way of life. To the contrary, it resembles more the way of the demons.

This is because people are relational, communal beings. We need one another, even to repent. Sin ruptures the "I-Thou" relationship with God and among human beings, and this same sacred relationship is the way of return. It is natural and healing for persons to live in loving communion with one another and with God. It would not be an exaggeration to say that the Church exists for this very purpose. There cannot, however, finally be harmony among human beings without God at the center and periphery of our communion. In the sixth century, Abba Dorotheus used an illustration of a compass to describe how our bonds with people affect our bond with God:

> Suppose we were to take a compass and insert the point and draw the outline of a circle. The center point is the same distance from any point on the circumference... Let us suppose that this circle is the world and that God is the center; the straight lines drawn from the circumference to the center are the lives of human beings.

In order to move toward God, says Dorotheus, human beings must move from the circumference to life's center:

> The closer they are to God, the closer they become to one another; and the closer they are to one another, the closer they become to God.... Such is the very nature of life. The more we are turned away from and do not love God, the greater the distance that separates us from our neighbor.[6]

We need people who care for us and who receive our care. "Human beings are God's language," according to a Hasidic saying. We repent by turning to people, and God responds by sending people to whom we may turn in repentance. Sometimes we need people because the wounds are too deep to admit by ourselves, the evil too painful to confront alone. Sometimes we need people to help us name and own our past. We may need a gentle companion who accompanies us on the spiritual path, to whom we can express the pain we feel, or the abuse we have suffered, or the addiction which ensnares and enslaves us. Perhaps we first need to learn to trust before we can begin to believe – in others and in God. Invariably, the ability to share with someone else is a sign that we are on the right track.

Our pain, our problems, our passions – these cannot be concealed and should not be denied. Potentially, they are, in fact, resources for spiritual vitality and renewal. If we listen to them, they may tell us something about where we are going in relation to others and in relation to God. In the film *Good Will Hunting*, Robin Williams plays a therapist counseling a young college-aged man, Will. In one poignant scene, they discuss personal quirks, the particular vulnerabilities and peculiarities that characterize each of us. The therapist says to Will: "People call these things imperfections. But they're not. Oh, that's the good stuff... The bad ... will always wake you up to good things you never paid attention to before."

When I can confess my peculiarity, my brokenness to someone who does not shame me, who will stand as a representative of the community and as a witness before God, then my healing can begin. When I take off the mask, and – together with at least one other person – look clearly at my vulnerability, then my recovery and restoration has begun. This, of course, is not easy; it is much easier to continue to hide. Repentance is a risk. It can be a painful process, much like bearing a child. In this process the will is not mortified. Rather, it is "buried alive" in a tomb that becomes the womb for new life.[7]

Repentance takes time – it moves at glacial speed. It takes toil – one has to really want to heal. It takes tears – but, "blessed are those who mourn" (Mt. 5:4). So, let us thank God for our weaknesses and breakdowns. They are reminders to us to turn to God and live. The tears of one who has begun this move are the promise of new life, like the cries of a new-born. The attendant emotional combustion is something like the burst of a rocket's fire just before its ascent. The grain of sand which irritates the oyster can be the start of a precious pearl. As in the case of St. Peter who broke down and "wept bitterly" (Mt. 26:75), tears are a sign that we have begun to cross the frontier of repentance and are gradually entering into the vast expanse of holiness. We repent, therefore we weep. We mourn, therefore we heal.

In the spiritual elder, the Church offers us someone with whom we can share our heart. This person is a benevolent companion who accompanies us on our spiritual journey. The spiritual father or mother is a fellow-traveler, not a tour guide. The bond that forms can be very intense, the relationship very intimate. This is made possible, in part, by the spiritual mentor's own purified condition and intense, intimate connection with the Holy Trinity. Though perhaps not yet fully glorified by God, ideally he or she possesses a purified heart in which the passions have been set aright and illumination has begun. With such a person we will be able to surrender safely and most easily to the process of spiritual direction.[8]

When one mortal consults another in total sincerity and openness, then the depth of immortality is revealed to both. To paraphrase St. John Climacus: "one [mortal] and one [mortal] make – not just two mortals, but – immortality." In the spiritual life, one plus one equals infinity. The spiritual elder, then, is a person who counsels us without compelling us. We depend on this person for nourishment, for encouragement, for insight, as well as for contrast and even contradiction, for criticism as well as opposition. It is with and through him or her that we will attain resurrection. This occurs simply by expressing our heart, by confessing our thoughts and by following the guidance and example of the one whom God has sent to us to be our living icon. There is something healing and life-giving in the simple act of verbally sharing one's private burden with one's elder. The rule in the desert of Egypt was that doing by sharing is always better than doing alone. A monk who once visited Abba Poemen: "told the abba all about his [demons], and immediately...he was relieved."

So we learn repentance from another person, and this learning is not optional for us. Our very salvation depends on it. Through consultation, we learn to let our burdens be borne by another person and, in the process, to bear the burdens of others. We learn to be forgiven, and thereby also to forgive. We learn to be loved, and thus we begin to love ourselves[9] and others. Learning to receive the repentance of others is as much a Christian discipline as learning to repent ourselves. We are, after all, members one of another.

It is very important that we be brutally honest with ourselves before our spiritual elder, otherwise "we have not even begun to repent."[10] We ought to be wary of any dishonest "niceness" – in our relationships, in our marriage, and in our churches – which undermines the process of consultation and the sense of community. We are called to love, not to pretend; to be holy, not to be "nice."[11] Often we convey the message that we do not want to speak or do not want other people to talk, for example, about our anger toward our children, our resentment toward our parents, our disappointment in our spouse, our fear of loss or our anxiety about death. Yet mutual love cannot exist where we do not share our real lives. We cannot know resurrection without knowing first the death of false pride through repentance. The "communion of sinners" is the other side of the same coin that we call the "communion of saints."

Clearly, repentance involves much more than simply remembering the past. Let us now consider how it implies "remembering" in the sense of becoming again members of one another in God.

### (v) Community: Repentance as Re-membering

For one to live in harmonious communion with God and with all creation, it is necessary to establish peace and harmony within oneself through conscious self-awareness. That which is in conflict, that which is restless, that which desires *something more* must be heard and appreciated. Our pathos is integrally related to our *penthos*, and so the former must be discerningly attended to in order that the latter may fully evolve.

It is crucial at the outset to recognize that passions are something beyond one's control, in the sense of happening to one "from the outside." This is implied in the literal meaning of the term "pathos." In Greek philosophy, just as in the Greek Fathers, passions are viewed in one of two ways. Some tend to see them as an irrational disorientation or infectious diseases which are extrinsic to our nature, intrinsically evil, and must be eradi-

cated. Alternatively, passions are considered to be neutral or
even positive impulses which depend on our free will. According to this second view, they are not to be eliminated, but
illuminated as powers which we possess and which constitute
an intrinsic part of human nature created "in the image and
likeness of God" (Gen. 1:26).[12] The latter view shall be conveyed
here.

Passions should not be equated with vices. Vices do indeed
need to be uprooted and eliminated, like weeds from the gar-
den of our heart. Passions, however, are "necessary and useful
for our spiritual nature"[13] and growth. They are a reminder of
our limitations and of our natural need to love one another and
God.[14] The aim in repentance is not to suppress these passions,
but to purify and reorient them. This, for instance, is the sensitive perception of the eighth-century champion of Church art
and music, St. John of Damascus. He defines repentance in his
work *On the Orthodox Faith* as: "the return to the natural state
from the unnatural state, through much ascesis and toil."[15] Other
Church Fathers dare to speak in terms of "holy passions" or
"blessed passions."[16] Our objective, then, is not to mortify the
passions, but to resurrect them and transfigure them into constructive and edifying forces in our lives and for the sake of our
community.

The Church as divine-human community offers us forgiveness and spiritual healing. As members of the body of Christ
and the communion of saints, we are a people dependent upon
one another and upon God. We support one another in our trials, for "if one member suffers, then all suffer together with it; if
one member is honored, all rejoice with it" (1 Cor. 12:26). To
view life as interconnected means recognizing that no one is
fully independent. This is not because we are inherently weak,
but because by nature we are intimately interconnected, innately
interdependent. The mysterious interrelatedness of life constitutes a fundamental factor in our healing and resurrection. We
are created *to be with*, to *live with*, and to be *saved with* others.
Death is the unhappy lot of all living beings in this fallen world,
but death has been invaded by life. The door of our tomb has,
through Christ, become the portal to life eternal.

The Church is the place where we confess and celebrate the
fact that we are called, in our imperfection, to become merciful,

"even as our Father who is in heaven" (cf. Mt. 5:48, which is here interpreted in the light of Lk. 6:36). The Church is the place where we are accepted as who we are and adopted as children of God. The Church is the place, in this culture of individualism and loneliness, where dependency is validated and interdependency is valued. The Church is the place with room enough for all, with all of our faults. Here we are welcomed, validated and affirmed as children of God. Here we are encouraged to become great in spirit. Here we can be "in the same space with one another," which is implied by the literal meaning of *syn-choresis*, forgiveness. Here earth becomes as roomy and spacious as heaven. Here each one speaks one's mother tongue, feeling "at home" in the embrace of the *pantokrator*, the "One who holds all." The Church is the "land of the living," *chora ton zonton*, the place of love and reconciliation. If Christ is the living water, the subterranean river which nourishes and sustains the earth, then His Church is the well where this water can be drawn.

The power of the resurrection is made known in the transfiguration of our lives through the healing touch of the community of believers. This community opens up new possibilities, even in – or especially in – the experience of failure. When the disciples ran to the tomb of their risen Lord, they discovered not an emptiness but a fullness. There is no mention of a vacant tomb; the angel pointed to the signs of death, the linen wrappings, which had become signs of life. The tomb was not empty; it was, and remains, open for each of us. It is an open invitation to overcome our fear of failure, of sin, of disease, and even of death.

In the community of the Church, we learn to share our weaknesses and to shed our tears, to love and to be loved. We recognize that we do not have to be perfect for people to welcome us. Repentance is the act of our re-integration into the healing body of the faithful, our way toward reconciliation with the "communion of saints." "Therefore," St. James encourages us, "confess your sins to one another ... that you may be healed" (5:16).

Forgiveness needs to be sought as well as given, accepted as well as offered.[17] In this way we feel at home, speaking openly and freely. We can begin to make sense of the voices of our parents and of our past. If we are wise enough to understand our limitations, and generous enough to share, and strong enough to forgive, then we are in a position to achieve wholeness. By widening "the gates of repentance," we can open the doors of paradise.[18]

This healing aspect of community invites a sense of responsibility from us all. Interdependence acknowledges not only our dependence on God and on one another, but also God's reliance on us. We are required to assume responsibility as agents of forgiveness, as ministers of divine healing and compassion in the world. "Above all things, have fervent charity...," we are told. Forgiveness through repentance does not alienate us from the weaknesses of others, but, in fact, welcomes such weaknesses, for we are all responsible one for another. The author of *The Ladder of Divine Ascent*, St John (Climacus) of Sinai, is quite clear on this:

> I have seen an infirm person who has, through faith, healed another's infirmity .... And as a result of the other's healing, his own soul too was healed.... If you have been redeemed by God, redeem others.... One who wipes away and cleans the impurity of others through the purity given to him by God ... becomes like a coworker of the angels.[19]

In the words of Abba Anthony of the desert, Christ has gathered us – indeed still gathers us

> ...out of all regions, 'til He should make resurrection of our hearts from the earth, and teach us that we are all of one substance, and members of one another. For the one who loves one's neighbor, loves God; and the one who loves God, loves one's own soul.[20]

St. Anthony expresses this succinctly when he says that "our life and death lie with our brother and sister." A more recent saint, Silouan of Athos, puts it even more concisely: "your brother is your life." We are saved together, by working out our salvation together as members of the body of Christ and as members of one another. How we relate with one another has everything to do with how we relate with God. As imperfect, perfected people, our only hope lies in the forgiveness which God has made possible for us in Christ and in offering that forgiveness to one another. The Lord's Prayer sums it up well: "for-give us our debts as we forgive our debtors." We repent, ultimately, by forgiving others.

### (v) Conclusion

Repentance is the joy of resurrection spilled over into our life. Yet, it is not a way that is simple and happy, without any complexity and pain. In this, we have – as the *Sayings of the Desert Fathers* remind us – "Christ as our pledge, our example, and our prototype."[21] When Jesus appeared to Thomas after the Resurrection, He did not show Thomas any healed and anti-septic scars. He said to him: "Put your finger here and see my hands. Reach out your hand and put it in my side. Do not doubt, but believe" (Jn. 20:27).

Jesus rose with His wounds; and we, too, rise with our wounds. In repentance, we are able to realize a resurrection of the heart before the final resurrection of the dead. The key to this mystery is given to us at the moment of our baptism, which offers the possibility of repentance and the foretaste of resur-rection. Through baptism, we find that our resurrection through repentance is not a denial or a disparagement of our past wounds and vulnerability. It is not a rejection of our own past, no matter how painful and broken this may have been. The resurrection is not an abandonment of the cross, but the reinte-gration of all our crosses, the reconciliation of all sinners, the incorporation of all suffering into the life-giving death of Christ. As we open up through repentance to all that has ever hap-pened to us, we know that nothing is finally wasted. Rather than casting aside the unwanted parts of our selves, we instead discover that childhood pain and adult humiliation, our expe-riences of sorrow and of joy, our confusion and our many losses all are gathered in and somehow being healed. We feel new life, and see new light – the life and light of the risen Christ. We become enabled to look at our own past with love, not in order to forget our past but in order to measure just how far we have come by God's grace and to appreciate precisely where we are called to go. Where, before, we could only see a wasteland of pain, we can now witness the crops that have been watered by the grace of God.

In our journey toward resurrection through repentance, we

are never left alone. We have our spiritual elder, we have our pastor (who, perhaps in most cases, will be our spiritual father) and, much more, we have one another. Yet, the beginning and the completion of this transformation that we call repentance is God, the God who loves us and delights in us, "in whose light we see light," who has assumed all the darkness, and pain, and ambiguity, and vulnerability of what it means to be human. This God is closer to us than we could ever imagine. Through Him, all broken relationships are resolved. To repeat the words of St. Paul: "My strength is made perfect in weakness. All the more gladly, therefore, will I render glory in my weakness, that the power of Christ may dwell in me" (1 Cor. 12:9).

God's grace is sufficient for us, His mercy infinitely greater than our sin. The light of His resurrection is able to dispel any darkness in our heart and in our world. The power of the resurrection can alone finally change this world. Christ's resurrection is the seed of new life, of life which is greater than sin, corruption and death. This divine life transfigures all that receive it. It can transform the cosmos into heaven, as well as my heart and yours. Repentance is the beginning.

NOTES

[1] *The Divine Liturgy of St. John Chrysostom.*

[2] *Step* 5, 1.

[3] *On Baptism* PG 65: 1025.

[4] Cyril of Jerusalem, *On Repentance*, ch. 6.

[5] See the fascinating study of the influence of the demonic in modern Greek culture by C. Stewart, *Demons and the Devil* (Princeton University Press: 1991).

[6] See E. Wheeler (trans.), *Dorotheos of Gaza: Discourses and Sayings* (Cistercian Publications: Kalamazoo, 1977) 138-9.

[7] Cf. John Climacus, *Ladder* Step 4, 4 PG 88: 680. See also *Sayings*: Sisoes 3, Zacharias 3, and Hyperechios 8.

[8] Choosing a spiritual mentor is an important decision which requires the guidance of the Holy Spirit. In places where the availability of such persons is limited, we must do the best we can given our circumstances, trusting always in the great providence and mercy of God. See chapter IV.

[9] Self-love can be an ambiguous concept in Christian spirituality, meaning both selfishness, which is sin, and love of one's soul, which

is holy (see Mt. 16:26). I am referring here to the latter.

[10] Abba Sisoes, *Sayings* PG 65: 369.

[11] Obviously, most often the two go together.

[12] See Kallistos Ware, "The Meaning of 'Pathos' in Abba Isaias and Theodoret of Cyrus", in *Studia Patristica* 20 (Leuven, 1989) 315-22. Also see Kallistos Ware, "The Way of the Ascetics: Negative or Affirmative?", in V. Wimbush and R. Valantasis (eds), *Asceticism* (Oxford/NY, 1995) 3-15.

[13] Theodoret of Cyrus, *The Healing of Hellenic Maladies* V, 76-9.

[14] Cf. Abba Isaiah, *Discourse* II, 1-2.

[15] Book II, ch. 30 PG94: 976A.

[16] Cf. Maximus the Confessor, *On Love* III, 67; also Gregory Palamas, *Triads in Defense of the Holy Hesychasts* II, ii, 22 and III, iii, 15.

[17] Cf. C.S. Lewis, *The Problem of Pain*, ch. 8.

[18] Hymn from the Sunday Matins of the Lenten or pre-Paschal period.

[19] *Treatise to the Shepherd*, ch. 76-9.

[20] *Letters* 6.

[21] Amma Theodora, *Saying* 10.

# II

## Repentance and Confession

### the forgotten mystery

#### (i) Introduction

Repentance precedes reconciliation and renewal. Having tasted the bitter fruit of sin eaten at another master's table, the repentant soul wants nothing more than to return to the house of the Lord. The whole host of reconciled sinners which form Christ's broken body cry in one voice with the Psalmist: "Have mercy upon me, O God, in accordance with your great mercy; according to the abundance of your compassion blot out my offense ..." (Ps. 50). It is through the faith not simply of the repentant sinner but of the repentant community of sinners that the individual is readmitted and forgiven: "When Jesus saw their faith he said, 'your sins are forgiven'" (Lk. 5:20; cf. Mt. 9:2 and Mk. 2:5). Repentance is a continual enactment of freedom, a bold movement forward leading toward greater spiritual liberty. To repent is "to accept with joy," in St. Isaac the Syrian's words, "the humility and humiliation of nature." The aim of repentance is not self-justification, but reentry into that consuming fire of love where all sin and imperfection and selfishness are burned away.

Repentance is not to be confused with mere regret, remorse, guilt, shame or feeling sorry for wrongs done. These are appropriate and necessary in so far as they lead to and reflect new insight into reality. Repentance is more than this, however. It is death and life – death to one's former, sinful ways and new life received from the Source. In the end, it is only repentance that matters. For this reason, the Church eschews the common division between the "good" and the "wicked," the pious and the rebellious, the believer and unbeliever, "them" and "us." All bear the image of God and in all this image is tainted. The question is not "Are you good?" for only One is good. The question, rather, is "Will you repent?" If so, then the "last" may become the "first," the prostitute of today may become the saint of tomorrow, and the thief may become the first to enter paradise thanks to the great mercy of God.

One repents not because one is virtuous, but because human beings have the freedom and the power and the will to change with the help of God, because what is impossible for us is possible for God. Passions are conquered by greater passion, and many desires by stronger desire. The motive for repentance is always humility, resulting from the deep awareness of the truth of our own insufficiency and neediness for God. Just as the power of God is revealed in the extreme vulnerability of His Son on the Cross, so also the greatest strength and glory of the human being is manifested when one embraces one's weakness: "for my strength is made perfect in weakness. Most gladly, therefore, will I render glory in my infirmities, that the power of Christ may rest upon us" (2 Cor. 12:9).

The Greek term for repentance, *metanoia*, denotes a change of mind, a reorientation, a fundamental transformation of one's outlook and vision of the world and of oneself. Repentance, ultimately, means a new way of loving, that is, of loving others and of loving one's deepest self, one's soul. It involves not mere regret of past wrong but also recognition and reversal of a darkened vision and version of our own condition. As we repent we begin to see how sin, by dividing us from God and also from God's creation, has reduced us to a separated, pseudo-autonomous existence and deprived us of our true freedom and our natural glory. "Repentance," says Basil the Great, "is salvation." And he adds, "...but lack of understanding is the death of repentance."[1] It is clear that what is referred to here are not discrete acts of contrition, but an enduring attitude, a way of being. "For this life," states Chrysostom, "is in truth wholly devoted to repentance, *penthos*, and tears. Thus it is necessary to repent, not merely for one or two days, but throughout one's life."[2]

Any division within oneself or distinction between the "time to repent" and "the rest of one's time" is false and, in the language of the Church, attributable to the demons.[3] Demons are extortionate, offensive, deceptive and divisive. *Diavallo*, the root of the word "devil," means to tear asunder. The demons may work even through virtue, conspiring to produce a kind of spurious repentance. We are by nature destined to advance and ascend spiritually, but the demons divert our course so that, instead of making steady progress, we wobble like crabs from side to side. One can test the quality of one's repentance by observing whether it is lasting and consistent or fleeting and fluttering. Endurance and steadfastness bode well whereas inconstancy and inconsistency signal spiritual instability. One is being played upon by demons when one is caused "at times to laugh; and at other times to weep."[4] In the end, these enemies of our salvation only have the power over us that we give them. Christ and the saints have shown us how, through humility and faith in God, we may protect ourselves from being duped by them.

### (ii) The Two Dimensions of Repentance: Divine and Human

The chief initiative for reconciliation has been made by God in Christ, but the fulfillment of Christ's sacrifice in our lives depends upon our response. Openness to God is the precondition for God's dwelling within us. Such openness is the mark of our willing presence before God in the abundance of divine mercy, and of God's willing presence before us in the abyss of His weakness. A heart that is open to God is able, with the Psalmist, to cry: "Set your compassion over against our iniquities, and the abyss of your loving kindness against our transgression."[5]

Repentance is not a self-contained act: it is, as we have seen, a passing over from death to life, and a continual renewal of that life. It is the reversal of what has become the normal pattern, which is the decline from life into death. To experience this reversal is to have tasted during this life the glory and beauty of eternal life in God. The more one tastes of God, the more one wants of Him, and so repentance deepens. This is what the Apostle calls "sorrow working repentance to salvation not to be repented of" (2 Cor. 7:10).

Every manifestation of life has an eschatological dimension. Every matter of the here and now, tends toward and anticipates the "end." To repent is not merely to restore lost innocence, but to transcend altogether the fallen condition.[6]

Spiritually, one may be "enriched" by one's experience even if it has been painful and crippling. The greater the fall, the deeper and more genuine the awareness of the need for God. The Fathers express great love – almost a preference, at times – for the sinful person who repents, inasmuch as thirst for God increases in proportion to the experience of one's estrangement and debasement (Rom. 5:20). "I say to you," says our Lord, "there will be more joy in heaven over one sinner who repents than over ninety-nine just persons who need no repentance" (Lk. 15:7). Indeed, the worst of sinners is welcomed by Christ and His Church with open arms, so long as one genuinely repents.

The word for "confession" in Greek (*exomologesis*) suggests something more than simply accepting, acknowledging and bearing witness to an event or fact. More than a matter of admitting a hitherto unacknowledged sin, to confess means to accept and submit to the divine Logos (*ex-omo-logesis*) who is beyond and above the nature and condition of humanity.[7] It is this Logos, the Word of God, in whom the repentant soul seeks salvation. To repent and confess is not so much to recognize and expose a failure as it is to respond from within to the call of God in whose image and likeness every person is created.

Repentance, then, is also a way of self-discovery: "Open to me the gates of repentance."[8] *Metanoia* is the gateway to one's soul, to one's neighbor and to heaven. It leads inward, but it in so doing opens outward. One's realm of consciousness ceases to constrict upon one's self and expands more and more to embrace the other – the divine Other and all others which are images of Him. Sin has the opposite effect. It blocks the way both inward and outward. To repent and confess is to break free from the restrictions of sin. In my repentance, my world ceases to rotate around "me" and begins to turn toward the other, centering on God. Then, everyone and everything no longer exist for my purposes but for the glory of God, in the Divine Liturgy of life. One then becomes more deeply aware of the love of God which is stronger than sin, suffering, death, the devil, and hell. One is amazed to discover the depth of love crucified, the presence of Christ in our midst – even "when the doors are shut" (Jn. 20:19, 26).

We are not asked to love God from the outset, but rather to hear that "God so loved the world, that He gave His only begotten Son" (Jn. 3:16). God's love is implicit in His triune,

communal nature. It is made explicit in the creation and suste-
nance of the cosmos, and emphatically again in the creation,
redemption and on-going restoration of all things in Christ.
"Herein is love," writes St. John the Theologian, "not that we
loved God but that He loved us" (1 Jn. 4:10).

"God is love" (1 Jn. 4:8,16), the Theologian further declares,
implying simultaneously that love is the true being of humanity as well, created in the very image and likeness of God. "Out
of extreme erotic love...the creator of all...moves outside
Himself...burning with great goodness and love and eros. He...is
"the fullness of erotic love," St. Dionysius tells us,[9] while St.
Maximus notes that "As Lover, He creates; and as Lover He
attracts all toward Himself."[10] "As a mad Lover," St. Nilus adds,
"He desires the human soul that was beloved to Him."[11] All
human beings need to know that they are loved by the greatest
Lover of all. They need to be told and they need to be shown, so
that they can see, sense, and feel God's love in the midst of this
fallen world. The love of God for us and for all needs to sink
into our awareness and saturate our consciousness, so that we
can proclaim with St. Ioannikios: "The Father is my hope, the
Son my refuge, the Holy Spirit my protection, Holy Trinity, glory
to you!"

The best response to God's indescribable outpouring of love
"in every good and perfect gift"(Jas. 1:17) – the greatest gift of
all being Christ – is simply to accept this love wholeheartedly
and gratefully. The honest realization of human inadequacy and
divine sufficiency properly evokes, not guilt, but gratitude. One
becomes aware of one's estrangement from God, from one's
self and from one's neighbor, and desires that this not be so.
Why else does one not partake of Holy Communion, then, after
committing sin, except as an acknowledgment that sin itself is
the denial of communion? In such times, repentance and confession are in order, constituting the first acts of communion.

God is not only at the end of the journey of repentance but
also at the beginning (Rev. 1:8). "In my end is my beginning,"
says the poet.[12] One seeks Him whom one already possesses. In
all one's sinfulness, one is still loved by God. Although God is
constantly being chased away by humanity, yet He returns again
and again.[13] In the words of the Psalmist, "the mercy of God
runs after us all the days of our lives...for His mercy endures

forever" (Ps. 26:6, and 135). One will come to realize God's love if only one will call to Him with one's whole heart in repentance. Then, Christ will come to that person and reveal Himself to him or her. Then, one's fall will not be into nothingness but into the arms of God, stretched open once and for all upon the Cross.

Repentance is a way of on-going transfiguration for which one must struggle continually, in which one's heart and mind continuously receive illumination by the Holy Spirit. It is a continuous pathway, a perennial striving, an all-embracing motion, and not merely an occasional emotion. Though it is a mutual, cooperative endeavor between the human being and God, ultimately repentance, like faith, is a gift, a gift that a person either accepts or rejects. If a person is open to God and desires Him above all else, the Holy Trinity will come to dwell in that person and gradually transform the "heart of stone" into a "heart of flesh."

### *(iii) Repentance and Tears*

"Passion or [longing] for God gives rise to tears," teaches Theodoret of Cyrus.[14] There is an intimate link between repentance and tears.[15] There are other criteria,[16] but *penthos* (mourning) is essential. *Penthos* consists in mourning for the loss of God's presence. It entails sorrow at His absence and thirst for Him. *Penthos* engenders *katanyxis* (compunction). Etymologically, the words *penthos* and *pathos* (passion) both stem from the Greek verb meaning "to suffer." Just as passion may be subsumed in God, so may mourning. "Like a woman suffering in childbirth,"[17] the repentant soul cannot but mourn in the midst of its regeneration.

St. Gregory the Theologian considers tears to be an integral part of the soul's purification: "All must shed tears, all must be purified, all must ascend."[18] St. Symeon the New Theologian is even more definite: "Remove tears and with them you remove purification. Without purification no one is saved."[19] This is why the Desert Fathers can say: "Truly you are blessed, Abba Arsenius, for you wept for yourself in this world![20]

There is a thirteenth-century French tale, "Le chevalier au Barizel," according to which a knight was supposed to fill up a barrel with water. He travels all over the world to do this, but the water always passes through the barrel. Seeing that his efforts achieve nothing, he weeps. Only then is the barrel filled, by a single teardrop.

Humanity is in a state of grief. Orthodox liturgical hymns, like the Church Fathers, speak of Adam sitting opposite paradise in mourning over his estrangement from God. The *Macarian Homilies* say that humanity must "weep its way back" to paradise.[21] Tears demonstrate the frontier between now and the future. In the longing to return home from exile, the homecoming feast is already "tasted." This is why we fast and why we feast. It is also why tears of repentance are welcomed. They are a sign of homecoming, a pledge of return, and a first fruit of its joy.

While there is no doubt something healing in the various kinds of weeping that give expression to emotional grief, the gift of tears is something different. This is "up to God," and not something we should try to force or induce in ourselves. It does not come as the result of an emotional wrenching. Rather, this spiritually healing stream of tears comes gently, softly and effortlessly, in the way that certain icons begin to weep. In those who have received the gift it may flow virtually continually. Their faces are carved with the paths of their tears. Their countenance bespeaks not anguish or depression, but sensitivity and insight. Their eyes shine and their words comfort. Perhaps the best way to characterize the disposition of such people is to use the expression "joyful sorrow" which is often used to characterize the quality of compunction in Orthodox icons, music, and worship, particularly during the Great Lent. Joyful sorrow is the natural emotional expression of resurrection through crucifixion, of life through death.

"Blessed are they that mourn, for they shall be comforted," says our Lord (Mt. 5:4). In a surprising way, those who fall into sin and then mourn are almost preferred to those who neither sin nor mourn. In the words of the *Ladder* of St. John Climacus:

> I consider those fallen mourners more blessed than those who have not fallen and are not mourning over themselves; because as a result of their fall, they have risen by a sure resurrection.[22]

And in the desert of Egypt, Abba Sarmatas agrees:

I prefer a sinful person who knows that one has sinned and repents, to a person who has not sinned and considers oneself to be righteous.[23]

Tears of repentance are a symbol both of mourning and of comfort. They are a sign of sins repented and of forgiveness received. Moreover, they carry the promise of good things to come, namely, the tears of joy that all who love God shall shed on the Day of the Lord.

### (iv) The Mystery of Confession

Repentance is a dynamic act of responsibility to God and to others. Although it implies self-knowledge and self-examination, it is not a matter of pining away in narcissistic self-absorption. Sin itself is a relational rupture – a fissure in the "I-Thou" relationship. When the prodigal son "came to himself" in the Gospel parable (Luke 15), he did so in relation to his father: "I will arise and go to my father, and will say to him, 'Father, I have sinned against heaven and before You'" (v. 18). We repent in the face of God, and we repent in communion with others, as members of the Church. Repentance in the early Church was in fact a solemn public act of reconciliation, through which a sinner was readmitted into the worshipping community (Mt. 3:6; Acts 19:18).

Confession, therefore, takes place *within the Church*. It is not a private procedure, a treatment of some guilt-ridden individual. It is not based on an admission of guilt and cannot be reduced to a feeling of guilt or liability for conduct contrary to norms or laws. It is not motivated by fear of punishment. Confession is related, rather, to what is deepest in humanity, to what constitutes human *being* and human *relating* with one another and, above all, with God: "against you only have I sinned, O Lord..."(Ps. 50:3-4). Confession seals one's change of direction from individualism to communion. It is a sacrament, "the visible form of an invisible grace," as the Blessed Augustine put it, which re-establishes the bond of union between God and humanity. This is why confession also takes place *within prayer*, because it is in and through prayer that personal relationship with God and with God's world is realized in all its intensity.

Confession and prayer are means and opportunities offered by the Church for overcoming sin and death. Repentance is in-

deed the foundation and cause of prayer as well as its consequence. "True prayer," according to St. Anthony, "[occurs when]
one forgets that one is praying."[24] Likewise, genuine repentance
enables one to forget oneself and simply long for God, who is
present in the very depth of human repentance.

The supreme act of communion is the eucharist, the communal sharing in Christ's broken body and spilt blood which he
offers "unto the forgiveness of sins and life eternal." The
eucharist celebrates, manifests and advances the reconciliation
of all in Christ which lies ahead but which has already begun in
Christ's body, the Church. Christ is perfect and to commune
with Him sinners must also become perfect: "Therefore you shall
be perfect, just as your Father in heaven is perfect" (Mt. 5:48; 1
Pt. 1:13; 2 Pt. 1; Eph. 4:13). This is possible only by the grace of
God whose strength is made perfect in weakness (2 Cor. 12:9).
The eucharistic prayer contains penitential elements, therefore,
in preparation for communion.[25] Conversely, many Christian
writers, as, for example, the influential third century
Alexandrian theologian, Origen, emphasize the significance of
eucharist for the forgiveness of sin.[26]

Perhaps the eucharistic aspect of confession was more apparent in the early Church when penance constituted a public rather
than a private act. [27] It was only after the fourth century that
private confession became widely practiced.[28] Even then, penance did not have the legalistic and ritualistic character which
it later acquired.[29] Very few Church fathers make reference to
absolution as a formal procedure. What is even more unheard
of in patristic literature is the reduction of sin to a punishable
legal crime inviting a penalty.[30] St. John Chrysostom is typical
in this regard. "Have you committed a sin?," asks St. John, "then
enter the Church and repent of your sin... For here is the Physician, not the Judge; here one is not investigated but receives
remission of sins."[31]

Unfortunately confession can be used, or rather, misused, in a
way that undermines or even replaces genuine inner repentance.
People, for instance, may come to feel "entitled" to communion following confession. This sense of entitlement contradicts
the true nature of repentance. Perhaps it is a result of the sacrament being narrowly and juridically reduced to "absolution."
Scholastic theology tended to transpose the concept of sin, re-

pentance, and forgiveness into a forensic idiom, placing the emphasis on the priest's power to absolve. In the Orthodox tradition, however, the priest is seen as a witness of repentance, not as a detective of misdeeds or a recipient of private secrets. He is not a power-wielding, forgiveness-dispensing authority. Such misconceptions externalize and distort the function of the confessor and of confession, which is to be an act of re-integration *of penitent and priest alike* into the Body of Christ.

The declaration, "I, an unworthy priest, by the power given unto me, absolve you," is unknown in the rites of the Greek Orthodox Church. The practice is of later Latin origin, and was adopted in some Russian liturgical books in an era when Franco-Latin thought and practice unduly influenced Russian Orthodox theology.[32] The emphasis on "power" served to bring confession into disrepute, turning it into a procedure of justification and exculpation with respect to otherwise punishable offenses. The Orthodox prayer of absolution, by contrast, witnesses to faith in the mercy and forgiveness of God upon all who are sincerely repentant. Absolution or forgiveness is not "administered" by the priest. It is a freely given grace of God given within and through Christ's body, the Church, "for the life of the world."[33]

A word must be said, finally, about "general" confession as distinct from a face-to-face confession between penitent and priest. General confession, in certain circumstances, may be an authentic form of repentance as a communal act, involving the whole body of the Church. As such, it manifests the very essence of confession.[34] It is not, however, a substitute for personal confession, which involves intimate self-examination and disclosure on the part of the penitent and the potential for guidance on the part of the confessor. As in all sacred mysteries, the function of the presbyter should neither be exaggerated nor minimized. As Bishop Kallistos Ware writes:

> All who have experienced the blessing of having as their confessor one imbued with the grace of true spiritual fatherhood will testify to the importance of the priest's role. Nor is his function simply to give advice. There is nothing automatic about the absolution which he pronounces. He can bind as well as loose. He can withhold absolution – although this is very rare –

or he can impose a penance (*epitimion*), forbidding the penitent to receive Communion for a time or requiring the fulfillment of some task. This, again, is not very common in contemporary Orthodox practice, but it is important to remember that the priest possesses this right... Not that the penance should be regarded as punishment; still less should it be viewed as a way of expiating an offense... We do not acquire "merit" by fulfilling a penance, for in his relation to God man can never claim any merit of his own. Here, as always, we should think primarily in therapeutic rather than juridical terms.[35]

The most significant effect of confession is due neither to the penance nor to the penitent, but to God who "heals the broken-hearted and binds up their wounds" (Ps. 147:3). It is not a matter of clearing a moral debt. It is about making the penitent whole. Such healing can only come as a gift. "Let us apply to ourselves the saving medicine of repentance," says Chrysostom. "Let us accept from God the repentance that heals us. For it is not we who offer it to Him, but He who bestows it upon us."[36] The Greek word for confession *exomologesis*, implies not only confession but also thanksgiving (cf. Mt. 11:25; Luke 10:21): "I shall confess to the Lord with my whole heart, and tell of all His wonders (Ps. 9:11).

### (v) Confession and Guilt

Reference has previously been made to the cloud of *guilt* which at times shrouds the sacrament of confession. This is by no means a theoretical question, for guilt is part of the human condition and tragedy. We experience guilt in the wake of the mistakes we have made and in the face of the appalling sufferings and misery which afflict many people today, and for which we all share a degree of responsibility. Yet, in the specific context of repentance and confession, guilt can be a highly misleading emotion.[37]

There is no mention in Scripture of the word "guilt" (*enoche*) per se, although, the adjective "guilty"(*enochos*) is occasionally used. Instead of "guilt," Scripture and the Church speak of sin (*amartia*) – failure, loss, a break-up in relations, resulting in a kind of false consciousness. Even the root verb of the term for "guilty" (*enechomai*) implies, in the Greek, a positive bond of holding fast within, or cherishing, as distinct from being ashamed in the face of a deity who inflicts retributive punishment.

The distorted emphasis on guilt originated within a hypertrophied, individualistic culture, with its self-regarding view of sin, repentance, and salvation, and its attendant legalistically oriented penitential system. Orthodoxy, when it has been most true to itself and to the Gospel, has always resisted any form of individualism and legalism, whether in repentance or in confession or canonical application. The Church eschews both undue confidence in one's achievement or merit, and the overharsh sense of guilt for one's failures. The latter, after all, is simply another way of being centered upon oneself and seeking some means to propitiate a wrathful deity. The Orthodox alternative is to accept in gratitude and faith what God has revealed in Christ and to respond with works of love for God and for God's world.

Breaks in communication or communion can lead to pathological forms of guilt. However, there is guilt born of a sense of responsibility for others as well as for oneself, leading one to a fuller awareness of rights, needs, and feelings of other people. The Christian view of humanity is largely a social one. Where there is a breakdown in personal love and a rise in impersonalism or institutionalism, one finds a thickening of the atmosphere of guilt. A saint might confess daily without a trace of neurosis, because she or he is in constant communion with God, humanity, and creation. Such persons know their need for others and, especially, for God. They know that they cannot overcome their sins alone. They freely and gladly admit these as the truth of their condition, shamelessly confessing, at the same time, the truth of God's all-powerful, redeeming love in Christ who "takes away the sin of the world." Acknowledgment of one's limitations leads to personal communion with God who alone can erase sin: "I acknowledged my sin to You and I did not hide my iniquity ...," cries the Psalmist, " ... Then You did forgive the iniquity of my sin" (Ps. 32:5).

In the spiritual teaching of the Orthodox Church, God is believed to declare His love for human beings alike at their greatest extreme and worst disgrace, indeed perhaps especially at their most extreme weakness: "while we were still sinners, Christ died for us" (Rom. 5: 18). God does not run away from our sins, but meets us in them. Rather, it is we who have difficulty facing them and Him. God's identification with humanity and His loving acceptance of us, despite the worst that human beings can do, makes repentance and confession not a desperate bargaining for forgiveness but a personal celebration of what God has already done for us in Christ:

> There is therefore now no condemnation for those who are in Christ Jesus, who do not walk according to the flesh, but according to the Spirit. For the law of the Spirit of life in Christ Jesus has made me free from the law of sin and death (Rom. 8: 12).

Together with the Apostle, "we also rejoice in God through our Lord Jesus Christ through whom we have now received reconciliation" (Rom. 5: 11). We now have been offered a way of rediscovering God and ourselves, and thereby of being set on the road to full and loving relationship with God, with other people, and with all creation.

* * *

Repentance and confession constitute a way of rediscovering God and oneself. They are the way out of the impasse caused by sin. Through the forgiveness of sins in confession, the past is no longer an intolerable burden but rather an encouragement for what lies ahead. Life acquires an attitude of expectation, and not of despair. In this respect, repentance is also an eschatological act, realizing in our very midst, here and now, the promises of the age to come. "No one who puts his hand to the plow and looks back is fit for the kingdom of God" (Luke 9:62). Looking backward would be to invite the fate of Lot's wife (Gen. 19:26). Instead, God Himself is revealed before us and walks beside us:

> [we] do not consider that [we] have made it on [our] own. But this one thing [we] do, forgetting what lies behind, and straining forward to what lies ahead (Phil. 3:13).

We see the crucified, risen Lord Himself revealed before us, awaiting us. Therefore, "with the fear of God, faith, and love, [we may] draw near."[38]

NOTES

¹ *De Perfectione Spirituali* 4 PG 31: 636.

² *De Compunctione* I, i PG 47: 395 and I, ix: 408.

³ The four lenten periods of the ecclesiastical calendar highlight the theme of repentance, as do various lectionary readings throughout the liturgical year. These special events serve to draw our attention to that which ought to be part of our life every day in the crucified and resurrected Christ. Repentance, as we have argued, must be understood not only in terms of fasting but also as a manifestation of resurrectional celebration and joy. Indeed, fasting, too, is, in Christ, an act of joy (see Mt. 6:16-18).

⁴Abba Isaias, *Logos* 29,4. John Climacus, *Ladder* 26: iii, 30 PG 88: 1088.

⁵First Prayer of Kneeling, Vespers at Pentecost.

⁶Cf. John Climacus, *Ladder* 4, 125 PG 88: 725 and 5, 19 PG 88: 780.

⁷Cf. Archbishop Stylianos Harkianakis, "Repentance and Confession," in *Akropolis Newspaper* (in Greek), Athens, April 10, 1980, p.6.

⁸Hymn of Great Lent.

⁹Dionysius, *On the Divine Names* 4, 2 PG 3: 712 and Maximus Confessor, *Commentary on the Divine Names* 4, 17 PG 4: 269.

¹⁰Maximus, *ibid.* , and *De Ambiguis* PG 91: 1260.

¹¹PG 79: 464.

¹² T.S. Eliot; *Four Quartets (East Coker*, 209). The second quartet ends with these words, having started with their inverse: "In my beginning is my end." The same theme appears memorably in the fourth quartet with these words: "We shall not cease from exploration / And the end of all our exploring / Will be to arrive where we started / And know the place for the first time."

¹³*On Love* 3, 2 in *Philokalia*, vol. 2.

¹⁴Theodoret of Cyrus, *Philotheos History* XXX, Domnina 2 PG 87: 1493.

¹⁵The tradition of the Christian East gives special prominence to the "gift of tears." The tradition can be traced to the New Testament, through the Desert Fathers, to John Climacus, through to later times, with Symeon the New Theologian standing out as one of its most significant witnesses. The gift of tears is by no means unknown in the Christian West, but it seems to have been accorded a higher place in the East, probably on account of the greater emphasis on the *heart* as a vessel of the Holy Spirit.

¹⁶John Climacus, *Ladder* 7, 25 and 48 PG 88: 805 and 809.

¹⁷John Climacus, *Ladder* 7, 60 PG 88: 813.

¹⁸*Oration* 19, 7 PG 35: 1049-1052.

¹⁹*Catechesis* 29.

²⁰*Sayings*, Arsenius 41 PG 65: 105.

²¹15, 17. Cf. Kontakion and Oikos of Cheesefare Sunday in *Triodion*

*Katanyktikon* (Rome, 1879) 105. Cf. also the prose poem by Staretz Silouan in Archim. Sophrony, *Wisdom from Mt Athos* (London, 1974) 47-55.

[22] Step 5,5 (PG 88:776B).

[23] *Apophth.* Sarmatas 1 (PG 65.413B).

[24] In Cassian, *Conferences* 9,31. Cf. also Evagrius, *On Prayer* 120 PG 79: 1193.

[25] The early forms of confession were apparently derived from liturgies or other communal rites related to the eucharistic celebration. Later forms may also be related to matins or compline. Cf. F. Nikolasch, "The Sacrament of Penance: Learning from the East," in *Concilium* 1,7 (1971) 65-75.

[26] *On Prayer* 28 PG 11: 528-9.

[27] "Therefore confess your sins to one another, and pray for one another, that you may be healed," exhorts St. James (5:16). This originally took the form of confession before the entire Church and, subsequently, before a spiritual father serving as a representative of the Church. Cf. *Apostolic Constitutions* 8, 8-9; Gregory of Neocaesaria, *Canon* XII. For confession before a spiritual father, cf. Socrates, *Ecclesiastical History* 5, 19 and 7, 16; John Chrysostom, *Sermon 4 on Lazarus* PG 48: 1012.

[28] For a detailed description of this order, see N. Uspensky, *Evening Worship in the Orthodox Church* (SVS: New York, 1985) 22

[29] The earliest extant order of confession, ascribed to John the Faster, Patriarch of Constantinople, is of relatively late origin (10th century). This text may well be the source of later Greek and Slavonic services of Confession.

[30] Cf. J. Meyendorff, *Byzantine Theology: Historical Trends and Doctrinal Themes* (London: 1974) 195.

[31] *On Repentance* 3,1 PG 49: 292.

[32] Cf. A. Schmemann, *Confession and Communion: A Report* (New York: 1972) 13-16.

[33] From *The Divine Liturgy of St. John Chrysostom*.

[34] St. Nikodemus of the Holy Mountain (d. 1809) underlines the fact that it is God, not the priest, who forgives. Cf. *Exomologetarion* (9th ed., Venice 1885) 77-8.

[35] Bishop Kallistos Ware, "The Orthodox Experience of Repentance," in *Sobornost/ Eastern Churches Review* 2, 1 (1980) 24-5. See Bishop Kallistos Ware, *The Inner Kingdom*, Collected Works, vol. 1 (St. Vladimir's Seminary Press: N.Y., 2000) 43-57.

[36] John Chrysostom, *On Repentance* 7, 3 PG 49: 327.

[37] Timothy Ware, *Eustratios Argenti: A Study of the Greek Church under Turkish Rule* (Oxford, 1964) 20f.

[38] From *The Divine Liturgy of St. John Chrysostom*.

# III

## Ministry and Brokenness

### healing the heart and the world

*(i) Introduction*

Repentance and confession are closely related to the apostolic ministry. The authority of ministry in the name of the crucified and resurrected Christ is rooted precisely in the Cross. "We preach Christ crucified," says the Apostle Paul. He continues:

> God has chosen the foolish things of the world to put to shame the wise, and God has chosen the weak things of the world to put to shame the things which are mighty; and the base things of the world and the things which are despised God has chosen, and the things which are not, to bring to nothing the things that are, that no flesh should glory in His presence. (1 Cor. 1:23, 27-29)

Christian ministers and ordained clergy must learn to acknowledge the authenticity – and thereby the authority – of our own weakness and woundedness, and not our supposed strength; we must accept our brokenness rather than feigning wholeness; we ought to admit our disease rather than pretending to be healthy. Genuine strength, wholeness and health can only come after weakness, brokenness and disease are cured, and to be cured they must be admitted. Even when standing tall in the dignity of the image of God which every person bears, the disciple of Christ and particularly the ordained servant of Christ's Church should be kneeling internally, in sincere repentance and in hopeful prayer to the Triune God. How might deacons, presbyters and bishops of the Church embrace brokenness? How might we make others aware of it? How might all members of the Church learn from and grow through increased awareness of our weakness? These are among the questions addressed in the following pages.

The problem of "role" is faced by many in ministry today. People feel "called" to do one thing, yet find themselves thrust into something else. Some are effective administrators, others become liturgical specialists, others focus on theological instruction, and others, on pastoral counseling. A fewer number, among the Orthodox clergy at least, take on the important roles of social workers, community activists and witnesses to the gospel of Christ in the wider public. Many of us eventually experience symptoms of spiritual and emotional "burn out." A certain percentage become disillusioned, particularly with the institutional, "political" aspects of Church ministry. Nearly all, it would appear, aim or have aimed for success in one area or another, striving hard to produce positive results for the common good of the Church.

With the many, seemingly overwhelming challenges and demands that ministry often entails, it is easy to lose sight of the Cross. It is easy for Christian ministers – and all Christians are called to "ministry" in one form or another – to become distracted from the centrality of humility and the significance of vulnerability in the Christian life. Yet, the priestly vocation arises precisely from and leads precisely to the Cross. It is identified with the broken Body of Christ, which the priest is called not only to celebrate ritually, but to mystically *become* and to existentially *be* in this fallen world. On the night of His Passion, the Lord said to His disciples: "I have given you an example, that you also should do as I have done to you" (Jn. 13:15).

The priestly authority lies not simply in the commission to break the bread and share the wine, invoking the transfigurative power of the Spirit; it lies equally in obedience to the command to do as Christ did, which means to be broken and shared as body and as blood. Although the power of the world may be expressed in a struggle for the survival of the fittest, "it should not be so among you" (Mt. 20:26). The power of the Kingdom is the authority to give of oneself and indeed to give one's very self in imitation of Him who said: "Take, eat, this is my body [broken for you]; drink of this all of you, this is my blood which is shed [for you and] for many for the remission of sins" (Mt. 26:20-30; Lk. 22:14-22). And when Christ commanded: "Do this in remembrance of me" (Lk. 22:19), He was "instituting" not merely a liturgical service but a way of life. In remembrance, in imitation, and in succession of Him, we are to be broken for others and shared with others. The task is quite simple, and yet far from easy.

This concept of woundedness or brokenness may, to some, sound negative or discouraging. Yet the idea of the priest as a "wounded healer," as a person who – before all else and beyond all else – is aware of his own personal weakness as being the very occasion of divine strength through him, deepens and broadens the notion of the authority of ministry as service (*diakonia*). The late Henri Nouwen (d. 1996) describes this profound spiritual axiom in this way: "Making one's own wounds a source of healing...does not call for a sharing of superficial personal pains but for a constant willingness to see one's own pain and suffering as rising from the depth of the human condition which all men share."[1]

The human experience of brokenness is universal. Moreover, from an Orthodox Christian ascetical perspective, the awareness of one's imperfection and brokenness can, paradoxically, become a source not only of personal blessing but also of ordained vocation. In order to see how this can be so, it may be helpful to consider the theme of brokenness in terms of three interrelated conditions or realities: first, the reality of personal sinfulness; second, the reality of physical and emotional brokenness; and, third, the reality of cosmic fallenness. With regard to the first, I should like to emphasize that the acknowledgment of sin can actually lead to communion with God, if only we can avoid what may be called "the cult of piety." As regards the second, I would propose that the acceptance of disability can lead to a deeper sense of belonging to one another, if only we can avoid what may be called "the cult of perfection." And as for the third, I wish to suggest that our assuming responsibility for the distortion of the world's image can lead us to a deeper connection with the world, if we can only avoid what I shall refer to as "the cult of pride."

These realities are not easy or pleasant ones to face and, perhaps for this reason, they are not often discussed in detail by clergy and ministers. Yet, they are central to the pastoral identity, authority and vocation. I believe that all of us who hope to be witnesses to the gospel of Christ are called to appreciate fully the imperfection and woundedness we experience within and among ourselves. In this way we may enable others to appreciate the brokenness which they, too, experience as members of the human race. Only then, when the soil is broken and soft, may the seed of new life be deeply planted. For, in the words of W. B. Yeats: "nothing can be sole or whole / that has not first been rent. ..."

### (ii) Sin and Brokenness

Perhaps one of the main reasons we often feel uncomfortable and remain silent about our weaknesses, failures and sins is that we are afraid of them and feel shamed by them. We fail to see that, through the wonder of God's love in Christ, our weaknesses are, in fact, opportunities for the divine strength which is "made perfect in weakness." Our reticence to own our own weaknesses and yet to step courageously forward in faith, like the Apostle Paul, the "chief of sinners," reflects and fosters a false sense of humility and independence. Instead of leading toward greater solidarity and interdependence in the truth which sets us free, fear, shame and pietistic timidity lead ultimately to the dis-memberment of the community and to the dis-integration of our own souls.

It is precisely here where the Church as community offers a life-giving alternative. The Church identifies us as a people who are interdependently related to one another and to God. As Church, we are the "communion of saints" who acknowledge our sin. We are members of that "Body of Christ" which is ever broken and poured out upon the altar of this world for the salvation of all. We are imperfect and we know it. Yet, we also know that He is perfect, and that we are perfectly loved. Therefore, the community of believers welcomes and supports each person in his or her unique trials: "if one member suffers, then all suffer together with it; if one member is honored, all rejoice with it" (1 Cor. 12:26).

At the same time, we live within the context of a western culture that places a high value on independence. We are told that we must pull ourselves up by our own bootstraps. Independence is encouraged and expected of us; dependence is considered an evil to be avoided. To be dependent is to be weak, something tolerable only for children, the elderly, or the unhealthy. Dependence signifies dis-ability; it indicates dis-ease.

Regardless of these cultural messages, the tradition of the Church shows us that, in some mysterious way, we become more whole when we recognize that we are incomplete. We may become more complete once we see that we are missing something significant. Paradoxically, we are given the opportunity to gain something far greater when we lose or surrender something that is dear to us – whether voluntarily (through an ascetic discipline or effort) or involuntarily (through death, or divorce in the family, or some other form of brokenness, brokenheartedness, or breakdown). Only when we confess the hole in our soul, can we be filled to overflowing. Only when we are brave enough to *let go* and to acknowledge our limitations, our neediness and our imperfection does the possibility and promise of our lives then become limitless in Christ:

> Listen, I will tell you a mystery! We will not all die, but we will all be changed, in a moment, in the twinkling of an eye, at the last trumpet ... when this perishable body puts on imperishability, and this mortal body puts on immortality. Then the saying that is written will be fulfilled: 'Death is swallowed up in victory.' 'Where, O Hades, is your victory? Where, O death, is your sting?' (1 Cor. 15: 51-2, 54-5)

Some time ago, my younger son, Julian, read a book entitled *The Missing Piece* written by the well-known contemporary children's author, Shel Silverstein. The book tells the story of a circle that was missing one of its pieces. So the circle traveled widely in search of this missing piece. This incompleteness, however, caused it to move rather slowly. And as a result, the circle was able to enjoy the scenery: it admired the flowers and the oceans, it chatted with the butterflies and the worms, it soaked in the sunshine, the rain, and the snow. When at last it discovered its missing piece, it was naturally able to roll along at a more rapid pace – but much too quickly to be able to notice or appreciate anything in its environment. So, the circle stopped, left its piece on the side of the road, and moved on, rejoicing in the fact that it was missing a piece.

The irony is that, in repentance, we are not called to look for our missing piece. We are called to search for "the one thing that alone matters" (cf. Lk. 10:42), for "the pearl of great price" (cf. Mt. 13:45-6) which is Christ. We discover Him, together with our own true selves, in one another, in community, in His Body on earth.

In the communion of the Church, the members that seem to be weaker are, in fact, invaluable and indispensable. God has so constituted the Body of Christ that everyone is necessary and important. Each person contributes to this divine-human community, not simply by the service that each renders but by the sacred mystery that each one is. This is the way that St. Paul describes it:

> There are many members, yet one body. The eye cannot say to the hand: 'I have no need of you;' nor again the head to the feet: 'I have no need of you.' On the contrary, the members of the body that seem to be weaker are indispensable, and those members of the body that we think less honorable we clothe with greater honor, and our less respectable members are treated with great respect; whereas our more respectable members do not need this. But God has so arranged the body, giving the greater honor to the inferior member, that there may be no dissension within the body, but that the members may have the same care for one another. (1 Cor. 12:20-5)

The *ecclesia* is the place where we recognize that we are called not to be invincible but to be vulnerable, not to be perfectionists, but to be perfectly merciful, "even as our Father who is in heaven" (cf. Mt. 5:48, interpreted in light of Lk. 6:36).[2] In the ecclesial liturgy – "the work of the people" – we learn to share our lives with one another (*koinonia*), to give thanks together (*eucharistia*), and to be mindful of how loved we are by God (*anamnesis*). The liturgy "begins" in the temple of the Lord, expanding from that temple to claim the whole earth as temple and all of life as worship of the one true God.

The liturgy, too, is not afraid to refer to our imperfection. It speaks repeatedly of our failings, our neglect, our hardheartedness. This is not because we are unaware of these, nor because the Church finds joy in contemplating them, but because they are real, and only in community can we fully face them and overcome them. We misunderstand the message of the gospel and of the liturgical services if we hear it as criticism, or correction, or condemnation. The gospel speaks to what is best in us. It is a message of communion and love, the love that is true and costly. By allowing ourselves to be challenged by this love, by courageously facing our imperfection and our weakness, we allow genuine healing to take place and new life to awaken within us. This is the "great understanding" that is repentance, according to *The Shepherd of Hermas*.[3]

All too often in the Church, however, particularly among clergy, an unhealthy pietism obscures the gospel message. This has occurred, in part, because we have identified sin and weakness with guilt and condemnation. As a result, we have sought to conceal the reality of our imperfection; we have tried to hide the brokenness of our existence, presenting a false image to others and to ourselves. As clergy we often feel that we have to be strong for others. We feel obliged to heal the wounds and bear the burdens of our people, forgetting that others may heal our wounds and bear our burdens as well. We fail to recognize, moreover, that our tragic ability to sin is a sign, not only of our imperfection but also of our dignity as beings who have been granted the gift of free will, and who can choose to repent. The human capacity to sin points also to the great mercy of God who has the even greater capacity to forgive sins. In the Church, in repentance, our sin becomes an opportunity, therefore, to encounter the living God. Sin is the measure of our estrangement from God, but our awareness of our sin can be the occasion for our return to Him. This is the joyful and hopeful good news of the Church. We can be healed. We can be saved. In the crucified and death-defeating Body of Christ, fear gives way to love (cf. Jn. 4:8).

### (iii) Disability and Community

In addition to spiritual brokenness, there is another dimension that is not always readily appreciated in our communities. I am referring to the reality of physical, emotional, and intellectual disability. We do not talk about these matters much in society and, perhaps, even less within the Church. We belong to an age and culture that can accept only with great difficulty the reality of human mortality, vulnerability, and frailty. Nevertheless, we stand judged by the way we treat the weak, needy and disabled among us. And who, among us, is not, at some point in life and in some way, weak, needy and dis-abled? The disabled show us and our relationships and values for what they are. They remind us of our priorities and our choices.[4]

I shall endeavor not to analyze mental or physical disability in abstract terms. Each person is unique and faces his or her own particular set of challenges. Likewise, each possesses his or her own set of strengths and talents. My own son, who has cerebral palsy, is a constant reminder to me that I have far less to teach him than I have to learn from him. I shall avoid here entering too deeply into the question of terminology: "disabled persons" or "persons with disabilities" or "differently-abled" or "challenged." Rather, I should like to address what I shall call "the cult of perfection" which is prevalent in our culture and which acts to stigmatize disability and to distort reality. As an alternative to this, I invite readers to consider an ecclesial way of life which emphasizes spiritual wholeness and communal interdependence.

So let us begin with a simple question: Is a disabled person a whole person? Surely the immediate response of most people, particularly of Christians, would be "Of course!" Yet, the issue becomes less clear when we critically examine certain historical Christian traditions and continuing practices, including those of the Orthodox Church. Even the witness of Scripture seems ambivalent. The Old Testament, for instance, presents a diversity of views on the matter. On the one hand, the disabled must not be mistreated or oppressed: "You shall not revile the deaf nor put a stumbling block before the blind." (Lev. 19:14; cf. also Deut. 27:18-19.) On the other hand, persons with disabilities are forbidden to undertake sacred roles:

> No one of your offspring...who has a blemish may approach to offer the food of his God. For no one who has a blemish shall draw near, one who is blind or lame, or one who has a mutilated face or a limb too long, or one who has a broken foot or a broken hand, or a hunchback, or a dwarf, or a man with a blemish in his eyes or an itching disease or scabs or crushed testicles. (Lev. 21:17-20)

Even animals that appeared lame or sick were deemed unacceptable before God (cf. Mal. 1:6-8, Lev. 22:21-5). Central to such prohibitions are the concepts of pollution and sin, or conversely, of purity and perfection. These important concepts may be, perhaps, best understood in terms of the brokenness and pain which arise "from the depth of the human condition which all people share," as Nouwen put it. The exclusion of such persons – whether from a community or from some sacred activity – signifies their less-than-acceptable status before the altar of God. Those who serve at the altar are seen as close to God, indeed as representing Him. There can surely be no "flaw" in the image of God, it is assumed. The presumption in this way of thinking, however, comes closer to a Hellenistic worldview than to the Patristic understanding. The idealization of physical beauty and external wholeness, frequently at the exclusion of difference and brokenness, is more characteristic of classical Greek aesthetics than of Christian asceticism.

One of the reasons for excluding disabled persons from priestly service was the assumed conjunction between disability and sin. Under the old covenant, disability was sometimes presented as God's punishment for sin (cf. Deut. 28:15, 28-29). This view is apparent, for example, in the account of Christ's healing of the blind man in the Gospel according to St. John: "As he walked along, he saw a man blind from birth. His disciples asked him: 'Rabbi, who sinned, this man or his parents, that he was born blind?'" (9:1-2). Christ's response, in fact, debunks the identification of disability with sin: "Neither this man nor his parents sinned. He was born blind so that God's works might be revealed in him."(v.3). Christ's "gentle touch" (cf. v. 6, 11) allows us to move forward into a world where humanity is no longer torn or divided.

The idea of sin is no longer often used with reference to disability. Yet, in many cultures, the cult of external perfection prevails and there is frequently stigma associated with disability. This is evident, it seems to me, even in the way people respond to the question: "should disability be healed?" Most would, without hesitation, say "yes," regarding healing as necessary, thereby implying that disability is wrong and unacceptable. Yet our Lord did not heal everyone with an illness. Remember His words: "he was born blind so that God's works might be revealed in him." I was born with sight so that God's works might be revealed in me. My child was born with cerebral palsy so that God's works might be revealed in him. Each of us is as we are, as clergy or as laity, so that God's works might be revealed in us.

In terms of human rights, persons with disabilities are entitled to services that enhance their well-being. In a political sense, they deserve a fair share of community resources. Socially, they ought to be accepted as full participants in the community. However, there is another sense, the spiritual sense, according to which they should be accepted as they are.

What is, perhaps, of more serious spiritual concern is our notion of perfection. The disabled present an uncomfortable challenge – especially for us who are clergy – to the illusion of human greatness, perfection, and progress. We must cease imagining God in our own image, for it is we who are made in His image (Gen. 1:26). We have already recalled that, when Jesus appeared to Thomas after the Resurrection, He said to him: "Put your finger here and see my hands. Reach out your hand and put it in my side. Do not doubt, but believe" (Jn. 20:27). The risen Lord presented His impaired feet, His wounded hands and His pierced side. Disability does not contradict divine-human integrity. Rather, it becomes, in the crucified and resurrected Christ, a new model of spiritual wholeness. Jesus rose with His wounds; so, too, shall we.

Returning to the notion of community, we might once again note our dependence on one another and on God. Often we prefer to speak of interdependence, which suggests mutuality and the ability to give and receive. While there is truth to this, it is crucial in the spiritual life to understand that the situation is not one of parity. God gives, we receive. We are indebted to Him (cf. Lk. 17:10).

Dependence is, in fact, a defining characteristic of the human person. It is an essential quality of the spiritual life and the quintessence of freedom in Christ. Such thoughts are not congenial to the modern mind which looks on humility as abasement rather than as the rational response that it is to an honest and accurate appraisal of our place in the world. Dependence, as a dimension of humility, is our true nature without pretense. We should, then, pay closer attention to the disabled and to our own disability, because it is in them that we discover models of spirituality and ways of salvation. They can show us what true humanity is in this world – far from perfect, and yet fully and totally loved by God. The reality of disability, like the Cross itself, must serve as a critique of our illusions and ambitions.

Spiritual growth is not gained or obtained by individual effort or achievement. Gifts are bestowed, not earned. Salvation is a gift which comes by way of the Cross. Silence before the saving word of the Cross – as the word about God's unfathomable love for every detail of His creation – is the proper corrective to our incessant activity and our clerical busyness. It provides an authentic measure of our spiritual standing.

The notion of prayerful waiting brings me to the third and final expression of our brokenness which I shall now address. I am referring to the shattered world around us as we stand – or kneel – before the twenty-first century. The brokenness of creation, I am convinced, reveals a further aspect of the role of clergy.

### (iv) The Shattered Environment

There is a paradox in our concern for the environment. In spite of our efforts to respond to the global eco-crisis, the situation is deteriorating. We are becoming all the more articulate about the contributing factors to the destruction of the ozone layer, much more informed of the alarming statistics. So why is it that we are still so far from any solution? A simple answer, at least from a theological perspective, is that we are not doing that which we are "ordained" to do. As an ordained clergyman of the Orthodox Church, I am called to preach the death and resurrection of Christ, to hear confessions of fellow sinners, to shed tears for the world, and to bury the dead.

The first step in ecological repentance is precisely confession. Perhaps the most mystical of all experiences is the profound realization of who we are and what we have done. With regard to the environment, we are not the "good Samaritans" but the "highway robbers" (Lk. 10:29ff.). It is self-righteousness to imagine that it is otherwise. We have not properly cared for this world. God has granted us life upon this beautiful earth and we are crucifying it even as we crucified Him. The least that we can do now is repent, confessing rather than repressing our sin. When we assume responsibility for our sin, just as God took responsibility by "assuming the sin of the world" (cf. the Great Doxology) in all its horror, cruelty, and pain, then the environmental crisis may be gradually transformed. Then restoration may begin.

Think of it in this way: I cut down a tree. I want, in all fairness, to be creative, to build a home. But I simultaneously create a problem. And so in making a home, I have – perhaps unwillingly, possibly even unwittingly – prepared a coffin. This is not a far-fetched image. It is the startling revelation of the interconnectedness of all things. For in cutting a tree, I have cut down the level of oxygen. I have buried not just the tree and the earth, but my own child. Now I behold my own soul and my own child laying in the coffin, in the earth's very soul. How can I dare preach repentance without repenting? How can I speak on behalf of the environment without first bearing responsibility for the tragedy of its brokenness? How can I become part of the solution until I cease to be part of the problem?

Instead of preaching, I must kneel silently; I must weep. The dismissal hymn of the ascetic fathers and mothers tells of the way that "the stream of tears gives fruit to the sterile desert." St. John of Damascus (d. 749) reminds us that "the whole earth is the living icon of God's face." And Dostoevsky exhorts us to embrace the earth: "the whole of it and every grain of sand." So I must venerate the earth. I must desire back my child. I must grieve the loss, perceive the sin, sense the decay, sincerely want back even the tree. I must ask forgiveness. This is my only hope of resurrection. And so it is death that teaches me about life; it is the acceptance of brokenness that once again brings about healing.

So when I hear that there is a hole in the ozone layer, I feel nothing unless I sense the hole, recognizing my own child in that hole. Only then can God's hand reach through the hole and transform the emptiness into the openness of His grace. It is only when I can see in the face of the world the face of my own child, and the face of all faces – the image of Jesus the Christ – that I also recognize in each tree a face, and a name, and a time, and a place, and a voice, and a cry that longs to be heard. "Can we," asks St. Augustine (d. 430), "ask for a louder voice than that?"

My confession before the environment then becomes a conversion. And so I can change my attitude to and my treatment of nature. I know that I should not treat people like things; but I need now also to learn not to treat things like things. My presence in this world must enhance and embrace nature, not threaten or destroy it.

Pride is a uniquely human quality; it belongs to Adam. All other species seem to know – instinctively, in fact – where they fit in the order of things. Human beings alone seem unable to understand how far to go, how much to gather, when to stop. There is a "cult of pride" that characterizes humanity, and the only remedy for our excess consumption is *ascesis*, an ascetic restraint and discipline, which acknowledges that the earth belongs to heaven, not to us. It is a matter of doing with less – in terms of food, clothing, work, entertainment and all manner of consumption. It is a question of simplifying, of "traveling light." We can almost always manage with a lot less than we imagine. An ascetic approach helps us not only to be more sensible in our attitude to the world, but also more sensitive to the people around us. For the truth is that we respond to nature with the same delicacy, the same tenderness with which we respond to people. By some connection that we do not always understand, the willingness to exploit one becomes the willingness to exploit the other.

St. Nikephoros of Chios (d. 1831) once preached that "people are poor if they do not love the trees." "If you do not love trees," he said, "you do not love God." As clergy, we are called to serve at the altar that is the heart of our community. Likewise, we are called to minister at the altar of the heart of others and to celebrate God's presence in the cathedral of the universe. We must communicate the truth that if we lose the forest, then we lose not just an aesthetical but an essential quality of life: we lose our imagination and our inspiration, we lose the mystique of nature and the mystery of life, we lose our sensitivity and our soul. The most endangered species is not the whale. It is not even the human being. It is the very earth that we all share. This is our home, our *oikos*, where we, whales and people alike, live and die.[5]

### (v) Conclusion

As we stand at the threshold of the third millennium, it seems fitting that we clergy review our past achievements and failures and set our agendas for the future. As we do so let us remember that the scriptural model of the priestly vocation should not be sought in the arrival of Moses into the Promised Land, but rather in the departure of Abraham into the dark

unknown. This is the dark side of discipleship. Let us not forget that the Church fathers speak of God Himself in terms and
images of darkness, for it is in darkness that we see light. "The
darkness," says the Psalmist, "is no darkness with you, but the
night is as clear as day. The darkness and the light are both
alike" (Ps. 139: 12). When we clergy are prepared to face the
darkness that is within and no longer anxiously concerned to
validate or justify our authority through external means, then
we come to understand what the Greek poet Nikiphoros
Vrettakos describes in his stunning poem, "The First Thing of
Creation:"

> I don't know how
> But suddenly there is no darkness left at all
> The sun has poured itself inside me
> From a thousand wounds.

NOTES

[1] Henri Nouwen, *The Wounded Healer: Ministry in Contemporary Society* (Doubleday: New York, 1972) 90.

[2] See C. Yannaras, *The Freedom of Morality* (St. Vladimir's Seminary
Press: New York, 1984) and his *The Privilege of Despair* (in Greek: Athens, 1973).

[3] *Mandate* IV, ii, 2.

[4] Cf. N. Eiesland and D. Saliers (eds.), *Human Disability and Service of
God: Reassessing Religious Practice* (Abingdon: Nashville, 1998).

[5] See T. Berry, *The Dream of the Earth* (Sierra Club Books: San Francisco, 1988); and C. Birch, *Feelings* (University of NSW: Sydney, 1995).

# IV

## The Spiritual Elder

### fundamental principles

#### (i) Introduction: From Apostle to Abbot

Repentance and confession are not identified exclusively with the priestly ministry. There is a need to see apostolic authority in the context also of the prophetic tradition of the people of God. Spiritual leadership must be seen in the light of its eschatological character, as a refreshing and illuminating transformation of prophetic authority in the Church. As Gregory the Great wrote:

> What of Peter the Apostle?.... All those who govern the church in matters of faith and morals exercise the same power of binding and loosing that he received. In fact, the Creator's very purpose in coming down from heaven to earth was to impart to earthly people this heavenly power.[1]

Through his relationship with his disciples, the spiritual elder hands down Christ Himself, in His relationship with His disciples. In this relationship, the holy Tradition of the Church is shown to be nothing other than interpersonal love in Christ. The elder's loyalty to and love for his children are a creative way of tradition, a striking – even if inconspicuous – embodiment of spiritual authority as foundational and formative. In him, they encounter a paradigm of integrity and of authenticity. He seeks to give nothing of himself, for it is Christ who lives in him (cf. Gal. 2:20). "I give only what God tells me to give," said St. Seraphim of Sarov, a beloved staretz of the Church.[2]

The figure of the spiritual elder illustrates the two levels on which the Church exists and functions in this world: the hierarchical and the spiritual, the outward and the inner, the institutional and the inspirational, ultimately the organizational and the charismatic. In this sense, the *geron* (Greek) or *staretz*

(Russian) exists alongside the Apostles. Although not necessarily ordained to be a presbyter through the episcopal laying-on of hands, the spiritual father is a prophetic person who has received his charisma from the Spirit of God. There is no formal act of appointment for the spiritual elder. Although he seeks the blessing of the Bishop, it is his disciples who point to and reveal the elder as a human being pregnant with God.

The dialectic or tension between establishment and charisma, between priestly and prophetic function, has never really been resolved, but has in fact characterized the life of the Church at least since the age of Constantine. If not always harmonious and easy, this tension has been a creative force. The monastic flight to the desert and the parish planted in the world are equally essential and complementary. Neither is without its weaknesses: the world continues to be an unadmitted temptation and idol for those in the city, whereas monasticism may give rise to individualism and to extremism. Nevertheless, together, they preserve the integrity of the Gospel. Monasticism remains a symbol of the Kingdom which is not of this world, while the parish reminds the Church that Christ is present "wherever two or three are gathered in His name" (Mt. 18:20).

Thus Orthodoxy gives rise to charismatic leadership within her embrace. The charismatic atmosphere especially prevails in the desert, where personal obedience to a chosen elder precedes all formal power relations. The spiritual elder's authority is legitimate inasmuch as he in turn subjects himself to and embodies the spiritual tradition of the Church in its entirety. In this regard, it has been noted that:

> there is one thing more important than all possible books and ideas, and that is the example of an Orthodox staretz, before whom you can lay each of your thoughts and from whom you can hear not a more or less valuable private opinion, but the judgment of the Holy Fathers.[3]

### (ii) The Spiritual Elder

The great Russian Orthodox writer, Fyodor Dostoevsky, offers us this description of the elder, such as he had experienced in the person of Father Ambrose:

> What is such an elder? An elder is one who takes your soul,

your will, into his soul and his will. When you choose an elder you renounce your own will and yield it to him in complete submission, complete self-negation. This novitiate, this terrible school of abnegation, is undertaken voluntarily, in the hope of self-conquest, of self-mastery, in order after a life of obedience, to attain to perfect freedom, that is from self; to escape the lot of those who have lived their whole life without finding their true selves in themselves.[4]

Such an elder merits the title *pneumatophoros* or "Spirit-bearer" because he strives to be led as perfectly as possible through the immediate guidance of the Holy Spirit, rather than through his own individual powers or ambitions. His authority was promised by the Lord Himself who said: " ... what you are to say will be given to you when the time comes, because it is not you who will be speaking, but the Spirit of your Father will speak in you" (Mt. 10:19-20). The genuine spiritual elder in turn becomes a spiritual leader, assisting in the rebirth and regeneration of others into the life of the Spirit. As an ascetic and martyr, he gives "[his] blood and receives the Spirit."[5]

Orthodox tradition knows only one Father "who is in heaven" (Mt. 23:9), "from whom every family, spiritual or natural takes its name" (Eph.3:14). It likewise affirms the bond of sharing and solidarity which develops through the spiritual begetting of others into the Body of Christ. Thus Arsenius the disciple of Symeon the New Theologian (d. 1022) is able to describe his relationship with his spiritual father as a lifegiving bond:

I am dead to the former world. How should I return backwards? ....I have a father according to the Spirit, from whom I receive each day the very pure milk of divine grace. I refer to my father in God. He is also my mother since he has begotten me in the Spirit, and he warms me in his embrace as a newly-born baby.[6]

The spiritual father gives birth to disciples through and in the Holy Spirit. He is, in this way, the servant of the Spirit – ever invoking and ever waiting upon the Holy Spirit. "Without the Holy Spirit, shepherds and teachers would not exist in the Church," claims St. John Chrysostom.[7] For it is the Holy Spirit that legitimates the authority of the elder, or rather reveals his authenticity as love. The Spirit is the Giver of life in all its forms: personal, interpersonal, communal, ecclesial, hierarchical. "God is love" (1 John 4:16), and reveals Himself as personal communion, in a person-to-person relationship. The Spirit of God makes possible true unity in diversity, reconciling freedom and authority in the Church.

### (iii) The Relationship with the Spiritual Father

The Christian meets God by way of the margins of self-renunciation, in the paradox of self-subjection to a spiritual elder. "Whoever seeks to save his life will lose it, and whoever loses his life will preserve it," says Christ in reference to His return (Lk. 17:33). The Christian lives in light of this day. One gives oneself away in Christ; and one learns how to do this through a relationship with one's elder.

Obedience, however, to one's spiritual father is not like the submission that one is subjected to in the world, for the former exists in the context of love. Without this special personal relationship, one gains nothing but a feeling of guilt from obedience. Such guilt defeats the purpose of obedience, which is spiritual liberation.[8]

As in the case of one's biological parent's, the spiritual child loves and respects his or her spiritual father or mother. Their relationship, however, is not biologically but spiritually based. Barsanuphius, the "great *geron*," observes that the spiritual father and child are "of one soul" in eternal love. For the monk or nun, the spiritual life becomes one's whole life and the monastery one's home. The diverse virtues constitute one's family, and one's father or mother is the one who toils with one, one's friend and "accomplice." Barsanuphius goes still further and claims that the elder does more for us than we do. He is the person with whom one must not be ashamed to confide everything. To confide is to confess, to throw off all disguise in the search for truth. In this way, cleansing and purification occur.

The relationship with one's spiritual elder may also include confession in the sacramental sense, if the elder is also a presbyter. However, ordination is not taken for granted in the tradition. Nowhere, for example, does St. John Climacus, the author of the great spiritual classic entitled *The Ladder of Divine Ascent*, indicate that the spiritual father should be in priestly orders, and there is no evidence that the author of *The Ladder* himself was actually ordained, though he clearly was a spiritual father. Similar cases are to be found in fourth century Egypt, where Abba Anthony and many other Fathers were not priests.

The same applies to Symeon the Pious, the spiritual father of Symeon the New Theologian, and in this century Staretz Silouan, who were not presbyters. In the West, too, there is no evidence that, for example, Benedict of Nursia was in orders, while Francis of Assisi was a deacon.

The spiritual father does not aim at imposing rules and punishments, even in his admonitory role. Although he is called "a [good] manager" he is, for his disciple, above all "an archetypal image," "a rule," and "a law": he does not prescribe rules but himself becomes a living model, not so much through his words as through his personal example. "Be their example, not their legislator,"[9] advises Abba Poemen, and Barsanuphius writes to a disciple: "I have not bound you, brother, nor have I given you a commandment, but an advice; so do as you wish." This freedom characterizes the geron, who need not necessarily be old in age if his attitude shows that "everything he says and does is as a law and a rule for the brotherhood."[10]

### (iv) The Spiritual Father as Sponsor

In a unique and refreshing passage, St. John Climacus describes the spiritual leader as *anadochos*, which is the term used for the sponsor or god-parent at Baptism and signifying the one who assumes responsibility for another.[11] The source of this doctrine is Pauline: "We who are strong ought to bear the failings of the weak" (Rom.15:1). Barsanuphius writes to a disciple: "I assume and bear you, but on this condition: that you bear the keeping of my words and commandments."[12] The spiritual elder does nothing less than to take on full responsibility for the souls of others, writes the author of the *Ladder of Divine Ascent*:

> Thus, there is an assuming of spiritual responsibility (*anadoche*) in the proper sense, which is a laying down of one's soul on behalf of the soul of one's neighbor *in every way*.[13]

Such *anadoche* may be complete, as Sts. Barsanuphius and John Climacus suggest, but it may also be partial. The spiritual elder may choose to undertake responsibility only for the sins of the past or those of the present.[14] In the *Apophthegmata Patrum*, Abba Lot says: "I will carry half of your fault with you." Barsanuphius responds to one spiritual child: "I care, then, for you more than you do; or rather, it is God who cares. ... But if you want to cast *everything* on me on account of obedience, I accept this too."[15]

Thus the spiritual leader lifts burdens, bearing them as his own. This is strikingly illustrated by the following anecdote recounted in the *Ladder*:

> The old man read it, smiled, lifted the brother, and said to him: 'My son, put your hand on my neck.' The brother did so. Then the great man said: 'Very well, brother. Now let this sin be on my neck for as many years as it has been or will be active within you. But from now on, ignore it.'[16]

The gesture may point to a ritual practice of penance in the early Church, preserved in the present custom of the priest laying his hand on the penitent's neck during confession. The act implies love and human solidarity, for the elder assumes the suffering of others, and thus "bears the cross" (Lk. 14:24) of Christ. The spiritual elder should not, however, lift burdens which exceed his powers. He will have to account for all his spiritual children at the Last Judgment (cf. Ezek. 3:20).

> 'If it is a difficult struggle to account for oneself,' states the *Life of St. Pachomius*, 'how much more so is it to account for many?'[17]

Still, the spiritual father would prefer his own damnation to that of his disciples. Although John Climacus himself does not develop this argument, it is certainly implicit in the *Ladder* and can be found explicitly both in the earlier and later Patristic tradition. The Old Testament precedent is Moses' petition to God on behalf of the people of Israel:

> Oh these people have committed a great sin, and have made for themselves a god of gold! Yet now, if You will, forgive their sin; but if not, I pray, blot me out of Your book which You have written (Ex. 32:31-32).

In like manner, the Apostle Paul writes to the Church in Rome:

> I wish that I myself were accursed from Christ for my brethren... (Rom. 9: 3).

Echoing this sentiment, St. Barsanuphius prays to God:

> Master, either take me into your Kingdom with my children, or else wipe me also off your book.[18]

Symeon the New Theologian likewise guarantees to his disciples that:

I will die if God overlooks you [my child]. I will hand myself
over to the eternal fire in your place if He deserts you.[19]

Such utterances, of course, not only echo God's reply to Moses
in Exodus (Ex. 32: 32-33), but especially highlight the power of
the loving prayer of a righteous person, as the spiritual father or
mother should be. Thus, the prayer of the elder "avails much"
(Jas. 5: 16). In particular, however, these passages reflect the aton-
ing love of the perfect One "who knew no sin to be sin for us, that
we might become the righteousness of God in this" (2 Cor. 5: 21).

### (v) Spiritual Direction as a Way of Love

In opening up to a spiritual elder, one allows the divine Other
into the whole of one's life. One cannot achieve this alone. It is
necessary to allow at least one other into the deepest recesses of
the heart and mind, sharing every thought, emotion, insight,
wound, and joy.

For most people this is a difficult venture. One is today taught
and encouraged from an early age to be strong and assertive, to
handle matters alone. Certainly, the capacity of appropriate
assertiveness is a sign of maturity. In life, love, at times, requires
it. Indeed, Christ Himself demonstrated such assertiveness
when He confronted the moneychangers at the temple (cf. Matt.
21:12). In addition to calling His disciples to a level of spiritual
strength wherein they could "turn the other cheek" (Matt. 5:39)
to other persecutors, He also modelled for them assertiveness
and boldness *not* to turn the other cheek, after being struck by a
religious official. Instead, He responded with the bold question: Why…?" (John 18:21:23). Moreover, there were many
occasions when Christ preferred to remain silent before His ac-
cusers – yet another response requiring inner strength and
genuine humility. At the same time, there is in the Orthodox
spiritual tradition a keen awareness of the interconnectedness
and mutual dependency of all living beings. We are members
one of another and we need one another. We are not islands; we
are not isolated..

We need others because often our wounds are too deep to
admit, the evil too painful to confront by ourselves. The sign, as
we have seen, that one is on the right track is the ability to share
with someone else. This is precisely the essence of the Mystery
of Confession. To seek God may be an abstract search; to ac-

quire purity of soul may be an arbitrary goal; but to seek and find one's neighbor is to discover all three: God, purity, and the other. "Life and death is found in one's neighbor."[20] This is why, in Confession, one discovers the abyss of sin and the mystery of grace alike.

Repentance should not be seen in terms of remorse, but rather in terms of reconciliation, restoration, reintegration, wholeness. Confession is not some transaction or deal; it defies mechanical definition and cannot be juridically reduced merely to the act of absolution. Thus Confession is no narcissistic self-reflection. While sin involves a rupture in the "I-Thou" relationship of the world, otherwise *metanoia* will lead to paranoia, confession is communion; it is being able to say, together, "our Father." It is the eucharist lived out day by day.

During the Reformation in the West, the emphasis was placed on guilt and remission; previously, the problem was obedient submissiveness to institutional authority; and today, although death, guilt, and institutionalism are less obvious and threatening, yet they gnaw away in the form of frustration and anxiety. This is the age when people die of boredom and meaninglessness. Yet, life is inherently meaningful. The ultimate content and reference-point of meaning lies in direct knowledge of the Logos, in the vision of God in and through the other.

We all have a need to overcome the fear of death. The answer is to be found in the God of light and life, in the resurrected Christ. Everywhere that we see light and life, it is the resurrected Christ who is experienced. So when a parent says to its child that "everything is all right," it is actually making a metaphysical statement; when you confess to an elder, you are resurrecting the crucified Christ; and when you believe in God, you are no longer "afraid, for He has overcome the world" of death through His love.

### (vi) Concluding Remarks

In the absence of a spiritual elder, one may turn to religious communities with an established tradition of prayer and silence. Much discipline and personal formation may be received from an ordered daily rule of prayer and liturgy, of labor and recreation . This appears to have been the chief way in which many persons in the past have gained inner maturity. The powerful presence of spiritual elders – who have passed away and whose memory still guides and guards a particular monastic community – can be evoked at all times and in all places by those who know how to trust and who wish to learn to love.

It is, in this respect, especially significant to recognize the *flexibility* in the relationship between elder and disciple. Some spiritual leaders may be endowed with rare gifts of the Spirit, while others are simply able to provide the fundamental guidance required. Some disciples may need to contact their spiritual elder frequently, whereas others may be inspired by infrequent visits. One must never forget the dynamism of each personal encounter: Symeon the Elder held Christ only once in his arms; John the Forerunner met Christ once; and Mary of Egypt took communion but once in her life.

Of course, if a suitable elder cannot be readily found, then the Patristic tradition encourages one to turn to the reading of Scripture and the writings of the Church Fathers.[21] The crucial point is always to look outside and beyond oneself, to open up oneself, to begin to trust another. Healing comes only once one learns to love and to be loved, when one is willing to bear the burdens of others and assume responsibility for them.

Through such openness to love, one receives the power to transform the whole world. Nothing is any longer trivial: everything is perceived, in the light of Mt. Tabor, as uniquely contributing to one's spiritual formation and salvation. Then one no longer places undue expectations on a spiritual elder, imagining him to be perfect. Rather, one places all one's hope and trust in the God who is love.

A spiritual elder is to be sought in prayer and repentance. Should one not find such an elder, then the call to prayer and repentance still remains. For if there is a certain identification drawn between Christ and the spiritual elder, yet it is always Christ who remains the true icon of the Father. It is to Him ultimately that one is opened, laid bare for diagnosis and therapy. If you find a spiritual guide, writes St. Symeon the New Theologian, tell him your thoughts; if not, then simply raise your eyes constantly to Christ.[22] The spiritual elder is the living image of Christ and begets us into the life in Christ. Symeon concludes:

> Secure a father ... through love and faith .... and desire, become

attached to him as to Christ Himself, so that you may be united
by him and in him to Christ and show yourself to be a partaker
and co-heir of His eternal Kingdom and glory, praising and
magnifying Him with His Father and His All-Holy Spirit.[23]

NOTES

[1] Gregory the Great, *Dialogues*, O.J. Zimmerman, trans., (New York:
1959) II. 91-93. For a general introduction to spiritual guidance as a way
to wholeness and holiness in the Eastern and Western traditions, see
(ed.) J. Sommerfeldt, *Abba* (Cistercian Publications: Kalamazoo, 1982).

[2] V. Zander, St. *Seraphim of Sarov* (London: 1975) 32.

[3] See Kallistos Ware, "The Spiritual Father in Orthodox Christianity," in *Cross Currents* (Summer/Fall, 1974) 296. See Bishop Kallistos
Ware, *The Inner Kingdom*, (St. Vladimir's Seminary Press: N.Y., 2000)
127-151.

[4] *The Brothers Karamazov*, C. Garnett, trans., (New York: Modern Library, n. d.) 27.

[5] Cf. *The Sayings of the Desert Fathers*, Longinus 5.

[6] Cited by I. Hausherr, "Vie de Symeon le Nouveau Theologien", in
*Orientalia Christiana* (Rome: 1928) 61. Cf. also G. Maloney, "The Elder
of the Christian East as Spiritual Leader," in *Studies in Formative Spirituality*, III(1982) 78 ff.

[7] PG50: 463.

[8] Regarding such guilt, cf. *Ladder*, Step 4:42 (PG88: 705B).

[9] *Sayings*, Poemen 174.

[10] Basil, *Sermo Asceticus* 3 (PG31:876BC).

[11] Step 4:104 (717B).

[12] Barsanuphius, *Letter* 270.

[13] *Letter to the Shepherd* 57 (1189AB). *Sayings*, Lot 2.

[14] Barsanuphius, *Letter* 39 and 169.

[15] For carrying half the weight, see Barsanuphius 168; for forgiveness of all sins since birth, cf. 202 and 210.

[16] Step 23:14 (980AB).

[17] *Greek Life* 132.

[18] Barsanuphius, *Letter* 110.

[19] Symeon the New Theologian, *Catechetical Oration*, 30. Cf. also
John Climacus, *Ladder*, Step 4:126 (728A).

[20] *Sayings*, Anthony 9.

[21] See St. Nil Sorsky, "The Monastic Rule," quoted in G. Fedotov, *A
Treasury of Russian Spirituality*, (London:1950) 96.

[22] *Ethical Discourse* VII. 399-405.

[23] *Epistle* III. 824-834.

# V

## Obedience to the Spiritual Elder

### the way of the will

> "Before your feet are able to stand in front of your Spiritual Father, they must first be washed in the blood of your heart."
> "Before your tongue is unable to hurt any person, you cannot converse with your Spiritual Father."
> (Traditional sayings of Asia Minor Greeks)

#### (i) Introduction

The issue of obedience, along with the attendant matters of authority and forgiveness, of free will and self-will, are central concerns in the spiritual direction of the human person. What is at stake in the matter of obedience is a person's ability to experience freedom in communion with God, as opposed to pursuing a separated, autonomous, non-communal existence. In the ascetic tradition, the monk is a solitary, but his solitariness is one of ascending spiritual communion and inward fulfillment, not a decline into inner emptiness and outer isolation. This chapter is based primarily on the *Ladder of Divine Ascent*, a seventh-century text authored by St. John Climacus who lived as a hermit in the desert and an abbot of the monastery of Mt. Sinai.

For St. John Climacus, obedience is so significant that he devotes to it the second longest chapter in his *Ladder of Divine Ascent* – the Fourth Step. He does not discuss obedience in terms of compliance with rules – whether these be regulations or refutations. In fact, although the Pachomian monks did have a written rule, Climacus never mentions the word "rule" in this sense. Rather, he speaks of obedience as a deeply intimate relationship with a chosen person, namely one's spiritual father, in which one is no longer engulfed by one's self. In this as in other respects, St. John Climacus does no more than follow the monastic tradition, especially as it is expressed in the Desert Fathers of fourth century Egypt and by the elders Barsanuphius and John of Gaza in the early sixth century. The first thing Pachomius himself is told to do is to find a *geron* or spiritual father.[1] And in Diadochus' *Century*, obedience is regarded as "the first introductory virtue."[2] Similarly, for Climacus, obedience constitutes the *alpha* of the first among the two mystical alphabets – that for beginners, since without obedience one cannot advance spiritually.[3] Thus, the teaching of obedience toward a specific person is present in the monastic tradition from the start.

These points are preliminary to our consideration of the meaning of obedience to one's spiritual father as a path of liberation in Christ. Let us now examine the isolating effects of self-will, obedience as a means toward spiritual communion and harmony, and the various roles played by the spiritual father in achieving this desirable end.

### (ii) Idion Thelema

"Self-will" (or, *idion thelema*) is the technical term used in ascetic literature to denote the will of our fallen nature (cf. Eph. 2:3). Climacus sees nothing wrong with free will as such, but believes that it has broken away from God's will, with which it was originally at one. What must be given up by the monk, and indeed by every disciple of Christ who wishes to know the reign of God in this world, is the "way of willfulness" (*idiognomon rythmos*), the "idiorhythmic nature" (*idiorrythmia*), and the "self-trust" (*oikeiopiston*) of human nature. The latter word is used by Climacus to describe the self-sufficient, self-regarding will which any humble person can recognize as deviant, as having "gone astray."[4] Obedience, then, means, first of all, cutting off the self-will, the elimination of *idiorrythmia*. All people are seen to be rebelling against God, by attempting to satisfy their needs apart from God and apart from their fellow creatures. Through giving up our own will and surrendering to the will of God as mediated through a spiritual father, we proclaim, in effect, that we have no part in this rebellion; we tear up the parchment of our will as a claim to our "rights," as an exaction. Paradoxically, we exercise our will – in an act of discipline and education

– in order to surrender and conform our will to the will of God. This surrender is no easy task. The ascetic needs at times to go to extremes in cutting off his own will and acquiescing to the will of God. He must go to extremes because of the extremity of his fallen, self-enclosed condition. A limitative situation requires limitative measures.

It may appear commendable to give up certain personal or egoistic pleasures, but the human person becomes holy and shares in Christ's divine-humanity only by giving up entirely his separated will. Such a person, says Climacus, will not merely be rewarded but "will inherit eternal life." This teaching accords with that of other ascetic writers who equate the denial of one's will with salvation itself, for God wills that all people be saved. Dorotheus of Gaza goes still further in saying that "he who wishes to be saved, must have no will in any matter at all."[5] The "narrow and hard way" (Mt. 7:14) of renunciation begins as a slow and painful process, like bearing a cross (cf. Lk. 22:42); but as we stand beside Him who was crucified, "we know that we will be resurrected."[6]

In the Old Testament, disobedience is seen as death (cf. Num. 16 and Ex. 14); the Fathers knew this and often spoke of "the death of one's own will" as the remedy for the death through disobedience. Yet, in placing our will before the feet of our spiritual father, we do not kill but bury it, as Christ was buried, knowing that it will be resurrected as He was. Its burial is "a willing punishment." For Climacus, "the tomb of the will" and the "tomb of the resurrection" are closely linked.[7] Thus the cutting off of self-will, while sounding negative, is in fact a most positive and life-giving event.

As disciples of Christ, our aim is to seek God's will and yield to it in all that we do (cf. Deut. 32:7) and are:

> every enterprise, utterance, thought, step, and movement (should be) in accordance with the Lord.[8]

This "accord" cannot come about unless we have previously surrendered our fallen self-will, shedding it like a garment and approaching God in our nakedness, or, as Barsanuphius says, in the "cold" nudity of a person who has nothing but God:

> Such a person dismisses one's self-will and hangs everything on the will of God.[9]

The transcendence of the self-will is a continual process throughout the spiritual life. Each detail of our life should aim to conquer our rebellious nature and surpass it as we move toward the condition of pristine harmony; each move we make should render us more humble or else we are liable to cut ourselves off from God's will. Some must be very patient in their self-abrogation in order to come to a perception of God's will; whereas the perfect come to know His will directly, in the personal encounter through prayer.

Finally, the *idion thelema* is not ultimately uprooted by one's own effort alone but, above all, by God's grace; God does the undoing with "the sword of the Spirit," in response to the humble in heart and body,[10] who no longer isolate themselves in impotent rebellion.

### (iii) Obedience

It is inimical to the life in Christ for one "to act in isolation," as Climacus attests; it is "less damaging" to do things wearing the garb of obedience and service, allowing Christ to govern one's life "without danger."[11] Obedience means carrying one's cross with joy, knowing that one is actually taking part in Christ's crucifixion – itself an act of obedience. Climacus adheres to the notion of obedience as expressed by Abba Hyperechios:

> Obedience is the best ornament of the monk. He who has acquired it will be heard by God, and he will stand beside the crucified with confidence, for the crucified Lord became obedient unto death (Phil. 2:8).[12]

Disobedience, on the contrary, forms a barrier between humanity and God (Eph. 2:14). Climacus characterizes obedience as a form of inward "martyrdom," while Barsanuphius speaks of "the shedding of blood." It is a "witness" or "confession" (*omologia*) which allows one actually to see God,[13] while the demons try to separate us from Him and render obedience useless.

Obedience is, indeed, "useless," as are all absolute, non-utilitarian commitments. Obedience is an absolute response: one gives everything away and receives in proportion to such giving, as a reciprocal gift, unmeritedly and effortlessly. Moreover, in the context of mutual love, obedience is blind. Even if the physician's prescription is wrong, taken in obedience it can heal.[14] At times, obedience seems to be taken to the point of the absurd and irrational but it is "not illogical." [15] The ascetic Fathers frequently stress blind obedience, even to behests that are ostensibly absurd – John the Dwarf is ordered to water a piece of dry wood – or even apparently immoral – Abba Saio is ordered to steal. By the same token, they stress fidelity and promptness in obedience: Abba Mark was copying the letter *omega* when his *geron* called him and he left the letter unfinished. [16] The pain experienced as a result of such obedience is likened by Climacus to an "anaesthetic" given by the physician while the patient undergoes the cure, and so the burden of obedience ultimately becomes a way of reconciliation and comfort to the monk. Obedience can only be efficaciously broken when it comes to questions of faith.

The liberating effects of obedience, which are enhanced by related disciplines, such as fasting and prayer, allow the monastic to "breathe" God, while at the same time simplifying the spiritual struggle against the vices. It also mitigates the effort in struggling. Ascetic authorities claim that those in obedience are attacked by only some of the eight classical vices, whereas hesychasts must face the challenge of the other five. It would seem that, for Climacus, obedience is a protective, preparatory stage, whereas *hesychia* marks the ideal, more advanced condition. [17] Still, obedience is understood to have a key role in undoing the destructive willfulness of fallen human nature, leading to *penthos,* repentance, and purification.

To repent is to redirect one's intellect, will, and actions towards God: it is an act of obedience to God, mediated by the spiritual father. It marks a new condition, a transformation. Obedience means obedience unto death, and even beyond death. The monk Akakios, in obedience to John the Sabbaite, overcomes the fear and barrier of death itself through obedience. He is said to obey even from his grave. Obedience becomes a promise of resurrection. To be thus resurrected is to be transfigured in divine light: "... I have seen those who shone in obedience." [18]

### (iv) The Spiritual Father

Some ascetic writers refer to the spiritual father as a "gymnast" or "trainer." Others prefer to use such words as "abbot," "guide," "shepherd," or similar pastoral terms. In what follows, I shall look at the spiritual father as guide, physician, teacher, and judge. I will then briefly consider his relationship with God and his role as priest in the world.

### a) The Spiritual Father as Guide

The spiritual father is one's precursor, a forerunner in the way of salvation, having first entered personally into heaven and seeing Christ, thereupon calling us to taste and see Christ for ourselves (cf. Ps. 34:8). If he himself has not encountered Christ, then in the words of St. Basil the Great:

> he is a blind guide, leading to the destruction both of himself and of those who follow him. [19]

In the *Ladder*, the spiritual father is likened to Moses who led the Hebrews out of Egypt; we, too, have need of "some Moses" to take us by the hand and guide us to the Promised Land of spiritual freedom. [20] It is self-deception to presume that one may rely on oneself in this endeavor, even if one possesses all the wisdom and strength of the world (cf. John 5:30), "for angelic strength is needed for the solitary life." Even in solitary life separation without obedience can be a way of self-servitude, whereas the seed and fruit of obedience is freedom in harmonious concord. For John Climacus' contemporary, Isaac the Syrian, only in obedience is one truly free. [21]

A number of recurring metaphors are used to express the idea of guidance: a guide for the blind (cf. John 29:15), a shepherd for the flock, a leader for the lost, a father, and mother (cf. 1 Thess. 2:7) for a child, a nurse for the needy, a friend for the desperate, and a navigator for a ship, even if the vessel is in peril:

> But I shall be surprised if anyone will be able by himself to save his ship from the sea. [22]

### b) The Spiritual Father as Physician

In speaking of spiritual direction, Climacus prefers therapeutic imagery:

> For we need a director who is indeed an equal to angels...a skilled person and a physician.[23]

The spiritual father is an experienced physician who knows, for instance, how to remove splinters without enlarging the wound. For Anastasius the Sinaite, the spiritual father must be experienced enough to heal. [24] Sin is equivalent to disease or illness, and so we must enter the hospital of confession where the spiritual father makes us inwardly whole by prescribing medication, by bandaging, cauterizing, even amputating when necessary. Trust in the spiritual father's judgment should be equal to confidence in the diagnosis of a physician. We are often incapable of detecting our own disease, as St. Basil observes. [25] Nevertheless, a physician can only heal us if we expose our wounds to him: the monks in the *cenobium*, visited by John Climacus at Alexandria, noted down every sin or sinful thought in a notebook which they showed to their *geron*. [26] One who confesses one's pain is near to health, says St. Isaac the Syrian. [27] The physician should be consulted immediately, and everything revealed to him unashamedly, lest the object of confession be defeated:

> If possible, sprinkle the feet of your judge and physician with your tears, like the feet of Christ. [28]

The physician prefers to inspect the wound while it is open. We must, therefore, reveal our sin and our repentance to our spiritual father without censorship or bias.

For his part, the spiritual father – impelled by "goodness" or "good pleasure" – must see his "patients" through to the completion of their healing process. Such goodness is identified by the author of the *Ladder* almost with "a good sense of humor" (cf. the reference to Moses in Acts 7:20, which is also cited by John Climacus). Abba Barsanuphius wants the spiritual father to be "free from anger." [29] Cases can occur, however, which will test the optimism of the spiritual father, when the physician will even cause despair. His powers are limited and certain degrees of illness cannot be healed but by angels or the Lord Himself. Not everyone is up the task of a confessor: "Not all of us are required to save others," says Climacus. [30] It is a vocation that presupposes vision – the gift of discernment or insight, and dispassion, without which the correct remedies cannot be administered. A spiritual father may also give away so much of himself that he is left spiritually dry, "empty handed" as it were, unless he is continually refreshed and replenished by God's grace. The fact, therefore, that one is spiritually gifted is not of itself sufficient for assuming the responsibility of a *geron*. The *Vita Antonii* illustrates well the notion that the spiritual father is called directly by God, or else indirectly through others. Anthony's door is broken down by those who have chosen him as *geron*. [31] Generally, the Fathers do not volunteer themselves for such a role and responsibility, recognizing that the guidance of others in the spiritual life presupposes a high degree of purification and of illumination. Even then, one should not undertake to heal or direct patients who are not entrusted to one's care (cf. 1 Cor 5:12-13).

> "Correct and judge justly those who are subject to you," says Abba Macarius of Alexandria, "but judge no one else." [32]

### c) The Spiritual Father as Teacher

As one who has received wisdom from above, the spiritual father is preeminently a "teacher" (*didaskalos*). He has need of no other books than the one he has received through personal experience, written "by the hand of God." [33] One might observe that, in the East, the Church never formally condemned unofficial, extra-ecclesiastical charismatic leadership. While accepting institutional authority, monks for example could challenge even Patriarchs in the name of the truth. In fact, a charismatic atmosphere seems to have especially prevailed in the desert, where personal obedience to an elder or teacher preceded all institutionalized ecclesiastical power relations.

The teacher should not only be adorned with the virtues of "guilelessness" and "zeal" but he should be, above all, rigorous and exacting, "for this also is the sign of a good Shepherd,"who is concerned that the Last Judgment not prove severe for his flock. [34] St. Gregory of Nyssa says of the paedagogue that he applies "wounds to one, to another advice, to one praise, and to another something else;" while St. Isaac of Nineveh corroborates: "He that combines chastisement with healing chastises with love." [35]

### d) The Spiritual Father as Judge

The shepherd cares for all the sheep all the time. He must be honored and remembered for his spiritual attainments and pastoral concern. He is not to be judged or criticized. All his counsels should be accepted with joy, even when they are not immediately to our liking, for he tests and "trains" us continually. Before one's spiritual father, the disciple is silent; one not only appropriates the teaching (cf. Matt. 3:9) but imitates the teacher. If the monk does not know the physician before placing himself into his hands, he might test to confirm whether he is experienced in healing and capable of curing the wounds. If he does know well the spiritual father, then he should not attempt to take advantage of "the condescension and indulgence of the superior." [36] In the words of Abba Isidore the priest:

> disciples must love as their fathers those who are truly their masters and fear them as their guides; they should not lose their fear because of love, nor because of fear should love be obscured. [37]

### e) The Spiritual Father and God

The spiritual father stands vicariously not only in the place of his child before God, but also in the place of God before his child. His desire for our salvation is Christ's very command. Envisioning thus the spiritual father as a living icon of the living God, ascetical theology regards obedience to him as though it were directed to God Himself. The spiritual father must be a servant of God, our real Father. As Scripture states: "call no man your father upon the earth: for one is your Father, which is in heaven" (Matt. 23:9). In the Orthodox tradition, the first part of this statement is understood not literally, but as giving emphasis to the second part, namely that God is the source of our existence. The spiritual father, then, does nothing more than speak the word of God to the sons and daughters of God. The desert fathers believe that God looks for nothing from beginners so much as renunciation of self-will through obedience to one who is advanced in the life in Christ. Thus, it is sometimes said that if someone has faith in another, and hands oneself over to him in complete submission, one does not need to worry about discerning God's will, but can entrust oneself fully to the care of the spiritual father. [38] God will honor the intent, which is not to reach mystical heights, nor to have command of prayer, but to mortify the will, to die to this world through obedience to a spiritual father who can, by God's grace, further our resurrection in this life. For Climacus, this remains valid even if the spiritual father is not a particularly "spiritual" person. God can speak through anyone he pleases:

> ...even if those consulted are not very spiritual. For God is not unjust, and will not lead astray souls who with faith and innocence humbly submit to the advice and judgment of their neighbor. Even if those who were asked were brute beasts, yet He who speaks is the immaterial and invisible One.[39]

This is the burden of "blind" obedience advocated by the ascetic Fathers. It is not blind in the sense of being pointless or misjudged. Rather, complete security and trust is implied. It is the risk of faith and the transparency of love which leads Abraham, "not knowing whither he went" (Heb. 11:8), to offer his son as a sacrifice because God asked him to. It was the same risk and transparency and trust in his father which led Isaac to cooperate with his own sacrifice, even carrying the wood to kindle the sacrificial fire. In a similar way, the relationship with one's spiritual father incarnates the relationship with God, a relationship which "allows" for unconditional obedience to the former as an offering to the latter.

As has been noted before, there is a "protective" element in this relationship. We are "covered" by its grace from pitfalls. The spiritual father, in fact, is present even in his absence; he protects even when he is not there. We surrender to him in imagination, or rather in trust, as we trust in God. Salvation depends on this. In the New Testament period, Christ was in person on earth. Now, following our Lord's ascension and the gift of the Holy Spirit to His Body on earth, we must obey Christ through and in others. We must surrender to one who is His living image, one who intercedes to God on our behalf. Indeed, it becomes, in a sense and most paradoxically, preferable to sin against God than against him:

> For when we anger God, our spiritual father can reconcile us; but when he is incensed against us, we no longer have anyone to make propitiation for us. But it seems to me that both cases amount to the same thing.[40]

There is, then, a continuity between God and the spiritual father. God is inscrutable, but He meets us face to face in another, in the spiritual father. In this encounter, all the ambivalent areas of personal commitment converge: obedience, trust, self-abnegation, recovery of oneself, and ultimate liberation. These areas always remain ambivalent, for none of them provide a basis for complacency and self-assurance. The link itself with the spiritual father provides no "guarantee" for unblemished spiritual life. That is a gratuitous gift of the Holy Spirit, which we may or may not receive, accept and cooperate with. If we receive and accept it, the gift commits us, and like all true commitment, this one cannot but be unconditional and enduring.

*f) The Spiritual Father as Priest in the World*

Finally, let us briefly touch on the priestly dimension of spiritual fatherhood. By presiding over our spiritual pathway, the spiritual father acquires a priestly function: he offers us to God in an act of sacrifice, preparing and leading us into the Holy of Holies. This is a form of consecration to a priesthood in the world. As "intercessor," the spiritual father expresses the ontological priesthood entrusted to all people by virtue of the divine image according to which we have been created and by virtue of the divine grace through which we have been baptized into Christ.

Whether ordained to the sacramental priesthood or endowed with the "royal priesthood" (1 Pet. 2:5 and 9), as all Christians are, the spiritual father is his disciple's supreme intercessor and guide. Thus, he is considered by St. John Climacus as being called to the highest and most arduous of orders:

> We can offer no gift to God so acceptable as to bring Him rational souls through repentance. The whole world is not worth so much as a soul.[41]

The calling is shown to be part of one's personal relation with God and with one's fellow-human beings. Whichever dimensions of spiritual fatherhood we look at – as priest, as intercessor, as healer, as teacher, as guide, as judge, as icon, or as proxy – it remains that the phenomenon of spiritual fatherhood, as indeed that of spiritual generation and spiritual direction, spells the supremacy of the personal over the impersonal. It is not by chance that St. John Climacus displays such a great interest in the spiritual father and his disciple as human persons having unique qualities and particular relations. The preeminence of the personal over abstract rules and ordinances has always been and will ever be a sign of life in Christ as this is known in the Orthodox spiritual experience and tradition.

NOTES

[1] *First Greek Life* 6. See also *Apophthegmata*, Isaiah 2.

[2] *Century*, ch. 41-42.

[3] *Step* 26, 14 (1017) and 45 (1028).

[4] See *Step* 24, 17 (981) and *Step* 4, 6 (680).

[5] *Doctrina* 21, 6 (PG 88:1817).

[6] Cf. *Step* 4, 5 (680).

[7] *Step* 4,4 (680).

[8] *Step* 27, ii, 31 (1113); *Shepherd* 50 (1188) and *Step* 26, ii, 1 (1056). Cf. also *Apophthegmata*, Anthony 37-38 (PG 65: 88), and Abba Isaiah, *Discourse* 1,2; 25,18; and 27, 8.

[9] Barsanuphius 40.

[10] *Step* 4,2 (677); *Shepherd* 50 (1188) and 100 (1204). For Cassian, too, obedience is a gift (*Inst.* IV, 29), and is linked with "simplicity of heart" (*Inst.* IV, 24).

[11] *Step* 8, 20 (832); 28, 27 (1133) and 56 (1140).

[12] *Apophthegmata*, Hyperechios 8. For the linking of obedience with the Cross, cf. Cassian, *Conf.* XIX, 6. This parallel is also found in later Fathers: Symeon the New Theologian, *Catechetical Discourse* 27, and Nicetas Stethatos, *Century* II, 54.

[13] *Step* 4, 10 (681); 15. 6 (881) and 33 (888). The reference to Barsanuphius is 254. The same notion is also found in *Apophthegmata*, Pambo (PG 65:369) and Symeon the New Theologian, *Cat. Disc.* 12.

[14] *Step* 26, 21 (1021); 25, 49 (1000); and 24, 14 (984).

[15] *Step* 4, 111 (720).

[16] See *Apophthegmata*, John the Dwarf 1 (PG 65:204); Cassian, *Inst.* IV, 27-28. Cassian also speaks of "indiscussa oboedientia" in *Inst.* I, 2, 4 and *Conf.* XVIII, 3. See *Apophthegmata*, Sisoes 10 (393), Joseph of Panepho 5 (229), Mark 1 (293), Pistos 1 (372), Saio 1 (420), Basil 1 (137). Further, see Palladius, *Lausiac History*, Didymus the Blind 4. Similar expression are found in the *Ladder*: *Step* 4, 32 (701), 70 (712) and 13 (681).

[17] *Step* 27, 11, 9 (1109).

[18] *Step* 4, 111 (720-721). See also *Shepherd* 67 (1192). Obedience unto death is stressed in Pachomius, *First Greek Life* 36 and 69. The notion

of obedience leading to resurrection is explicit in *Apophthegmata*, Nau 294 (1909, pp. 377-8).

[19] *Reg. Fus. Tract.* 25, 2 (PG 31: 985). See K. Ware, "The Spiritual Father in St. John Climacus and Saint Symeon the New Theologian," in *Studia Patristica* 18,2 (Peeters: Leuven, 1990) 299-316.

[20] *Step* 1, 14 (633); *Shepherd* 93 (1197) and 100 (1201).

[21] *Step* 27, 12 (1097); 26, 111, 45 (1089). See also Isaac the Syrian, *Mystic Treatises*, pp. 24 and 142.

[22] Step 15, 56 (892).

[23] *Step* 1, 15 (636). Symeon the New Theologian refers to his spiritual father as "equal to the angels": cf. *Cat. Disc.* 22. Medical imagery is found in *Step* 8, 23 (832); 23,1 (976); and 4, 28 (697). See also Athanasius, *Life of Anthony* 87 (PG 26:965); Greg. Naz., *Oration* II, 16 and 18 (PG 35: 425 and 473); Chrysostom, *On the Priesthood* I, 9 (PG 48: 630); Basil, *Reg. Fus. Tract.* 30 and 51 (PG 31:993 and 1040); Pachomius, *First Greek Life* 132; Cyril of Scythopolis, *Life of Euthymius* 9; Isaac the Syrian, *Mystic Treatises*, p. 51; and Symeon the New Theologian, *Cat. Disc.* 18.

[24] *Quaestiones* 6 (PG 89:369-372). The emphasis on experience is especially evident in later Fathers: Symeon the New Theologian, *Cat. Disc.* 14; and Nicetas Stethatos, *Century* 1, 73.

[25] *Reg. Brev. Tract.* 301 (PG 31:1296).

[26] *Step* 4, 32 (701), 70 (712) and 13 (681).

[27] *Mystic Treatises* (ed. J. Wensinck) 7. See also Basil, *Reg. Fus. Tract.* 46 (PG 31:1036).

[28] *Step* 4, 56 (709), 27 (697), 32 (701) and 39 (705).

[29] Barsanuphius 23. The reference to the *Ladder* is from *Step* 1, 33 (637-640).

[30] *Step* 3, 5 (664). See also 15, 74 (897) and esp. 26, 12 (1016). Cf. Pachomius, *First Greek Life* 126.

[31] Athanasius, *Life of Anthony* 14 (PG 26:864). See similar expressions in Cyril of Scythopolis, *Life of Sabas* 19 and Symeon the New Theologian, *Cat. Disc.* 20.

[32] *Apophthegmata*, Macarius 2 (PG 65: 304); and *Step* 14, 7 (865).

[33] *Shepherd* 5-6 (1165) and 20 (1177). The parallel here is with the tablets given to Moses on Mt. Sinai. Symeon the New Theologian speaks similarly in *Cat. Disc.* 18. In the Patristic tradition, the teacher is usually God: cf. Greg. Nyssa, *Against those who criticize* ... PG 46:309-312) and Chrysostom, *That we should not be satisfied* ... 2 (PG 50:655).

[34] *Shepherd* 30 (1180). The reference here is *Shepherd* 7 (1168). See also *Shepherd* 27 (1180), 94 (1200), 96 (1201), and 99 (1201).

[35] Gregory of Nyssa, *On ... two gods* (PG 46:300). Macarius adopts similar terminology in *Letter* (PG 34:424-5). See also Pachomius, *First Greek Life* 103. Chrysostom also adopts the image of the Last Judgment (PG 50:657 and 653).

[36] *Step* 4, 91 (716), 107 (717), and 122-3 (725).

[37] *Apophthegmata*, Isidore 5 (PG 65: 236). See also *Step* 4, 106 (717); Basil, *Const. Monast.* 4 (PG31:1408-9); Cassian, *Inst.* IV, 10; and Symeon the New Theologian, *Cat. Disc.* 3.

[38] *Apophthegmata*, Ares 1 (PG 65:132-3).

[39] *Step* 26, ii, 2 (1057).

[40] *Step* 4, 126 (728) and 1, 14 (633-636)

[41] *Step* 1, 14 (636) and *Shepherd* 90 (1196).

# VI

## Dynamics of Spiritual Direction

### the tradition of the desert

*(i) Introduction*

There is no subject more essential and at the same time more misunderstood than that of spiritual authority. The various dimensions and problems of spiritual authority comprise a central focus of the literature of early monasticism which has yet to be meticulously charted in both academic and ecclesiastical circles.

One reason for this vacuum of scholarship is the sparsity of information in the Patristic tradition on the aberrant attitudes and the inappropriate behaviors *on the part of the elders themselves* in the relationship of spiritual direction. The primary sources that discuss the particular qualities and charisms necessary for spiritual fatherhood[1] do not address in detail the potential dangers or consequences of mis-direction or pseudo-direction. The Christian classics of spiritual literature will not normally undermine the *responsibility* proper to the director, but they will rarely underline the *results* of improper direction. The early Christian writers provide only general advice on such matters, warning, for example, against the possible harm in:

> submitting oneself to a master without experience or to one still subject to the passions, because he might initiate one into the diabolical life instead of the evangelical.[2]

This chapter examines the theme of spiritual direction in relation to its abuse on the part of the spiritual elder, with particular reference to representative literature from early Egyptian (fourth-fifth century) and Palestinian (sixth century) monasticism. The purpose is to clarify the somewhat mystified concept of the spiritual director by turning to the early sources of this tradition.

The Fathers and Mothers who moved away from society into

the desert of Egypt in the fourth century acquired considerable spiritual authority among their contemporaries. By totally rejecting ordinary human structures and almost provocatively renouncing worldly institutions, they paradoxically came to represent another, different kind of power. Their advice was sought in matters of spirituality, salvation, doctrine, even social life and political action.

The monastic literature of Egypt in no way exaggerates the figure of the holy, charismatic elder. Egyptian monasticism consciously reacts to and opposes any form of "attachment" – whether to material things or to human persons. In the *popular* mind of that time, the desert ascetics clearly enjoyed a position of spiritual prowess and prestige, but the desert fathers and mothers did not accept this picture of themselves. First of all, their life was too *flexible* and their relationships too unorganized to allow for any strict regulation or formation of roles. Although Anthony and his contemporaries did constitute prototypes of spiritual direction for subsequent generations, throughout their lives they avoided any perception or promotion of themselves as *models*. Vainglory, they understood, was a temptation and a trap, going "against the grain" of the desert.

By the end of the fourth and the early part of the fifth centuries, the monks of the Egyptian desert are characterized by a sense of *movement*: not only have they increasingly been "discovered," but they now also begin to be "dispersed," for various reasons gradually becoming attracted to neighboring regions. For instance, after the death of the founding fathers of monasticism – the "great" Anthony (d. 356), Pachomius (d. 346), and Amoun of Nitria (d. c. 352) – Abba Silvanus moves to Palestine, via Egypt, around the year 380. Much later, after the death of Macarius in Scetis (d. 390), perhaps during the 430s, Abba Isaiah settles in Gaza. It is from here that we have a series of twenty-nine *Ascetic Discourses* attributed to Isaiah and written in the latter part of the fifth century.[3]

Abba Isaiah seeks in various ways to direct and promote the spiritual formation of the monastics for whom he is responsible. In his discourses, perhaps the primary means of protecting the sense of community is his effort to raise awareness in matters of relationships with one's elders and brothers. The implication is that community comprises continual exchanges of honest communication and humble reconciliation. Whether speaking of the power of the will, the manifestation of thoughts, the notion of obedience, the role of the spiritual elder, respect toward oneself and others, or even the inherent temptations in spiritual direction, Isaiah's is most definitely an asceticism of sensitivity, which aims ultimately at spiritual liberty.

Whether deliberately or not, the emphasis in Western Christianity on *the monastic Rule*, especially from the sixth century onwards with the influential work of Benedict, allowed far less room for individual discretion or direction, thus restricting individual judgment *on the part of both the elder and the disciple*. It was precisely during this period that Barsanuphius and John – steeped in a tradition which emphasized personal discernment and the role of the charismatic elder – indicated their awareness of the dynamics and even the dangers of spiritual direction. As they offer guidance to numerous visitors outside Gaza, they defy the romanticized picture that gradually develops in Eastern Christendom and becomes almost normative for the "spiritual director." These two "old men" never claim to be experts, nor do they expect those who seek their advice to bare their souls to them. They do not provide "wisdom" on request, nor do they attempt to solve all problems brought before them. What characterizes them, like the desert dwellers of Egypt, is a *flexibility* that is reflective of the Spirit of God which "breathes where it wills"(Jn. 3:8).

### (ii) The Desert Fathers Revisited

*a) The Apophthegmata: "Text" or "Tale" ?*

When we consider the *Sayings of the Desert Fathers* and Mothers, we must have in mind the "secret" of the spiritual relationship that is concealed, and the sacrament of spiritual mentoring that is conveyed in them. These *Sayings* – whether positively or negatively, either in constructive or even in seemingly destructive ways – tell the *story* of their spiritual journey. Like any story or text, they are not the history of the actual relationship. They constitute a kind of map which requires unfolding and careful reading. In order best to understand the story, correctly to follow the map, one needs to be on the same journey with a guide:

One who climbs a mountain the first time needs to follow a known route, and he needs with him, as a companion and guide, someone who has been up before and is familiar with the way.[4]

The ascetic inhabitants of the fourth-century Egyptian desert were well aware of the tensions and problems inherent in spiritual direction. It is, however, unfortunate that those who subsequently edited their "sayings" failed to pass on the rich texture and dynamics of these spiritual lives, conveying instead only the results of their knowledge. What, therefore, has come down to us through the centuries is the distillation of the wise words, without the description of the *process* of wise living. The "shift," observed by Columba Stewart, "from a free-flowing manner of transmission, based on telling and retelling stories, to a more static written form"[5] involved more than formal changes of a linguistic or stylistic nature. The revision and rearrangement of the "sayings" over generations inevitably meant a certain reduction in focus, even a distortion of the original, oral tradition that presumably would have conveyed a more comprehensive vision – "warts and all" – of the ascetic literature and lifestyle in the desert. The problem, therefore, arises for us today – as indeed it must have arisen for people in earlier centuries who read the *Apophthegmata* – as to what one ought to do about a failed spiritual relationship in the absence of any explicit teaching to be gleaned from the primary sources.

Now the *Sayings of the Desert Fathers* (the *Gerontikon*, in Greek) narrate many such legends of spiritual direction; they describe the leading figures, recount their memorable words, and portray their outstanding examples. Yet these tales must be understood within their context. No "abba" or "amma" declared himself or herself to be a spiritual authority or an oracle of wisdom.[6] They belonged to an ages-long tradition of spiritual authority and direction that is associated with the titles "abba" and "amma." Elders were themselves disciples of other elders. Derwas Chitty wrote of a "pedigree of spiritual authority."[7] There existed a kind of "charismatic succession" alongside of – and, to varying degrees, congruent and overlapping with – the more institutional "apostolic succession."

A deep awareness of the sacredness of this *tradition* helped to maintain a strong sense of *responsibility* and *accountability* on the part of spiritual directors, primarily to God and toward their own elders from whom and through whom they received the gift of spiritual authority. This *responsibility*, and this *capacity to respond* to the needs of the disciple, helped to engender in the disciple a similar response-ability. The spiritual elders understood that the very Spirit of God "taught them at that hour what they ought to say" (cf.Lk. 12:12). At the same time, they were very aware of their "mere humanity." Pachomius reminds his disciples that:

> when the Lord ceases to reveal Himself we are but human, like every other human being.[8]

### b) Idols of Power or Icons of Love ?

There is a temptation for contemporary readers and admirers to romanticize the lives and lifestyles of the early ascetics. It is important to avoid this temptation, for to idealize is to idolize, and both the scriptural and the patristic tradition forbid the creation of idols.[9] Discernment – a virtue highly prized among the desert elders – needs to be exercized by contemporary Christians, so that the true, inner meaning of spiritual authority and eldership may be discovered.[10]

Eccentricities unraveled and illusions unmasked, the desert dwellers in fact always remain fully human. In their stories and sayings, the intensity of their struggle reveals the love for their neighbor as the integrity of their heart, and the love for God as the intention of their life. So it is not so much the great fast or the impressive feat that matters in the desert but the principle of love.[11] This principle is supremely important for the evaluation of spiritual authority and the evasion of its abuses. The ascetics are not idols of supreme power, but icons of sublime love:

> They said of Abba Macarius the Great that he became, as it is written, a god upon the earth, because, just as God protects the world, so Abba Macarius would cover the faults which he saw, as though he did not see them; and those which he heard, as though he did not hear them.[12]

Fully conscious of their own limitations, the desert fathers were able to show great understanding for the weaknesses of others. Thus the sense of moral vertigo experienced when reading their *Sayings* is reconciled with the virtue of humble compassion.

*c) Ascetic Terminology*

There are certain terms in "the way of the ascetics"[13] that require unpacking in order to be properly understood. These terms constitute part of the heritage transmitted down through the centuries by the desert literature in relation to the dynamics of spiritual direction. In this section, two such ascetic terms will be briefly discussed: "obedience" and "dispassion."

*Obedience* is clearly very important for the desert fathers (cf. also Heb. 13:17). It was out of obedience that John the Dwarf watered a piece of dry wood for three years, and it bore fruit.[14] We have already examined the concept of obedience. Here, let us simply reiterate that it is not one's free *will* which one is called to surrender, but one's *willfulness*. The ascetic needs to go to extremes at times in cutting off altogether the fallen, individual will and in acquiescing to the will of God. Extreme measures merely reflect the extremity of our estrangement from God. The renunciation of the fallen will is undoubtedly a slow, painful process. It is likened to bearing one's cross (cf. Luke 22:42). It might also be paralleled with bearing a child, for the "death of one's will" is the first step to resurrection and new life.[15] The will is not killed but buried – buried alive, one might say – and the tomb is the prerequisite and precursor of the womb that brings forth life and light.

We must, of course, disabuse ourselves of the modern, Western notion of the "free individual" as this has developed from the nineteenth century. For the desert dwellers in Egypt, the notion of "free will" is inextricably linked with the sense of inter-dependence belonging to a community. It is not always easy to distinguish clearly between personal conviction and communal connection in monastic piety. And certainly after the rejection of Origen and his intellectual legacy by the monastic tradition of the Egyptian desert, the idea of individual free will lost some of its power and charm. The Council of Nicaea (325) further established this new direction theologically by sharply distinguishing between Creator and creation. Grace was henceforth understood to be transmitted more institutionally than individually. As Susanna Elm has demonstrated in her study *Virgins of God*, the significance of *public power* far outweighed the influence of *private will*.[16] And so, while the names of the desert fathers may not be associated with the formal monastic "rules," the founders of monasticism most certainly are: Pachomius and Basil in the East; Augustine and Benedict in the West. Perhaps even the editors of the *Apophthegmata* were constrained by the general institutional shift of their times. Yet the desert hermits themselves do not advocate compliance with rules and regulations. They never, in fact, mention the word "rule" in this connection, though they speak of obedience as an enriching relationship with a chosen person.

The biblical command holds true in the desert of Egypt: "do not become servants of human masters" (1 Cor. 7:23). Obedience, then, is neither submissiveness nor servility, at least not in a unilateral way. For, obedience is *also due from the elder*, not simply to abstract rules but to another specific person. This is once again the *tradition* of spiritual authority referred to earlier. Abba Mios clearly states:

Obedience responds to obedience,[17] and not to authority.

The desert tradition stresses the importance of eschewing priestly ambition. It does so to avoid the danger of a one-sided, unbalanced authority.[18] Provided the superior personally adhered to the rule, the principle of obedience served as a unifying principle in the wider community of the Church. The virtue of obedience was thus conceived in terms of a circle, that is, communally and not in a linear or institutional fashion. It was mutual responsiveness, not monological reproach.

The understanding at all times is that both elder and disciple are subject to the same conditions and commandments, both accountable before the living God. The two are traveling together, though they *may* not be on equal footing.[19] Unfortunately, the desert literature once again offers little explicit, helpful advice for when problems arise. The reader may be left with the false impression that all problems are to be swiftly "dispelled" by the unilateral practice of obedience on the part of the disciple toward the elder, bowing before the authority of the latter and submitting to the overwhelming burden of the tradition of ages.

The second term that needs clarification or demystification is *apatheia*, variously translated as "dispassion" or "passionlessness." In its negative significance, dispassion may be linked with mor-

tification of vices and purification of life through obedience; in
its more positive aspect, it implies resurrection and restoration
of the will.[20] In the Christian (as compared to the Stoic) practice,
*apatheia* is neither aloofness nor insensitivity. Rather, it is freedom from misdirected passions and the suffering they cause. It
involves, as Abba Abraham says, not the elimination of the passions but their "control."[21] This discipline of control is required
not only of the disciple, but also of the elder who must practice
"non-attachment" (*apotage*) in the exercise of spiritual authority. Such *apatheia* has nothing to do with apathy, as this term is
commonly understood. On the contrary, it is the ultimate expression of empathy for others. The greatest gift on the part of
the elder to the spiritual directee is in fact the least imposition
on his/her will. Dispassion is the ground of compassion and is
closely linked with charity:

> One of the Fathers used to say: Eat a little without irregularity;
> if charity is joined to this, it leads the monk rapidly to the thresh-
> old of dispassion.[22]

*Apatheia*, then, in the Christian ascetical tradition, is not static
but dynamic and creative; it is associated not with a cold, hardened heart, but with a heart that is free, open, and burning with
divine energy and compassion. This gives dispassion an extend-
ing, impelling significance. For no longer is it seen as a
self-regarding condition. Rather, it is identified with love, constituting the other side of the same coin, inseparable and
"distinguished [from love] only in name."[23]

### d) A Remarkable Model

When it is said of Abba Agathon that he was "self-sufficient
in all things,"[24] this should be understood not only in terms of
manual labor and material needs but also and more significantly
as spiritual freedom. The director is encouraged to empower
and the disciple is encouraged to exercise his or her own judgment, to assert his or her proper self-will. A striking example of
this may be found in the life of Abba Poemen:

> A brother asked Abba Poemen: I am harming my soul through
> staying near my Abba. Should I still stay near him? And the old
> man said: Stay, if you want. So he went back and stayed there.
> He came again and said: I am losing my soul. Should I leave?

But the old man did not say: Leave. He came for a third time and said: I really cannot stay any longer. I am leaving. Abba Poemen said to him: See, now you have been healed. Go, and stay no longer.[25]

This is much more than simply a license to escape a harmful spiritual relationship. It is a limit placed on the director and safeguarding the spiritual boundaries of the disciple. Abba Poemen here seems to be struggling to exclude his own will, while expanding that of the disciple. He knows that healing is found not through *what is done by others to us*, but in the final analysis through *what is done by us in ourselves*. He helps the disciple to take responsibility for his own healing and to honor his own limits.[26]

### (iii) From Egypt to Palestine: Abba Isaiah of Scetis

#### (a) An Asceticism of Sensitivity

Drawing on a rich monastic tradition that defines regulations for those living in a religious community,[27] as well as from the basic evangelical precepts of charitable conduct (cf. Mt. 7: 12 and Lk. 6: 31), Abba Isaiah is careful to delineate clearly the boundaries of respect in regard to personal and interpersonal relations. The *Ascetic Discourses* open with a firm clarification, indeed a "commandment," that "condemning" – in word or in thought – or even "correcting others" is in general to be avoided (*A.D.* 1). This was the primary task of the Scetiote monks, as reported by Abba John the Dwarf:

Such was the work of the monks of Scetis: [not to judge, but] to give heart to those who were in conflict.[28]

Abba Isaiah agrees:

Without charity, the virtues are merely an illusion (*A.D.* 21).

It is significant, however, that Abba Isaiah should observe this at the very outset of his monastic treatise because such charity and sensitivity is also deeply connected to the virtue of renunciation, which is the first step in the ladder[29] of ascetic spirituality:

Above all else, renunciation is the first ascetic struggle.

Sensitivity in brotherly relations is part and parcel of monastic detachment, the radical surrender of all sense of individual possession. For, the ultimate aim of giving up is learning to give; to give freely of one's own and one's self. The desert ascetic in Egypt – so Isaiah would have recalled from his own sojourn there – was called to let go of all material, verbal, and spiritual control:

Our fathers of old said that the flight is one from one's own body (*A.D.* 26).

"Letting go of oneself before God," "letting go of other people," and "letting be of things in general" are phrases often repeated in Isaiah's ascetic writings (cf. esp. *A.D.* 4). Such is "the power of renunciation" that is discovered in "the power of the cell" (*A.D.* 4). Without complete surrender, the act of worldly renunciation proves worthless and "vain" (*A.D.* 26).

*(b) The Power of Will*

Letting go of one's individual will and right, especially when one believes these to be according to God, is a great matter for a person (*A.D.* 8).

Yet the purpose of "surrendering the will of the passions" is "submission to the will of God" (*A.D.* 16). And the struggle is intense, precisely because the will is hardened:

Every person is either bound to hell or loosed therefrom through personal will. For there is nothing harder than the human will, whether it is directed toward death or else toward life (*A.D.* 18).

Repentance is a "blessed regeneration from above in the will of God, a bowing of the neck before the yoke of divine will" (*A.D.* 25). It is a "small breeze of refreshment" (*A.D.* 29), a "light ... that reveals to us how the [fallen] will is to be cut off, and how we are to be saved" (*A.D.* 21). Repentance is a personal choice between:

the way of life over the way of death ... of the glory of God over the bitterness of the enemy ... of the kingdom of heaven over the reality of hell ... of love over hatred ... of desire for God (*A.D.* 21).

And asceticism is not the denial of will, of life, or "of the will to live."[30] It is the liberation of passion, the redirection of desire, the transformation of power, and the transfiguration of choice. As such, it becomes the way of dependence and trust, the way toward confidence and concord.

This is why submission of the will is in fact a protest against, and not a prolongation of authoritarian structures. It is a contradiction, and not simply the continuation of institutional roles of power. At its depth, or height, there is nothing more contrary and shattering to the power of hierarchy than the vulnerability of submission. Obedience is subversion, not subservience. Or, as Abba Isaiah himself puts it:

The one who obeys is the great one (*A.D.* 3).

The most vulnerable, then, is the most powerful. And in the ascetic life, vulnerability is measured by manifestation of one's thoughts.

### (c) The Manifestation of Thoughts

Concealing one's inner life is a vice; manifesting the same "respectfully" and "confidently" (*A.D.* 16) is a virtue:

Do not hide your every thought and every sorrow and every desire, but proclaim them with respect and with freedom to your elder. And whatever you hear from him, strive to carry it out faithfully (*A.D.* 1).

Whether it is a question of "good thoughts or evil thoughts," the spiritual struggle is gravely jeopardized "when one is silent about one's thoughts" (*A.D.* 4).[31] John Climacus – some two centuries later – reports a striking anecdote about a monastery in Egypt where the person in charge of the refectory had the intriguing habit of carrying a small notebook, hanging from his belt, in which he used to jot down all the thoughts that came to him during the day, in order to show these to his superior.[32] In the spiritual life, anything "hidden" in darkness is in stark opposition to open confession and illumination (*A.D.* 5):

For even our enemy [i.e., the devil] is never silent (*A.D.* 21).

Renunciation, or manifestation, of evil thoughts is redemption thereof:

Being silent about, instead of confessing one's thoughts, signifies one's pursuit of worldly honor and shameful glory (*A.D.*
16).[33]

This is because Abba Isaiah identifies "confessing to one's fathers" (*A.D.* 16) with "confessing to one's heavenly Father" (*A.D.*
27), indeed with an "acquisition of an intimate relationship and
boldness or familiarity with God" (*A.D.* 27). Thoughts are our
wounds, which inhibit or prohibit us in our relationships with
others and with God. Disclosing our thoughts to a "physician"
is a step in the direction of trust and community. It is as much a
way of dealing with the past, as it is of directing our future.

*(d) The Notion of Obedience*

The evidence of "letting go of oneself" and of "surrendering
one's own" (*A.D.* 3) lies in the practice of obedience. Once again,
as in the manifestation of one's thoughts, the monastic is called
to obey the words of the elder, even when it comes to making
decisions on affairs that appear to be good:

> If some of the elders are speaking the word of God, ask your
> abba whether you should stay and listen, or else withdraw to
> your cell. And do whatever your elder tells you (*A.D.* 3).

Abba Isaiah is familiar with the ascetic tradition of Egypt,
where the desert fathers emphasized obedience to the utmost.
We have already seen how Abba Mark did not even complete
the letter "omega" when called away by his elder, Abba
Sylvanus;[34] this is a story which Isaiah may have either heard
or even experienced first hand in Scetis. In any case, Abba Anthony insisted upon sharing with one's elder every step that
one takes and every drop that one drinks.[35] Abba Isaiah trans-
lates this tradition to the region of Palestine with his own pithy
statements about obedience to one's elder:

> Neither add anything, nor take away anything [from whatever
> he tells you] (*A.D.* 3);[36]

> if your brother calls you, do not say: 'Wait a little, until I finish
> what I have started,' but obey at once (*A.D.* 5);

> we are to be obedient to our fathers in God *in everything* (*A.D.*
> 25; emphasis mine);

... even in the slightest details: whether it is a matter of speaking or doing something, of receiving or eating or drinking something, of sleeping, or indeed of anything at all. In order first to test whether something is according to God, you should confess the root cause of everything, and then do what must be done before God (*A.D.* 27).

The result of such radical obedience is not the ultimate expulsion but the spiritual expansion of one's personal conscience (*A.D.* 4). Rather than undermining the ascetic or the novice, obedience serves to underline personal integrity. For Abba Isaiah, as we have already noted: "the obedient person in fact becomes the great person" (*A.D.* 3); or in biblical terms: "the one who is humbled will be raised" (Mt. 23:12).

This is precisely why obedience resembles more an attitude of mind, than a discipline of life:

I should be obedient to my neighbor for the sake of God. ... And not just to my spiritual father who cares for me, but also *to any person*, even one who opposes me (*A.D.* 8).

Obedience transforms our entire life, consecrating every action and sanctifying every detail:

Attachment to material things disturbs both the mind and the heart. But obedience renews everything (*A.D.* 16).

### (e) The Role of the Spiritual Elder

Abba Isaiah adheres closely to the tradition of obedience to one's elder. His advice, as already indicated, is unwavering:

Do whatever he tells you. Neither add to it, nor subtract from it (*A.D.* 3).

And he recognizes that subjection to one's elder should be both confident and complete:

Bare all your thoughts to your elder with confidence (*A.D.* 4).

The elder is naturally someone "spiritually superior" (*A.D.* 4). A weak person can destroy one's own soul in presuming – or in prematurely assuming – the authority of spiritual direction (*A.D.* 5). The elder is also a "wise accomplice" (*A.D.* 8), who "remains with us" (*ibid.*) throughout the intensity of the ascetic struggle.

However, Abba Isaiah appears to be flexible in regard to the number of spiritual directors that one may consult. He understands well that the monastic life is not a life characterized by isolation, but rather one constituted by encounters. Thus, in *Discourse 9*, he refers to confiding in one's "fathers" (*sic*; note the plural), as well as "giving one's heart to the obedience of one's elders." This multiplicity of spiritual direction was practiced during the next century in the nearby monastery by the founder and abbot Seridos and by Dorotheus of Gaza, who enjoyed "dual fatherhood"[37] from the "great old man" Barsanuphius and "the other old man" John the Prophet. The aim is never "to be or to act alone" (cf. also *A.D.* 12), but always to act in consultation:

Always consult your elders (*A.D.* 16; cf. also 25).[38]

Sharing is not an exceptional, but in fact an essential aspect of the ascetic way. The monastic is always in the process of learning to share; the virtue of renunciation is experienced in the context of community. The goal is not so much dependence on others, as it is independence from self; and there can never be any rigid, any uniform way of achieving this purpose.

Abba Isaiah was perhaps one of the first monks to introduce into the monastic milieu of Palestine and Gaza a life-style that acquires prominence in the next generation with the peculiar practice of the popular "old men," Barsanuphius and John. From the seclusion of his cell, Barsanuphius directed a nearby monastery (formally, and nominally, supervised by Seridos). He may well have learned or liked this manner of spiritual direction from Isaiah and his own relationship to Peter (who may have acted as administrative superior in the nearby community). If this is the case, then with the most renowned disciple of Barsanuphius and John, Dorotheus of Gaza, and before these Isaiah and his own disciple Peter, we have four generations of an ascetic "pedigree," a monastic "succession" or evolution that begins in the Egyptian desert.

This context, then, of obedience to a spiritual elder is again, as Abba Isaiah understands it, of an ages-long tradition of spiritual continuity (cf. also *A.D.* 26). This context and tradition are able to protect the community from the inherent dangers of self-designated directors, from those who:

> want to have authority over others, who enjoy talking with ... and who enjoy teaching others, without themselves actually being questioned .... (*A.D.* 17).

Outside of this line of spiritual succession, the advice is to avoid teaching and counselling. Without the understanding that the power of authority is shared, or the assurance of an established tradition of spiritual direction, monastics knew that to function as a spiritual elder was but another temptation and illusion of self.

*(f) The Temptation to Counsel Others*

In *The Lord of the Rings*, one of J. R. Tolkien's immortal elves recognizes that:

> Elves seldom give unguarded advice. For advice is a dangerous gift, even from the wise to the wise, and all courses may run ill.

Abba Isaiah too warns against the temptation to counsel others:

> Again he said about teaching: 'There is a fear you can fall into that against which you teach. For so long as you submit to a weakness, you cannot teach others about it'... (*A.D.* 26).

We cannot teach or counsel others about a passion that continues to hold or control us (*A.D.* 26):

> For it is shameful to teach others, before one has been liberated from the passion about which one is teaching (*A.D.* 26. Cf. also 27).

Furthermore, Abba Isaiah is critical of any form of "self-reliance" or "self-righteousness." How can a person who is "holding onto one's own will ... either find rest or else see what is lacking" (*A.D.* 8)? There is a fundamental humility in the recognition that each of us must "repent for our own sins" (*ibid.*). The axiom – surely Isaiah would have recalled – of the Egyptian desert was that one should be a model and an example for others, not a teacher or legislator.[39] Indeed, the desert fathers

and mothers preferred to be taught, rather than to teach.[40] They
accepted the responsibility to direct the souls of others – in the
words of a later Byzantine text – "not by pursuing it, but by
being pursued themselves, spiritually."[41]

Conversely, if a disciple does not follow the advice of an elder, then the solution does not consist either in imposing one's
will or in insisting upon one's own way, but rather in desisting
and detaching oneself:

> So detach yourself, otherwise your own soul is in danger of
> dying (*ibid.*).[42]

This advice is again understood within the context of community and in light of Abba Isaiah's firm conviction that:

> all of us are in need of medical attention: someone feels pain in
> the eye, another in the hand; some require vaccinations, or other
> medical treatment (*ibid.*).

### (g) The Way of "Humi-limit-ation"

Abba Isaiah understands well the significance of self-disci-
pline and of setting boundaries. One of his favorite phrases is
"set boundaries for yourself" (*typoson seauton*: *A.D.* 4). This notion safeguards the ascetic from any excessive measures, which
are always described by Isaiah as demonic, or evil. For instance,
the monastic is encouraged to follow a disciplined, but delicate
fast:

> Allow the body whatever it needs to function properly, with-
> out forcing one to distraction (*A.D.* 4).

All of our actions should always be "measured" and moderate, never excessive (*A.D.* 4, 10, 17) or extreme. At all times, the
most striking feature and spiritual foundation of Isaiah's writing is "balance" (*A.D.* 4). Any excessive measure – even in the
treatment of his beloved topics, like the gift of tears – is attributed to the demonic, though Isaiah is mild also in his concept
of demons. Abba Isaiah clearly enjoyed a wide reputation for
discernment. He was moderate and modest, while at the same
time never mediocre in either his discipline or his doctrine. In
the fourth century, Egypt was the forging-ground and the test-
ing-place of all kinds of monastic life and all extremes of

monastic striving. Yet in the fifth century, it was the "royal way" that was transmitted to the middle East (to Palestine and Gaza) and the West (to Rome and Gaul). Much as Cassian did in "translating" Egyptian asceticism to the West, Isaiah introduced the same spiritual legacy to the Palestinian region.[43]

Limitation of oneself and moderation in one's discipline are connected with respect of the other; one is called neither to "betray oneself" (*ibid.*) nor to wound another, but to be "generous to one's body" (*ibid.*) and gentle toward others. Ascetic struggle ultimately implies an attitude of charity. This is precisely why Abba Isaiah treats the disciplines of diet and vigil as a prelude to his discussion about friendship. Abstinence is a way of *agape*; restraint is the other side of the coin known as respect.

If individual limits or measures are to be curtailed, it is in order that they may be tailored to a fullness according to the measure of Christ (cf. Eph. 4: 13). Curiously, however, for Abba Isaiah, this does not entail the maturity of adulthood, but the integrity of infancy. In the final analysis, one is called not to increase in spiritual complexity or appearance, but – paradoxically – to decrease in simplicity or nakedness. The aim of *ascesis* is "to come to the measure of a child," "to reach the measures of sacred infancy" (*A.D.* 25). This child-mindedness, or holy innocence, provides for Abba Isaiah the key to the heavenly kingdom (Mt. 18: 3) and holds the secret to his understanding of spiritual direction. The efficacy of spiritual direction depends more on the disciple's innocent trust than on the elder's spiritual maturity. Perhaps even the effectiveness of prayer and forgiveness – while deriving essentially from above – depend on the faith and obedience of the disciple, rather than on the power or charisma of the elder.

Ultimately, in the monastic community, discipline and discipling are interconnected; if we are to limit ourselves, it is in order to "liberate our conscience" (*A.D.* 4). Such is the meaning of obedience in spiritual direction, the privilege of submission to a spiritual elder – an ultimate self-dedication to God, in an act of giving away which alone attracts the fullness of life. To obey one's father in Christ is humbly to dwell on the margins of surrender, and there to discover the limitless space of freedom.

It is *a gift to be obedient*: the openness of the heart is a gift; the insight of an elder is a gift; the possibility of community is a gift. It is *a gift also to be free*. The paradox lies in the reality that the first gift generates the last: we grow in the spiritual way when we give in acts of sharing; we begin to live even as we are – "behold" – prepared to die (cf. 2 Cor. 6:9); and we attain genuine freedom only through total obedience and surrender:

> That which renders us free is abstinence. And what safeguards abstinence is bodily toil. Through all of this, Israel is finally liberated, and we are able to give thanks to God (*A.D.* 4).[44]

### (iv) The Palestinian Tradition

*a) The "two old men:" Barsanuphius and John*

The great age of Palestinian monasticism constitutes a link between the earlier Egyptian movements of the third and fourth centuries and the later Byzantine developments of the seventh and eighth centuries. Monastic life flourished in Palestine during the fifth and sixth centuries, coming to an end in 638 when Jerusalem fell to muslim Arabs and the centers of monasticism shifted to the West and to Asia Minor.

The two main regions of Palestinian monastic life were Judaea (from the Holy City of Jerusalem to the Dead Sea) and Gaza. It was in the latter region that, near the turn of the sixth century, a monk from Egypt named Barsanuphius settled to live a life of seclusion near a cenobium founded by a monk named Seridos. From his cell outside this monastery, Barsanuphius effectively directed the community's life through only Abba Seridos, the single person to whom he would open his door. Around the year 524-5, another hermit, named John – of whose background we know even less – assumed a similar life in a nearby cell. Barsanuphius, John, and Seridos all died around the middle of the sixth century, probably in 542-543.

Neither Barsanuphius nor John would see anyone in person; they preferred to advise people through letters dictated to their secretary, the Abbot Seridos. These letters were answers in response to questions addressed to them in writing. In this way they guided not only the nearby monastery with which they were associated but also numerous daily visitors from the surrounding area. Barsanuphius, known as "the great old man," is more *spiritual* in his responses; John, known simply as "the other old man," tends to offer more *practical* advice. Yet, they support each other's ministry, often advising people to: "go and ask the other old man."

Often contemporary scholars, indeed sometimes the primary sources themselves, tend to emphasize the more extraordinary qualities of the early desert dwellers. However, Barsanuphius and John are less spectacular. They are not eccentric miracle-workers,[45] but practical advisers. They are not extreme ascetics[46] or charismatic visionaries, offering instead simple teaching, encouragement, and hope to people in their struggle.[47]

Some 850 examples of this remarkable correspondence survive, a living testimony of people[48] inquiring at the time about diverse aspects of the spiritual and daily life. The questions addressed to the elders come from monks, ordained leaders, and lay people. They range in content from personal temptations to interpersonal relations, from spiritual issues of joy or depression to practical matters of property and employment, from social questions concerning Jews and pagans to superstitious themes such as magic, from theological and liturgical directions to questions dealing with talking in church or praying at bath.[49]

Barsanuphius and John have behind them two centuries of ascetic experience in the tradition of the desert fathers. Their spirituality is in the succession of the earlier inhabitants of Nitria, Scetis, and Kellia. Indeed in the wonderful expression of Lucian Regnault, the French translator of these as yet unedited letters:

> What the *Sayings of the Desert Fathers* let us glimpse only in the form of transitory flashes, is here played out before our very eyes like a film.[50]

### b) Direction and Submission: A course by correspondence

In their *Letters*, the two elders are very clear about the need for spiritual direction and for submission to a spiritual guide. We all need an adviser; no one can travel the journey alone. This legacy they bequeathed to their own disciple, Dorotheus of Gaza, who writes:

> Do you know someone who has fallen? Well, you can be cer-

tain that this person has trusted himself.[51]

Barsanuphius and John repeatedly stress the idea of non-attachment or renunciation, which occurs through the surrendering of one's will. To this end, we are advised to do very little without the counsel of a wise elder.[52] This they consider to be an absolute principle of salvation.[53]

The two "old men," however, take pains to underline the effort (*spoude*) required on the part of the spiritual directors.[54] The vocation of spiritual direction presupposes a life of continual prayer,[55] a temperament that is slow – indeed "foreign" – to anger,[56] as well as a nature that is both "gentle" and "generous:"

Not wounding one's neighbor, that is the way of Christ.[57]

One should not hasten to consider[58] – let alone to appoint – oneself an "abba." Barsanuphius writes almost lamentingly:

I do not wish to become either an elder or a teacher to anyone. For I have the Apostle who rebukes me: you, then, who teach others, will you not teach yourself? (Rom. 2:21)[59]

It is dangerous and tempting for the spiritual guide to overlook his or her own salvation by becoming distracted by the role of spiritual direction. Transferring concentration on one's personal struggle to apparent concern for others' weaknesses in the end proves self-destructive:

God knows, that if I ignore my own salvation, how will I find the strength to care for you?[60]

These two Palestinian epistolographers and professors of spirituality give great emphasis to the solidarity and mutuality involved in the relationship between elder and disciple. This *solidarity* is expressed in the respect[61] of the elder for the disciple, as well as in the elder's readiness to receive from the disciple:

The Lord has bound your soul to mine, saying, do not leave him. So it is not for me to teach you but to learn from you.[62]

The "oneness of soul" between teacher and pupil extends beyond this life to the next.[63] For the spiritual elder, there is a greater degree of *identity with* the disciple than there is *authority over* the disciple. Therefore, the emphasis is always on "consulting," and not on "compelling."[64] This insistence on not defining regulations for the spiritual life is a constant theme throughout the correspondence. A spiritual disciple should not be stuck on fixed rules; and a spiritual director must not be stuck on fixed roles. Barsanuphius continually appeals to the Gospel emphasis on free will (cf. Mt.16: 24; Mk. 8:34; Lk. 9:23):

> Never force a person's will, but simply sow in hope. For our Lord too did not compel but only evangelized; and whoever wanted to, heard.[65]

There is a profound respect for the free will, which cannot be restrained or constrained.[66] The elder stands beside the disciple as a soul-companion and, as we have already seen, merely accompanies the will:

> Do not conceive in your heart that I have given you a rule; it is not a rule but a friendly opinion.[67]

This opinion, however, is not mere external advice. The spiritual elder teaches primarily by personal example.[68] This is what accounts for the *authority of one's words.*

Barsanuphius believes that this form of obedience – as openness to divine grace and not simply conforming to human laws[69] – is the way of the saints whose accountability before God confirms their *authority from God*:

> The saints do not speak of themselves, but it is God who speaks in them as God wills – sometimes in a hidden, and at other times in an open manner.[70]

With his heart open for *communion with God in prayer* and for *communication with the disciple in care*, the spiritual elder does nothing less than accept full *responsibility* for the souls of others:

> Although you ask something beyond my strength, I shall show you the limits of love, that it is forced to move even beyond its limits. I admire you, and I assume responsibility for you, on this one condition, that you in turn bear the keeping of my words and commandments.[71]

Sometimes the elder will assume total responsibility,[72] while at other times the responsibility is partial.[73] On occasion the elder covers the disciple's sins from childhood and even from birth.[74] Always, the loving concern reaches far beyond death:

I will never abandon you, even in the Age to come.[75]

There is a sense in which the compassion involved in the spiritual relationship conquers not only the guilt of sin but the very power of death. This is why, as we have seen, the elder refuses even to enter heaven unless the disciple, too, is saved. The powerful words of Barsanuphius are worth citing once again:

Master, either take me into your Kingdom with my children, or else wipe me also off your book.[76]

This attitude of *vicarious transference* is legitimate inasmuch as it reveals an extraordinary ascendancy over individual human existence. It is rooted in a transcendent communion. The opening up that occurs between elder and disciple is the allowing of the divine Other into the whole of one's life. Reintegration presupposes reconciliation, and repentance requires relationship. It is this spiritual relationship – and not obedience to any outward rules or codes – that is unconditional and enduring. This is why the elder will in fact care for the disciple more than the disciple cares for oneself – quite simply, because God does![77]

### (v) Conclusion

If matters of general spiritual guidance form the central structure of these remarkable early documents, then one of their most critical and recurring themes is certainly that of spiritual fatherhood. The tradition of the spiritual father/mother is particularly important in Eastern monasticism which is less institutional and more personal than that of the West. Where in the West one is attached to a specific monastic order or community, in the East one seeks out an elder. Eastern Christians have always visited monasteries to encounter persons of profound prayer and spiritual experience, rather than to consult scholars and learned persons. Such is the chief social role of monasticism in the East.

Yet frequently, it is the privileges of spiritual direction and not its problems that are underlined among Eastern Christian authors. Throughout the centuries people have chosen to single out the advantages of such a spiritual relationship and to cover up the disadvantages. Therefore the idea of spiritual fatherhood has been somewhat idealized, and spiritual authority has been romanticized. We tend to ignore the fact that, according to the relentless truth of social relations in the ascetic tradition, "from our neighbor comes [not only] life, but also death."[78] This is a passionate conviction of the desert experience and expectation.

Obedience and submission are qualities which may be *soul-mending for the disciple*, but these very virtues of the disciple may become *soul-rending for the spiritual director*. The elder must at all times be aware of his or her limitations before God (whose divine will must be reflected), as well as of his or her boundaries in relation to the disciple (whose free will must at all times be respected).

This is why the Palestinian elders distinguish clearly between "command" and "opinion." The "other old man," John, writes:

> Simple advice according to God is one thing, and a command is another. A command has an inviolable bond; but advice is *counsel without compulsion*, showing a person the straight way in life.[79]

Authority and obedience are perceived by the Desert Fathers and Mothers in the light of a *continuity* in the tradition of spiritual direction, and in the context of *communion* between director and directee. Abba Isaiah of Scetis presents a spiritual dimension of authority identified with *conceding power* rather that with *controlling others*. Barsanuphius and John also stress the *correlation* between elder and disciple, as well as the importance of *consultation* instead of compulsion. In this respect, the Palestinian tradition is neither an innovation in desert spiritual literature nor a deviation from the way of the desert fathers and mothers. The sixth century teaching on this matter is very much a continuation of the fourth and fifth century desert practices. St. Barsanuphius sums up this profound tradition as follows:

> I have not bound you, brother; nor have I given you a command. I have simply offered you an opinion. Go then and *do as you will*.[80]

NOTES

[1] The basic study on spiritual fatherhood remains that by J. Hausherr, *Spiritual Direction in the Early Christian East* (Cistercian Studies: 1990; originally in French: Rome, 1955). See the introduction by K. Ware (pp. vii-xxxiii). See esp. ch. 8 on "the efficacy of spiritual direction" (pp. 243-266). The concept of spiritual guidance – from people and from books – as it developed prior to fourth-century Egyptian monasticism is the subject of an insightful work by Richard Valantasis, *Spiritual Guides of the Third Century: A Semiotic Study of the Guide-Disciple Relationship in Christianity, Neoplatonism, Hermetism, and Gnosticism* (Fortress Press: Minneapolis, 1991).

[2] Cf. Symeon the New Theologian, *The Practical Chapters* (Cistercian Publ: Kalamazoo, 1982) 33-34. One of the few works by contemporary Orthodox theologians that attempt to examine problems involved in spiritual direction is J. Allen's *Inner Way: Toward a Rebirth of Eastern Christian Spiritual Direction* (Brookline: Holy Cross Orthodox Press, 1999) esp. pp. 49-55. One of the only books that deals explicitly, though not exclusively, with the tensions in the spiritual relationship in the early sources of monastic life is G. Gould, *The Desert Fathers On Monastic Community* (Clarendon: 1993), esp. pp. 69-74. However, the book by Gould considers primarily the *abba's* endurance of "maltreatment" or a "bad relationship" (p.71). Other books will only briefly consider the possibility of "an immature director," as for instance the fine "manual" of spiritual direction by F.K.Nemeck and M. T.Coombs, *The Way of Spiritual Direction* (Wilmington: Liturgical Press, 1985) 165-6. A discussion of the "social" accountability or "political" consequences of holy men and women, with particular emphasis on the Syriac tradition, may be found in the study by S.A.Harvey, *Asceticism and Society in Crisis* (University of California Press: 1990) 94-107. Cf. Poemen 131 and Isidore 1. Indeed the stories related in the *Apophthegmata* generally encourage the experience of endurance as salvific in itself (p.72). Cf. John the Theban and Zacharias 4. References to the *Apophthegmata* are from B.Ward, *The Sayings of the Desert Fathers* (Mowbrays: 1975) and *The Wisdom of the Desert Fathers* (SLG Press: Oxford, 1975). The Greek Alphabetical Collection is found in *Patrologia Graeca* 65; the Latin Translation in *Patrologia Latina* 73; the Syriac version is available in E. Wallis Budge, *The Paradise of The Fathers*, 2 vols (London, 1907). In spite of one exceptional passage (which we shall quote later: see note 22), Gould is almost reluctant to admit "that strains or tensions do arise from only one side of the relationship" (p.73), or "that there will be times when it is impossible (despite the rewards that endurance brings) to endure a bad relationship" (p. 74).

[3] A complete English translation of the *Ascetic Discourses*, with intro-

duction, notes, bibliography, and indices has been prepared for publication by J. Chryssavgis and R. Penkett, and will appear in Cistercian Publications (Kalamazoo MI).

[4] K. Ware (Bishop of Diokleia), "The Spiritual Father in Orthodox Christianity," in *Cross Currents* 24, 1974, p. 296 [see also his *Inner Kingdom*, pp. 127-151]. B. Ward is aware of the difficulty in translating the mind of the desert fathers on the issue of spiritual direction; cf. *Wisdom*, p. xiii: "The Coptic monks were simple men, and their understanding of this relationship is difficult to recapture in a sophisticated society."

[5] Cf. *The World of the Desert Fathers* (SLG Press: Oxford, 1986) xi-xii. Exactly when the written tradition began is not certain, but a rudimentary *corpus* was already in circulation by the end of the fourth century: cf. Evagrius' collection in his *Praktikos* 91-100, in ed. A. & C. Guillaumont, in *Sources Chrétiennes* 171 (Paris, 1971) 692-710.

[6] Cf. P Rousseau, *Ascetics, Authority, and the Church in the Age of Jerome and Cassian* (OUP: 1978) 25. See his Part One, ch II on "Masters and Disciples" 19-32.

[7] *The Desert A City* (Mowbrays: 1966) 67-68. The tradition of spiritual direction is described in A. Hamilton, "Spiritual Direction in the *Apophthegmata*", in *Colloquium* XV, 2 (1983) 31-38.

[8] *Vita Pachomii (First Greek Life)* ed. F. Halkin, Brussels, 1932, p.48.

[9] Cf. Ex. 20; Deut. 4 and 5. See Gregory of Nyssa's doctrine of eternal progress in *The Life of Moses* PG 44:397-405.

[10] Cf. Antony 8, Agathon 5, John the Dwarf 34, and Syncletica 16: "We must direct our souls with discernment."

[11] Moses 2, Poemen 92, and 109. Cf. D. Burton-Christie, "The Call of the Desert: Purity of heart and power in early Christian monasticism," in *Pro Ecclesia* VII, 2 (1998) 216-234.

[12] Macarius 32.

[13] Title of a book by Tito Colliander (new ed. London & Oxford, 1983).

[14] *Saying* 1 . Cf. also Antony 36, Agathon 28, John the disciple of Paul 1, Mark 1, Poemen 103, Pambo 3: where obedience is classified as superior to fasting, poverty, and charity; Rufus 2: where obedience is exalted as "salvation of the faithful, mother of all the virtues, disclosure of the kingdom, food of all the saints, companion of the angels"; Sisoes 10, Saios 1, and Syncletica 16. See also *Wisdom*, pp. 45-47.

[15] Cf. John Climacus, *Ladder* Step 4, 4 PG 88:680A, Sisoes 3, Zacharias 3, and Hyperechios 8.

[16] *Virgins of God. The Making of Asceticism in Late Antiquity* (Clarendon Press : 1994, paperback 1996) 372-85.

[17] Mios 1. See also Poemen 65, Sisoes 45, and Psenthaisios 1.

[18] *Pachomian Koinonia* (Cistercian Publ: Michigan, 1980). See "The Bohairic Life" 28, 52. See also *Sayings*, Basil 1.

[19] Cf. J.Aumann, *Spiritual Theology* (Christian Classics : Westminster MD, 1987) 391-393.

[20] Cf. *Ladder*, Step 15, 4(881A) and 65 (873CD), as well as 29, 1-4 (1148).

[21] Abraham 1. Abba Theophilus underlines the eschatological prospect of dispassion understood as the opposite of disquiet: cf. *Saying* 4.

[22] Evagrius 6. Cf. Alan Jones, *Exploring Spiritual Direction* (Harper and Row: San Francisco, 1982) 77-79. See also *Ladder* Step 30,4 (1156B).

[23] *Ladder*, Step 30,4(1156 B).

[24] Agathon 10 (Read in context of preceding and consequent words).

[25] Quoted in Gould, *op.cit.*, pp. 73-74. The text is from the collection edited by J.C. Guy, *Recherches sur la tradition grecque de Apophthegmata Patrum (Subsidia Hagiographica* 36: Brussels, 1962; repr. 1984) 29-30.

[26] Poemen 174.

[27] Cf. Pachomius, *Canons* 8 and 9 PG 40: 948; John Cassian, in PL 28: 860; and Palladius, *Lausiac History* 7 PG 34: 1019. References to the *Ascetic Discourses* of Abba Isaiah are cited in parentheses *(A.D.)*.

[28] Ward, *Sayings*, John Colobos 18 PG 65: 209-212 [p. 76-77].

[29] Cf. John Climacus, *Ladder of Divine Ascent*, Step 1 PG 88: 632-644. Step 3 (664-672) also precedes Step 4 "on obedience," which is the longest step in the *Ladder* (677-728). Abba Isaiah feels that "we must learn to love our renunciation (*xeniteia*)" *(A.D.* 25). On renunciation, cf. E. Clarke, *Reading Renunciation: Asceticism and Scripture in Early Christianity* (Princeton University Press: 1999).

[30] See P. Van Ness, "Asceticism in Philosophical and Cultural-Critical Perspective," in ed. V. Wimbush and R. Valantasis, *Asceticism* (Oxford University Press: 1995) 590.

[31] Cf. Ward, *Sayings*, Poemen 101 PG 65: 345 [p. 152].

[32] See his *Ladder*, Step 4 PG 88: 701.

[33] This silence is not the silence of prayer and humility (cf. *A.D.* 27).

[34] Ward, *Sayings*, Mark (disciple of Abba Sylvanus) 1 PG 65: 273-296 [p. 123].

[35] See Ward, *Sayings*, Anthony 38 PG 65: 88 [p. 7].

[36] Cf. also Barsanuphius, *Letter* 305.

[37] The phrase belongs to L. Regnault in his introduction to *Maitres Spirituels au Désert de Gaza: Barsanuphe, Jean et Dorothée* (Solesmes: 1967). A translation in English of the correspondence by Barsanuphius and John is currently being prepared for Cistercian Publications by John Chryssavgis and Robert Penkett.

[38] Cf. also Symeon the New Theologian, who encourages his monks to disclose their thoughts to a brother whom they trust in the monastery, even if this is not the Abbot. See ed. I Hausherr and G. Horn, *Un grand mystique byzantin. La Vie de S. Syméon le Nouveau Théologien par Nicétas Stéthatos*, in *Orientalia Christiana* 12 (Rome, 1928) xlix-xlxx.

[39] Ward, *Sayings*, Poemen 174 PG 65: 364 [pp. 160-161].

[40] See *Vitae Patrum* V, 81 PL 73: 967. Also Ward, *Sayings*, Sisoes 16 PG 65: 397 [p. 181], and Macarius 2 PG 65: 260 [p. 106].

[41] John the Deacon, *Life of St. Joseph the Hymnographer* 7 PG 105: 945.

[42] Cf. Ward, *Sayings*, Theodore of Pherme 20 PG 65: 192 [p. 65].

[43] Cf. C. Stewart, *Cassian the Monk* (Oxford University Press: 1998).

[44] Cf. also *A.D.* 27 and 17, where a connection is also made with "dispassion."

[45] There are nonetheless certain miracles attributed to their power: see *Letters* 1, 43, 47, 124, 171, 227, 510, 581, and 781.

[46] Yet they do also lead a rigorous and disciplined life as recluses: see *Letters* 72, 73, 78, and 97.

[47] Although there are instances of clairvoyance: see *Letters* 1, 27, 31, 54, 163, 777, and 800. For an example of mystic experience, cf. *Letter* 110.

[48] Certainly of men, since there is no evidence of correspondence from women.

[49] The letters are in Greek, though Barsanuphius himself was certainly a Copt. For the letters of Barsanuphius and John, see the Greek text cited by S. Schoinas, *Biblos Barsanuphiou* (Volos, 1960), originally edited by St Nikodemus of the Holy Mountain (Venice, 1816); the incomplete English translation by D.J. Chitty, *Barsanuphius and John: Questions and Answers*, in *Patrologia Orientalis* 31 (Paris, 1966); and the French translation and introduction by L. Regnault, *Barsanuphe et Jean de Gaza: Correspondance* (Abbaye de Solesmes: 1972). References in this chapter are to the Schoinas/Volos edition, which is not identical to Regnault's. A brief yet insightful account of the life and letters of Barsanphius and John may also be found in D. Chitty, *The Desert A City* (Mowbrays: 1966, esp. pp.132-142), where Chitty informs us that he was "engaged on a critical edition" (p.133) of the questions and answers, a project sadly cut short by his own death in 1971 .

[50] Quoted in P. Brown, *The Body and Society: Men, Women and Sexual Renunciation in Early Christianity* (Faber and Faber: 1990) 233.

[51] *Teaching* 5, 6 PG 88: 1680B. Indeed, the context within which Barsanuphius and John lived included many layers of spiritual direction: the two "old men" guided the monks of the nearby monastery at Thawatha; the monastery, however, had its own Abbot in the person of Seridos whom the spiritual "dyad" had appointed; and even one of the more renowned members of this monastic community, Dorotheus, was assigned by Abba Seridos spiritual charge over the monk Dositheus, whose *Life* Dorotheus composed. See ed. L.Regnault, in *Sources Chrétiennes*, vol. 92 (Paris,1963) 122-45.

[52] Cf. *Letters* 162, 344, 356, 551, 558, 583, 694, 703.

[53] Cf. *Letters* 144, 242, 243, 614. See also *Letters* 192, 209, 227, 262, 263.

[54] Cf. *Letters* 109, and 206.

[55]*Letters* 17, 80, 109, 129, 208, 216, 235, 255, 353, 365, 645.

[56]*Letter* 23.

[57]*Letter* 26.

[58]*Letter* 570.

[59]*Letter* 162.

[60]*Letter* 77.

[61]*Letter* 208. Cf also *Letters* 1, 119, 121. In his article, "A Form of Charismatic Authority," in *Eastern Churches Review* VI, 1 (1974) 52-65, F. Neyt refers to a balance or mutuality in the spiritual relationship between elder and disciple, particularly as this experienced by Dorotheus in his contact with Barsanuphius and John, with Abba Seridos, and with the other monks. Neyt underlines the need for obedience or for the "opening of the heart" on the part of Dorotheus, *even as an elder himself.* Nonetheless, Neyt still yields to the temptation of idealizing spiritual authority: "We should not speak of a 'blind obedience': the person who lets himself be guided by a man with charismatic clarity of vision does not think of himself as blind" (p. 56). This perception, however, must form the perspective behind the command of Abba John to Dorotheus of Gaza: "You must obey in all things, even if it seems to involve sin" (see *Letter* 288, quoted by Neyt, p. 56).

[62]*Letter* 164.

[63]*Letter* 5, and 305.

[64]*Letter* 187. The subject of spiritual direction in relation to "forcing" another person's will is admirably developed by S. Tugwell in one of a series of articles: cf. part V, in *Doctrine and Life* (Dublin,1983).

[65]*Letter* 35.

[66]*Letter* 51.

[67]*Letter* 160.

[68]*Letter* 344.

[69]Cf *Letter* 344.

[70]*Letter* 778.

[71]*Letter* 270.

[72]Cf *Letters* 48, 169, 231, 239, and 614.

[73]Cf *Letter* 168.

[74]Cf *Letters* 202, and 210.

[75]*Letter* 239. See also *Letter* 647.

[76]*Letter* 110. Cf also *Letters* 212, 217, 573, 645, and 790.

[77]Cf *Letter* 39.

[78] Antony 9.

[79]*Letter* 368.

[80]*Letter* 56. Italics are mine.

# VII

## Obedience and Authority

### dimensions of a hierarchical church

#### (i) Introduction

Authority in the Church is never the monopoly of an ordained few (cf. Eph. 4:11-12) – whether bishops or other clergy. Authority is the responsibility of all (cf. Eph. 5:34). Likewise, obedience is not the obligation of an "inferior" laity or lower clergy, but a requirement of all faithful, lay and ordained. In the history of Christianity, centuries of institutionalism and clericalism, followed by the "lay revolution," in conservative and anti-hierarchical churches alike, have rendered the concepts of authority and obedience problematic – a point of contention and almost disdain. Nevertheless, clergy and laity cannot exist without one another; spiritual elder and child must be existentially united. Together they constitute the living body of Christ; together they experience the mystery of Christ. Any distinction between them is merely functional and provisional, not essential. What is essential is the relationship of love and trust in Christ. Unity lived out *even* in diversity is precisely the promise of God to His Church. Any form or expression of authority, then, must not be the expression of human pride but of humility before God, of assimilation to the divine hierarchy, and of obedience to the will of Him who alone is called Father (cf. Mt. 23:9). Such obedience is of the very essence ("esse") – not simply the well-being ("bene esse") – of humanity. Hierarchy exists in order to reveal the priestly vocation (cf. 1 Pet. 2:9) and function of all within a world that is beautifully ordered by its Creator as *cosmos*.

#### (ii) The Way of the Ascetics

Obedience is good, but (only) if it is done for God's sake.[1]

In the ascetic tradition and spiritual formation of the Church, obedience is considered "the first of virtues."[2] For monastics, in particular, perfect obedience, understood as "the mortification of the will" (cf. Phil. 2:8),[3] is integral to all ascetic endeavor. Monastic life would indeed be unthinkable without the basic notion of obedience.[4]

Etymologically, the Greek word *"thelema"* (will) is probably derived from the words *"theein lian,"* which denote "a clear vision" on behalf of the person desirous of something; the word may, on the other hand, originate in the phrase *"theletou lemma,"* implying the possession of that which is desired.[5] Either way, it is never intended that the human will be broken or crushed, but only that it be educated and guided. As creatures of the Triune God, "we are children ... of will."[6] The faculty of free, rational choice is an essential attribute of humanity.[7] Ignatius of Antioch writes:

> Will, in order that you may be willed.[8]

In the patristic writings, the only one who is sometimes considered *not* to have a will is the devil.[9] The faculty of will is a prerequisite for salvation. This implies cooperation with the Divinity who voluntarily chooses to risk moving out, "erotically," in search of the lost human being, who in turn responds to this divine initiative with a mutual return of love and desire.

It has already been noted that the Fathers do not speak of obedience in terms of normative requirements. Obedience transcends mere submissiveness, with which it is commonly confused. The virtue of obedience occurs within the context of loving trust and personal relationship between two people in Christ, which *in itself* reveals the presence of Christ (cf. Mt. 18:20). Without this special relationship, one gains nothing from authority but pride, and nothing from obedience but guilt. Such feelings, however, defeat the very purpose of spiritual authority and hierarchy in the Church.

The Church of Christ is *hierarchical,* and this hierarchy "corresponds to an imitation of God," reflecting the order of life "even among the celestial beings."[10] Yet the Church is not solely hierarchical in its ministry and service: the Holy Spirit is poured out on *all* the people of God. Each faithful is considered king, priest, and prophet, while the gifts of the Spirit are many and varied (1 Cor. 12:28-30), understood as being neither restricted to the ordained ministry nor reduced to the level of obedience alone (cf. 1 Thess. 5:19-20). One recalls the influence in the Christian East of unordained, "lay" or monastic elders, which has often proved far greater than that of any hierarch. The sacramental authority of the hierarchy always exists alongside the spiritual authority of the saints. Both are required and presuppose each other. Ideally, the two work together, like two wings of a bird. They counterbalance and complement one another when needed. The hierarchical order and dimension of the Church cannot be correctly interpreted except in relation to the priestly and prophetic ministry entrusted to the entire people of God (1 Pet 2:9), clergy and laity.[11]

Authority in the Church is always identified with the vivifying breath of the Spirit. There must be synergy, not tyranny. The role of the holy people does not replace the responsibility of the bishops. The bishops are called to lead their people in taking up the cross of love and freedom in Christ. Orthodoxy has never attempted to resolve this seemingly paradoxical twofold dimension. It has never reduced the Christian faith to a few charismatics, nor has it relied upon the bishops alone. On the contrary, it is the communal aspect of the Church which is constantly affirmed.

That the laity must obey clergy is a commandment from the earliest Apostolic times. Ignatius of Antioch encourages the Trallians to be:

> submissive to the bishop as to Jesus Christ ... and also to the presbytery as to the Apostles ... and to respect the deacons ... for without these no Church is recognized.[12]

This of course implies no comfortable theology – in either theory or in practice. Clement of Alexandria states clearly that "will" is taught, not given. To be educated in the knowledge of God, the human will must go through several developmental, pedagogical stages.[13] Obedience is clearly addressed to the "genuine" and "rational" will.[14]

### (iii) The Primacy of Freedom

"The glorious liberty of the children of God" (Rom. 8:21) is a freedom attained through *ascesis*. Perhaps the most tremendous thing granted to the human person is choice. It is true that this freedom may prove self-destructive for some, yet it is essentially and fundamentally a privilege that only humanity possesses.

It is precisely this vital emphasis on freedom through obedience in the Church that this chapter endeavors to shed light upon. For there is at all times the danger of corporate expediency and utility, the risk of leaving unanswered the vital problems of human relations that determine the reality of life.

The *Concise Theological Dictionary* offers one definition of authority:

> [Authority is] the palpable, demonstrable trustworthiness or legal claim of a person ... capable of convincing another person of some truth or of the validity of a command and obliging him to accept it, even though that truth or valid character is not immediately evident. The acceptance of a command on authority is called obedience; the similarly motivated acceptance of a truth is called faith. Both are modes of *indirect* recognition based on the authority of an intermediary.[15]

In an age when movements for securing human rights appear to have achieved so much for the improvement of living conditions, and when the "gulag archipelago," the abuse of vulnerable children and adults, as well as the exploitation of the earth's resources have shocked the world; at a time when freedom of thought and expression is emphasized, and when imperialism and totalitarianism are at all levels questioned, if not rejected; authority should neither be blindly accepted nor unquestionably permitted to be objectivized or institutionalized, and its representatives or ministers in the various structures to assume shades of "infallibility." Everywhere we are witnessing a breakdown of structures of authority and paternity. The duty of Christians is to search painfully for:

> a new reality in the light of the revelation of the Trinity.... The contemporary revolt against the father is not basically a denial of fatherhood as such but a search for a Trinitarian fatherhood lived in loving respect for the other, in order that the life-giving Spirit may be communicated.[16]

The primacy of freedom is difficult to understand. It determines the very limits of the Church, being incarnate yet without end. There is a temptation to objectify this freedom, to make idols of institutional or even individual authority. The problem of freedom, therefore, is one of discerning and discriminating between personal liberty and limitation, between genuine and utilitarian authority. The most appropriate language for describing such freedom is that of selfless love: it is the active love that is at all times prepared:

to find a leper, and to give him one's own body and take his.[17]

Desire for the image of God revealed in the human person led Isaac the Syrian to write:

Do not reprove anyone for any transgression, but in all things consider yourself responsible and the cause of the sin. Avoid laying down the law, as you would flee from an untamed lion. Do not join in this with the children of the Church, nor with outsiders.[18]

It is an exhortation to personal identification with the other and not to moralistic condemnation of the sinner.

Orthodox faithful, then, should not seek "refuge" in the simplistic belief that supreme authority lies in the hands of a patriarch, or in ecumenical councils, or in certain local synods, or perhaps in the local bishop. Such notions are not entirely erroneous, but they are surely limited, threatening to objectify and institutionalize the Church. Synods and Bishops are sources of authority which operate primarily in cases of conflict and necessity, that is in abnormal situations such as the condemnation of heresy or the establishment of disciplinary order and pastoral care. Authority in the Church is in the final analysis undefinable, never limited to an order or council or to any one individual or group of individuals. Ecclesial authority is the experience of the mystery of God in Christ through the Spirit who guides the Church.

This reality is incarnate and exercised as a *mutual subordination* of love deriving from the sharing in common of the saving mysterious life of the Church. This is the all-transcending and binding authority, the dimension of the Church beyond any kind of structure and institution and organization.[19]

In the final analysis, the Church can never be identified with authority, since authority as a worldly structure is alien to her very nature.

### (iv) The Spirituality of Freedom

All too often authority is confused with power, meaning the ability to compel others to do something. What happened in the case of Adam and Eve, where the harmony of mutual relationship was destroyed, also extended to the people of Israel, where the harmony of a people uniquely guided by the will of God degenerated into disobedience and unfaithfulness. By analogy, what frquently occurs in male-female relations may further occur in the Church, where obedience is turned into subjection and domination. Yet to be obedient (Greek: *yp-akouo*) is not to be subjected to the will of another who is more powerful; it is to wait upon God, *to listen* (Greek: *akouo*) *and to hear*, to be all ears; ultimately to obey is to love.

*Listening*, therefore, is a crucial virtue for those endowed and entrusted by others with authority. Often one will help others most not so much by what one says and advises, as by one's peaceful, silent presence and attentive listening. Yet the art of listening is not as easily achieved as one might at first suppose, and it is – according to the spirituality of the ascetic fathers – as infrequently to be found as the practice of pure prayer. Spiritual authority is often characterized by a plethora of words which can unfortunately conceal the Word revealed in *hesychia*.

Within such a dimension of silent prayer and open love, the ultimate goal of all authority becomes the sharing in the vision and depth of God. God never compels persons, but only redresses evil. God speaks with authority, but never imposes His will – even upon those who would reject, condemn, betray, crucify, and kill Him. God does not desire slaves, but friends (cf. Jn. 15:14-15). The whole life and ministry of the Church should be based on the *person* of Christ, whose Body it constitutes in space and time. Throughout history, it is *persons*, the saints, who have manifested this attitude of Christ. They have exercised their responsibility for the other and in response to the needs of the other "with all their heart and with all their soul and with all their strength and with all their mind" (Lk. 10:27). Authority, therefore, means, above all, love towards one's neighbor "with one's whole power" (Mk. 12:30). It is not *control over* others, but *commitment to* them, even to "the least of one's brethren" (Mt. 25:45).

Unfortunately, power in the Church is frequently manipulated. The end – the need to teach or the desire to spiritualize – is frequently used to bless the means and justify surrender to worldly categories. People maneuver the souls of those entrusted to them – even rendering doctrine and spiritual teachings "suitable" for the occasion – so as to fit them into a particular mold of "spirituality." Perhaps one is free to choose an elder with an understanding attitude, but the structure is at times so overpowering that there is little room or strength left to distinguish between the healthy and the ailing.

In the spiritual life, "easy" children tend to become "easy" adults who cannot think or decide, who are passive. Yet we are called not to passivity but to active love, to vision and *praxis*. Unfortunately, the hierarchy are not expected to respect the laity as they should, preferring instead to revere their own ecclesiastical elders. Still less are they able to make use of criticism from below. They are often so established that they cannot "step down" – these might perhaps be the negative implications of the notions of "indelibility" and "perpetuity" of ordination. Tradition is crucial, but always within its communal aspect of trust in and love of the other. The wrongful exercise of authority conceals many dangers, not least of which is that God Himself gets overlooked and ignored, relegated to the "third heaven," from where He cannot reach humanity except through a barrage of layers and levels, all of them so human. The ultimate abuse of pastoral concern is its transformation into spiritual coercion.

Admittedly, people sometimes feel secure in obeying and setting up idols of "our fathers." Here, no distinction is made between contemporary and classical elders, though people are unable to accept without reservation the weaknesses of current Church leaders. Which weaknesses, for instance, of Fathers in the past are readily expounded or easily accepted? And yet, as we have already noted in earlier chapters about the value of brokenness in ministry, these very weaknesses should be part and parcel of the dynamic legacy and living tradition of the Fathers. What defects in the character, morality, doctrine, or speculation of Church hierarchs are emphasized as positive and creative traits? And when a contemporary bishop sins, he loses all credibility; whereas, if a saint is described as erring, the misunderstanding is immediately justified. It is a formidable task to accept, respect and venerate – as God does – the fullness of humanity. We rely upon the "infallibility" of what stems "from above," instead of seeking knowledge of God through obedience to a pastor (cf. Jn. 10:14-15). So the aim of the Christian life is seen in terms of receiving, seldom in terms of maturing through questioning. Is it right, however, that authority in the Church overpowers and stifles every other aspect?

### (v) Conclusion

In briefly analyzing the concept of authority in Church life and spirituality, there has been no intention to question the significance of genuine authority for the integral life and theology of the Christian Church. The sacramental structure of sacred orders is unreservedly accepted and respected as the source of ecclesial authenticity and identity, finding its original and foremost expression in the priesthood of the "one mediator between God and humanity, the man Christ Jesus" (1 Tim. 2:5).

There is, furthermore, no intimation of "revolution" or "liberation" within the Church. A freedom which is asserted in reaction to "fallen" authority is a "fallen" freedom, a pseudo-freedom. There is no real freedom outside the Church.[20]

The aim of this chapter has been to bring to the fore certain fundamental deficiencies in the understanding of the notions of authority and obedience, especially in the practical life of the various institutions and structures. Solutions to such crucial issues should be sought in the God-established origins of the ministries, as well as in light of the ways those ministries have been exercised in history. A critical study of past and present structures can only lead to a clearer vision of what the Church is. Existing institutions are not to be abolished, but they must become less imperious, less patronizing, and more fruitful in service and ministry.

In contemporary western societies, people demand equality, rights of all kinds, freedom from domination and injustice. Without unquestioningly embracing these, the Church should be challenged by them. It is perhaps possible to review the established structures in their practical aspects. Above all, it is necessary to restore a healthy theological balance in the existing hierarchical and spiritual relations by encouraging greater co-operation, communication, and communion. Surely the dimension of *"koinonia"* is central to the Church. Ecclesiastical authority must be seen in terms of service and not rule; in relation to *"diakonia"* and dialogue, not domination. In order, however, for this to occur, the faithful must be regarded as gifted people of God, and not manipulated as objects or "sheep" to be taken for granted. The vision of endless personal freedom in the Holy Spirit (cf. Jn. 3:34) must be the measure of all relationships in the Church, the source of authority and obedience alike. In this manner, the whole dialectic of authority and freedom may be transformed into truth, life, beauty, and joy. In the words of that luminous saint of the nineteenth century, Seraphim of Sarov:

> When the Spirit of God descends and overshadows one with the fullness of His outpouring, then the human soul overflows with unspeakable joy, because the Spirit of God turns to joy all that He touches.[21]

The Church, then, must be the reality where the dualism of authority and freedom is ever transcended through *"obedience unto death"* (Phil. 2:8) and in love *toward one another.* If the issue of authority and obedience is to be examined creatively, we must, first of all, clarify our understanding about how we, as Church, can become a more loving and serving community. Obedience is a mystery revealed by the Holy Spirit and experienced as sacrament in the life of the Church.

Present realities and structures will continue to exist. Yet we must learn to *be more open,* allowing the Spirit to be more active in them. In the course of His ministry, Christ was asked on several occasions by what authority He acted. In fact He never explicitly answered this question. Rather, He responded by the way He lived, that is by the authority of love incarnate. Authority outside this Christ-like love is an arbitrary tyranny. Authority lived in the laying down of life for one's neighbor (cf. Jn. 10:11), on the other hand, is creative and life-giving.

NOTES

[1] *Sayings of the Fathers 19* (PL 73: 851-1024), quoted in O. Chadwick, ed., *Western Asceticism (Library of Christian Classics* XII: SCM 1958) 155.

110 SOUL MENDING

2 Cf. Diadochus, *Century* 41.

3 Cf. Basil, *Ascetic Sermon 11*, 2 PG 31:884B; Antiochus, *Homily 39* PG 89:1556A and John Climacus, *Ladder* 4 PG 88:680 and 717.

4 Cf. article by Archim. Sophrony, in A. Philippou, ed., *The Orthodox Ethos* (Oxford: Holywell Press, 1964) 270f.

5 See Athanasius, *Definitions* 2 PG 28:281 and Anastasius the Sinaite, *Director* 2 PG 89:61.

6 Clement of Alexandria, *Stromateis* III, 7 PG 8:1161. Cf. also Maximus the Confessor, *Anbigua* PG 91: 1085; Athanasius, *Against Arians* III, 64 PG 26: 457 and Gregory of Nyssa, *Against Eunomius* VIII, 2 PG 45: 781.

7 See Anastasius the Sinaite, *Director* 2 PG 89:64D and Maximus the Confessor, *Opuscula* PG 91:153A. See also Clement of Alexandria, *Fragment* 40 PG 9:752A.

8 *Romans* VIII, 1. For a balanced understanding of self-surrender and obedience from a Christian perspective, cf. M. McIntosh, *Christology from Within: Spirituality and the Incarnation in Hans Urs von Balthasar* (University of Notre Dame Press, 1996) 59-87.

9 See Heracleon, in PG 14:628C.

10 Dionysius the Areopagite, *The Celestial Hierarchy* III.

11 Cf. Metropolitan John (Zizioulas) of Pergamon, *Being as Communion. Studies in Personhood and the Church* (St. Vladimir's Seminary Press: New York, 1985) 214-225.

12 Cf. *Epistle to the Trallians* II and III. See also *Epistle to the Ephesians* XX, 2; *Ep. to the Magnesians* II; *Didache IV:* 11 and *Letter of Polycarp V, 3.*

13 *Stromateis* VII, 11 PG 9:485.

14 Cf. John Climacus, *Ladder* IV PG 88: 729B and *Scholion 4* in *Ladder* IV: 732D.

15 Ed. K. Rahner and H. Vorgrimler (Herder – Burns and Oates, 1965) 44.

16 From the article "Purification by Atheism" by O. Clément, in *Orthodoxy and the Death of God*, ed. A.M. Allchin (1971) 33-4.

17 Cf. Abba Agathon, *Apophthegmata* PG 65:116.

18 Quoted in C. Yannaras, *The Freedom of Morality* (Crestwood, N.Y: St. Vladimir's Press, 1984) 272. Prof. Yannaras describes morality not as obedience to external rules but as fulfilling one's personal nature, that is, as becoming what one truly is. The theme of his book is precisely the adventure of freedom (cf. 2 Cor 3:17).

19 N. Nissiotis, *Interpreting Orthodoxy* (Light and Life, n.d.) 29-30. See also A. Khomiakov in A. Schmemann, ed., *Ultimate Questions; Anthology of Modern Russian Religious Thought* (N.Y.:Holt, Rinehart and Winston, 1965) 50f.

20 Cf. A. Schmemann, *Church World Mission* (Crestwood, N.Y: St. Vladimir's Press: 1979) 184f.

21 Quoted in ed. G. Fedotov, *A Treasury of Russian Spirituality* (N.Y.: Harper Torchbooks, 1965) 275.

# VIII

# The Misuse of Spiritual Authority

## facing clergy misconduct

### (i) Introduction

In earlier chapters, we have explored the phenomenon of the abuse of personal freedom in the process of spiritual direction. In this chapter, we shall consider the misuse of spiritual authority within the institutional structures of the Church. In social and spiritual relations, just as in family structures, the misuse of authority is not always readily acknowledged. Unfortunately the same phenomenon of denial is also encountered in the Church.

As a field of study or research, at least in bibliography pertaining to Orthodox theory and practice, the issue of spiritual abuse has not been discussed at length. Details and statistics are minimal, and are not always available, possibly because one always runs the risk of appearing irreverent toward sacred institutions such as the parish, the priesthood, or monasticism. After all, it is normally the "critics" of the Church who are expected to sensationalize scandals or stigmatize ecclesiastical institutions. Therefore, up until the 1980s there exists no study or writing from an Orthodox perspective – at least to my knowledge – on this subject. The silence rather resembles the way in which problems of incest or child abuse have been handled within families and societies till recently: we know that they exist, but we do not want their existence to be known. From our appreciation of the available information, it is clear that we are not simply dealing here with "immoral conduct" or "perverted desires," but primarily and predominantly with the abuse of spiritual authority and responsibility. Any form of abuse – whether physical or emotional – is in its depth and in its essence a spiritual problem. The Church needs to break the code of silence, of embarrassment and of shame that surrounds this

111

issue. It is called to be ahead of and not behind secular institutions that care for those who have been hurt. The moral responsibility of spiritual fathers or elders does not essentially differ from the responsibility of other healing professions in society, irrespective of how inappropriate or insufficient it is to define a spiritual bond or the priesthood as a "profession." All other caring professions – such as teaching, psychology, psychiatry, medicine, social welfare, and various forms of counseling and therapy – have specific moral regulations which clearly define the *boundaries of the profession*. The purpose of the pages that follow is to offer a humble introduction to and an honest exposure of the problem, together with a description of the role that each of us has in the body of the Church.

Every group, nation, civilization, and family has its own *common points of acceptance* and its own *common points of denial*. There are certain aspects or details that are projected, if not polished and promoted; and there are others that are concealed, if not avoided. In the same way, there are certain social and personal "secrets" in the Church which are not betrayed without particular consequences. In fact, one of the secret rules that apply in groups is that no one may question the validity of the rules. Such conspiracy of silence is itself evidence of guilt. That the Church, furthermore, is suffering today, more than in the past, from ruthless criticism from without – as well as from within – is a metaphor and an opportunity that allows us to consider a deeper reality and meaning. It is this reality and this meaning that we ignore whenever we concentrate our attention solely on the "progress" or "promotion" of the Church without allowing or encouraging constructive and healthy criticism. We must at some point begin to disabuse ourselves of our denial in order to assume the responsibility for our failures within the institution of the Church. This is the only way through which we shall procure any profound change. It is unfortunate that, while as Christians and as clergy or theologians we have acquired some experience in identifying and confronting the evil that exists within society, we have not yet learned to understand and appreciate the evil that exists within the Church. And if we do not expressly name the evil, then we surely cannot hope to overcome it.

My purpose is not to blame. The warning given to us by our

Lord still remains inspiring, almost terrifying:

> let the one who is without sin among you, cast the first stone (Jn. 8:7).

Nevertheless, another scriptural verse states that "Rachel wept over her children, but she could not be consoled" (Mt. 2:18). These words are equally obliging in calling us not simply to avoid condemning, but in fact to comfort those who have been wounded. The silence must some day be broken. The lines that follow are dedicated to the "Rachel" that I have known, the Rachel who was abused in a cruel fashion by those to whom "Rachel" once entrusted herself. It is also dedicated to every other Rachel, known or unknown, for the purpose of sincere consolation.

## (ii) Priesthood and the Healing Profession – the Byzantine Heritage

A brief historical outline of the Byzantine heritage of the priestly ministry will be useful at this point in order to make today's reality more explicit. Specifically, it is helpful to explore the nature of the relationship in the Byzantine period between the spiritual authority of the clergy and the professional training in healing as practiced in other, secular professions. What were the boundaries and the criteria for priestly care by comparison with medical care?

The Byzantine Church was not an independent organization in itself – however autocephalous it may have been by standards of ecclesiastical jurisdiction. However, in Byzantium, the Church had a more general relationship and closer contact with the other areas of the Byzantine society.[1] Likewise, all governmental authority depended on the consensus of the people, without the moral claims of the people on a ruler bearing any necessarily metaphysical quality.[2] In other words, in Byzantium, we meet an "agreement" or "cooperation" (Justinian, *Institute* IV) between the earthly kingdom and the heavenly hierarchy which serves successfully to limit both sides. This argument defines the expression and extent of the Monarchy and the Patriarchate alike, while at the same time regulating both Society and Church. It is only after the destruction of Constantinople in 1204 and the ensuing collapse of the Empire that the boundaries of Church and State begin to become confused, and the former begins to lay claim to the privileges and rights of the latter. Earlier, and already from the 5th century AD, the Empire's legislation under Valentinian III offers clear directives to the clergy who were involved with affairs outside the realm of their priesthood – and this mainly implied and included business matters. Such legislation makes it clear that such clergy were subject to civil courts and not protected by any special privileges or "benefits of clergy." It appears that for much of the history of Byzantium, there were many examples of clergymen who held worldly professions, especially in the *legal* and the *medical* domains.

In Byzantium, medicine and religion were closely associated, just as physical and spiritual health are dependent upon one another. On this matter, the Byzantines agreed with the ancient Hellenes, as well as also being in harmony with the Hebrew tradition, which holds that the human person is a psycho-somatic being. In this way, then, Basil the Great had established, since the 4th century, the foundations for a theology of medicine [i.e., the healing profession], and the ancient Church recognized many and adept physician-priests who treated both the soul and the body. Impressive hospitals and philanthropic institutions appeared with the initiative and foresight of such leaders as St. Basil himself (in Cappadocia), St. John Chrysostom (in Constantinople), St. Andrew of Crete (in Greece) and St. John the Merciful (in Alexandria).[3]

Furthermore, of the ten most renowned for their healing, Unmercenary Saints of the Church, seven had received specialized training in the medical arts, and had practiced as physicians. Even Patriarchs, such as from the ecclesiastical throne of Alexandria, served as doctors. Only after the twelfth century, when the practice of medicine by those in religious orders became officially illegal in the Church, did the phenomenon of physician-priests begin gradually to desist. Until that time, however, specific legislation (civil) and prevailing customs (in monasteries) wisely regulated numerous details pertaining to the responsibility of doctors and other workers within ecclesiastical-social institutions.

Whether or not healing or wholeness is meant to be psychosomatic in no way implies a license for the spiritual guide to move or enter freely from one domain to the other. On the contrary, the additional accountability of the one toward the other is further underlined. Monastics-clergymen with the responsibility for the spiritual supervision and treatment of the afflicted were endowed with specific professional knowledge, even while functioning under the specialized administration of ecclesiastical authorities. This was not only because of the above-mentioned *cooperation* between Church and State, but also because of the clear and certain professional *correspondence* between the various vocational spheres such as medicine, pharmacy, and even psychiatry. Consequently, it is no exaggeration to claim that in the area of medical knowledge in particular, as in the whole area of healing in general, the East indisputably surpassed the West during the Byzantine period.

The Byzantine Church was extremely careful in regard to its responsibility toward society. It never adopted those roads that strayed far from its people, but rather sought always to express the social conscience of its people.[4] The holistic healing practiced by the Church of the Fathers aspired to integrate the pastoral responsibilities of the Church without segregating it from the professional requirements of society. The idea was to relate – not to alienate – the spiritual obligation of the clergyman with the everyday criteria and regulations of human behavior. The integrity of the human person is always diagnosed and preserved within an integrated spiritual formation, as well as with the participation of the other healing professions.

### (iii) On Selecting and Honoring Church Leaders

The Church is the body and bride of the divine-human Christ. In Christ's kingdom of love, everyone reigns because all are one in Him. The Church, as the symbol and advent of God's kingdom upon the earth, must be a place where equality and love prevail. Its paradigm is the Holy Trinity. The harmonious relationship that exists within the Godhead, among the Father and the Son and the Spirit, is to be reflected and enacted in the life of the Church on earth. There are distinctions among the three divine, hypostatic persons, in that, from the Father who is without beginning, the Son is begotten and the Spirit proceeds. Yet, all three together constitute the one God.

On account of the incarnation, life, death and resurrection of Jesus Christ, humanity has the potential to be incorporated into the life of God. Through the eucharist of Christ's resurrected body and blood, we are nourished for eternal life. No one in the Church is ultimately subject to imperfect human authority; all are subject to Christ who is the head of the Church. He is Lord. He calls Himself the true vine and His Father the vinedresser. He asks us to abide in Him and allow Him to abide in us by loving one another, that we may bear much fruit and bring glory to the Father (Jn. 15:1-17).

Orthodox piety rightly holds the ordained servant-leaders of Christ's Church in high esteem and in frequent prayerful commemoration. The task of pastoral service in the name of Jesus Christ is of such import and the responsibility so great that gratitude and respect is surely due to all who devote themselves to this sacred work. The gift of honor on the part of the faithful toward their leaders becomes all the more fitting when a deacon, presbyter or bishop reciprocates the commitment, proving himself to be a genuine instrument of God's peace and love in the lives of the faithful.

Sometimes, however, the formalities of appreciation can distance bishops and their representative presbyters and deacons from the people whom they are called to love and serve. It can feel as if they have been set high atop a pillar where they are kept out of the way, inaccessible and irrelevant to the faithful as they go about their daily lives. If pampered or overindulged, some leaders may come to regard themselves as entitled to special privileges and superior treatment. Such an attitude of entitlement, of course, contradicts the spirit of loving communion and humble service taught by Christ.

Unfortunately, our traditional teaching and piety places clergymen so high up on a pedestal, that either they are consequently rendered inaccessible and irrelevant for most people, or else they exercise tremendous authority over them. The result is that the clergyman is often respected by the pious faithful as being something super-human, as "equal to the angels," to quote St. John Chrysostom.[5] Yet it is extremely dangerous for a clergyman to regard *himself* as anything else or more than merely human. The power of a clergyman is extensive, inasmuch as it concerns the way in which people relate to

God, as well as revealing people's vulnerability. If the priest-hood constitutes an image of Christ's priestly nature and High-priestly ministry, nevertheless every priest must at all times be fully conscious of his limitations – both personal and interpersonal, physical and spiritual. The same Chrysostom explicitly rejects any form of "angelism" in the priestly minis-try.[6]

It is sometimes falsely assumed that those who are designated as confessors or spiritual fathers and mothers have already been fully healed and perfected. Would that this were the case! Did not our Lord say "first remove the plank from your own eye, and then you will see clearly to remove the speck from your brother's eye" (Mt. 7:5)?

Accordingly, some would like to see the three levels of priest-hood – diaconate, presbyterate and episcopate – correspond with the three levels of spiritual development – purification, illumination and glorification.[7] It would certainly be ideal if all candidates for ordained ministry first achieved the respective stage of spiritual development prior to their ordination. This, however, seems difficult to implement in the present context. How would these spiritual stages be assessed and measured? Would there be enough qualified candidates to meet the pasto-ral needs of the Church today?

While a candidate for ordination ought to have experienced a certain degree of spiritual catharsis, this does not mean that such a person has been fully cleansed, once and for all. The "fallen nature" of the human being is under constant attack, in every person, until the last breath (cf. 1 Cor. 9:27). Spiritual develop-ment is an ongoing, lifelong process, which must begin well before ordination but should continue after one assumes pasto-ral responsibilities up to the final moment of one's earthly life.

Clearly, the more holy we become, the greater service we will be able to give to God, the Church and the world. We become holy precisely through holy communion with God and humble connection with creation. It is in this sense that we should un-derstand the call to purification, illumination and glorification as a prerequisite to ordained ministry. The canonical require-ments regarding ordination ought also to be seen in this light, as should the practice of selecting confessors from among the brotherhood of presbyters.

In places where "the harvest is plenty but the laborers are few," selectivity unfortunately might sometimes be compromised. The work of the Church must be done. On the other hand, in order for our work to be the "work of the Church" it must bring glory to the Holy Trinity. The self-assurance and ease with which service in the name of Jesus and responsibility for the care of souls is frequently assumed suggests a certain lack of awareness of this.

All of us suffer from passions and weaknesses, to a greater or lesser extent. Like all people, deacons, presbyters, bishops and abbots are sinners in need of healing. When people whose inner wounds are unhealed assume authority over others, there is a greater risk that their spiritual ailment will afflict others and perhaps be passed on like a virus. It is also possible that they will attract people with similar wounds. Therefore, careful screening of potential leaders is very important. The Church should always seek the most spiritually mature, psychologically fit, talented and humble people available for such positions. Every effort should be taken to select the best candidates for ordination and to prepare them – and help them to prepare, themselves and others – educationally, psychologically and, above all, spiritually. Only when a certain standard is achieved should the "axios!" of ordination be pronounced.

Regardless, however, of how rigorous and careful the selection process is for electing, ordaining and appointing hierarchs, pastors, abbots, abbesses, confessors, spiritual elders, pastoral counselors and other ecclesial ministers, even the best are imperfect and have need of improvement. "There is none righteous, no, not one," quotes the Apostle (Rom. 3:10). All human beings are subject to temptation and must struggle with a fallen human nature. Only one is perfect; one alone is holy (cf. 1 Pet. 1:16).

Of course, without a doctor, no one can be cured. Everyone has need of some spiritual healer. This is the unequivocal teaching of the Saints of the Church, as we have seen in previous chapters. However something which is seldom remembered is that bishops, priests, and confessors too have the *same* need for continual therapy. Certainly no one claims to be perfect. Yet there remains the covert assumption that those who are designated as spiritual fathers or elders have somehow *already been healed*.

The ongoing purification is in accordance with the direction of St. Gregory the Theologian:

> Become clean before seeking to cleanse; become wise and thus teach wisdom; become light and so shine; having touched God, reach out to others; become holy in order thus to sanctify.[8]

We are all imperfect beings who are, none the less, called to glorification through God's grace and our willing cooperation. Everyone has need of another who can mediate God's healing love. Everyone deserves to have their own spiritual guide and confessor. This applies not only to lay people but also to patriarchs, bishops, priests, deacons, abbots, abbesses, confessors and spiritual elders. Church leaders are fellow-travelers with all the faithful on the way to holiness. This is a communal journey. None of us are saved or perfected alone. We all need the prayers, love, support and companionship of others who will encourage and affirm what is good in us while challenging us in areas where improvement is needed. This is all part of belonging to the body of Christ.

### (iv) Institutionalized Sin and Institutionalized Grace

In the Church, the misuse of authority may deprive us of communion, but it should never permit us to ignore compassion. The abuse of power should be clearly named and openly acknowledged as a reality in the Church's life. Sin is indeed the reality of life, though it is not its truth. So often we prefer to undermine the presence of sin in the human experience of the Church and to underline the priority of grace. "Institutionalized sin" is rarely confessed, while "institutionalized grace" is triumphantly proclaimed. Yet this constitutes an abuse of sin and grace alike. For, beyond any personal and cosmic dimension, both sin and grace have a corporate dimension. Just as we refer to wrongdoing and injustice in society, in economy, and in ecology, we must remember that sin or abuse may also be found in, and even caused by institutions that are traditionally identified with grace.

The apparent contrast lies not in the distinction between institution and inspiration, between law and grace in themselves, but in the discrepancy between "divine grace" and "sinful institution," between the charismatic element of the Church and the sinful expression of institutional authority. We have observed how the Church operates on two levels, which are complementary, together preserving the integrity of the Gospel: the hierarchical and the spiritual, the outward and the inner, the administrative and the prophetic. Between these two aspects, there need be no juxtaposition or contradistinction. Rather, the problem lies in the use – ultimately, the abuse – of the dimension of grace by the outward structures that surrender to sin and inflict suffering upon others.

Perhaps one reason for the misuse of institutional authority is the sharp line of demarcation drawn by Church leaders – often with such precision and apparent conviction – between grace and sin. The former is supposedly possessed, and even controlled, by the Church, while the latter characterizes the rest of the secular world. Yet, as we have seen in previous chapters, neither should grace (which is divine) be too sharply distinguished from human nature (which is all too sinful), nor should sin be too harshly identified with darkness, since it provides the challenge for our purification and the source of our illumination. Those who misuse or manipulate power, claiming authoritatively to control divine grace, present us with a profile of spiritual abuse: in their life, obedience and submission are on the one hand equated with communion of grace; on the other hand, disobedience is threatened with ex-communication, identified with "falling from grace."

Unlike physical and environmental abuse that leaves bruises on the body and on the body of the earth, spiritual abuse leaves permanent scars on people's souls and on the body of the Church. This occurs when grace becomes something *determined for you*, rather than something *discerned by you*. And it also occurs when sin becomes something for which you are disciplined, rather than something which you discipline and subsequently direct toward healing.

I am not suggesting that people in authority tend to distort the reality of sin and grace. Power, however, has a way of blinding the conscience. The result is that those who misuse spiritual authority deny having any control over others. They sincerely believe that they are acting in the name of some "ordaining" grace. Yet the call to grace always remains a call to caring and sharing. Responsibility and respect form an integral part of love and humility that alone prevent the abuse of grace and power by those in positions of authority. How paradoxical it is that, in many places, the Church has developed and fostered a mode of leadership that is essentially opposed to compassion and communion. In any healthy organism, sin and misuse of authority should become the stimuli for self-examination and self-transformation. In an unhealthy organism, self-criticism regarding sinful conduct simply cannot be tolerated.

The issue here is the unfortunate reduction of God's limitless grace to the institutional limits of the Church. The problem is the identification of divine grace with human representatives – whether one or many – of the Church. Ministers often feel that grace acts "mechanically," that "their way" is the "right way." Or else they think of the Church in terms of a "wizard of oz" model, wherein grace acts "magically."

The refusal to admit sin – primarily in ourselves, but also in our institutions – is itself the loss of grace. It is the conscious awareness of sin that opens up to divine grace. Otherwise, sin is established from generation to generation; sin becomes institutionalized. Openness to grace, however, is readiness to grieve for the institutionalization of grace. Institutions, too, like institutional leaders, must recover a sense of vulnerability and sensitivity. Institutions must weep for the hardening of heart (cf. Heb. 3:8) in their structures as well as in their leaders.

### (v) Pastor Idealization or "Transference"

The Church must avoid "idealizing" and "idolizing" its leaders. It is a mistake to turn our leaders into gods and worship them. We have but one Lord, a reality that the entire Church confesses each Sunday prior to holy communion. When idealization happens, ministers are subtly and unfairly set apart and, in this sense, excluded from the community. Invariably, such idealization is dehumanizing. It does not give the pastor or hierarch the opportunity to learn from his mistakes because he is not, in fact, permitted to make them. He is expected to be "perfect." Since none of us is perfect, some may feel the need to hide their weaknesses and pretend "for the people's sake" to be more virtuous than they actually are. In this way, hypocrisy sets in while inner wounds fester. It is important that we see our priests and bishops as whole persons, with strengths and weaknesses, as sinners and saints just like us.

In her illuminating book on clergy sexual misconduct, Candace R. Benyei discusses the phenomenon of pastor idealization using the psychological concepts "transference" and "counter-transference:"

> When a ... congregant ... comes to the clergyperson for help, he or she already perceives the pastor, by nature of the clerical position, to be kind, sympathetic, caring, affirming, long-suffering, strong, and godlike. This benevolent picture is called transference and may or may not be characteristic of the counselor in question. The clergy-person, as recipient of this rosy projection, feels competent, affirmed, and valued whether or not he or she is indeed capable of performing usefully as a counselor in an objective sense. This is called countertransference. Because caring and valuing are two of the most sexually arousing activities that can happen between people, this sort of transference/countertransference quickly develops into what is called transference love – the warm, gooey, filled-up, no-longer-lonely, safe, embraced, exhilarating, sexually powerful feeling that our culture has co-opted us into believing is true love...[T]he sheer force of the sexual attraction that arises from transference love cannot be emphasized enough... Transference/countertransference love is the stuff of all infatuations and all experiences of 'falling in love,' which are more accurately the wishful desire to possess the fanciful 'good object'... Real love [on the contrary] can only occur in a real relationship that has been, most often painfully, stripped of illusion so that we see one another face-to-face and not through a glass, darkly... It is very easy for emotionally starved, overworked clergypersons to fall into the trap of believing that these powerful feelings of transference/countertransference love are signals, finally, of the love that they have never had – true love to which they now abandon themselves with little thought of the consequences.[9]

Pastor idealization ("transference") should be recognized for what it is. The kindness, compliance, vulnerability and adoration of congregants and spiritual children must never be taken advantage of or manipulated by a spiritual leader to gratify one's own needs for power, love or adoration. In this light, I would venture to define the concept of abuse of authority as the *given difference* between two people which lends to the imposition of the will of one over that of another, whether physically, emotionally, or spiritually.

### (vi) Responsibilities of Church Leaders

The mystery of the priesthood has always been regarded in the past, by Christians both in the East and the West, as the supreme form of loving service.[10] The calling of spiritual leaders is to encourage, strengthen and affirm all that is beautiful, true, and good in human nature (cf. Phil. 4:8). A primary goal of the pastoral relationship is the undoing of sin and the restoration of life (cf. Jn. 10:10). On account of such transformative relationships, the world may discover in the Church the healing and spiritual equilibrium for which it yearns. In this way, the Church fulfills its mission to "preach the good news to the poor, to heal the spiritually troubled, to proclaim freedom to the captives, and to forgive the brokenhearted" (cf. Lk. 4:18-19).

Aware of their talents and abilities as gifts of God, those who take on the duties of pastoral ministry must remain ever conscious of their weaknesses and limitations, particularly of their personal, interpersonal and spiritual weaknesses and temptations. These they must be vigilant to address. Ministers of the Church have the responsibility to act always and only in a manner which is appropriate for the healing and spiritual progress of the persons whom they are called to serve. Any action which is contrary to this principle will have as an unavoidable consequence the wounding of others, perhaps also causing them to feel unworthy of the love and forgiveness of God whom the pastor is called to represent.

Recognition of the moral responsibility involved in ministry led St. Isidore of Pelusium to write the following in one of his remarkable letters on spiritual authority:

> the task is difficult, not easy; it is a responsible ministry, not an unaccountable authority; it requires supervision, to the detail of a medical science, not tyrannical control; it calls for sensitive care, not unrestrained power.[11]

"Unless you are converted and become as little children," says our Lord, "you will by no means enter the kingdom of heaven" (Mt. 18:3). This applies not simply to the faithful lay people but to every member of the Church. Church leaders must not let their position lead them to feel superior. St. Ignatius the God-bearer and Bishop of Antioch writes:

> Let no one boast in pride over his position, because faith and love are everything, and are to be preferred above all.[12]

### (vii) Power Dynamics in Pastoral Ministry and Spiritual Mentoring

Christian mentoring and discipleship has nothing to do with subjugation. All people bear the image of God. All are of equal and incalculable worth. All members of the Church have received the Holy Spirit and been ordained through chrismation into the royal priesthood of Christ. All deserve honor and respect. As St. John Chrysostom points out, it is a delusion for an ordained person to regard himself as superior to others. One is ordained to serve. For a genuine spiritual father, this means the "sacrifice of his own life for another" (Jn. 10:11), "even as Christ Himself loved" (Jn. 13:34). This – and this alone – is the "authority" of the truly Christ-like spiritual father (cf. Jn. 10:18). St. John Chrysostom describes the consequences of clergy who misuse their authority, and even claims that he would prefer anarchy to such sinful authority.[13] Contemporary reality can assist us in redefining and refining more specifically and more carefully the concept of spiritual direction and submission. It also guides us in discerning genuine from counterfeit spiritual authority.[14]

It sometimes happens that spiritual mentors require of their disciples near total obedience to themselves. The absence of humility on the part of such elders leads them to grasp for control over others. While imposing their authority, they may attempt to justify their un-Christlike behavior on the premise of a "spirituality" of the cross. A dysfunctional relationship is thus "rationalized" as they become "crucifiers." They may argue that the "self-will" of a spiritual child must be broken so that he or she may acquire the virtue of humility by which he or she may progress spiritually. In reply, one may ask how, in such an arrangement, is the self-will of the spiritual director checked and his or her humility preserved? The Patristic tradition equates this kind of "violation" with the sin of adultery, which occurs when a spiritual father imposes obedience in the form of orders which serve to appease his own desires. In the words of St. Mark the Ascetic:

one who gives orders so as to secretly fulfill his own will is an adulterer![15]

Such misuse of spiritual authority is more than adultery; it is a form of spiritual "autism," whereby everyone and everything are regarded in terms of how useful they are to the spiritual director. Such an elder, however, can never honestly express or experience the words of the Lord's Prayer: "*thy will be done*, as it is in heaven so also on earth."

A "one-way street" in spiritual relationships is never healthy. On the other hand, a certain commitment to the spiritual work on the part of both the spiritual guide and the disciple is necessary for the relationship to achieve its aim. That aim, however, is a fully liberated spirit, a purified heart and a will to love; the aim is never a broken will. The Apostle Paul teaches that a parent must avoid "exasperating his [or her] children, that they may not despair" (Col. 3.21).

If one does not possess a vital and strong will, it is quite likely that one will end up disrespecting oneself, for it is precisely by our will that we learn to love others and ourselves in the proper way. We do need to chasten the fallen will, which keeps us from genuinely loving our neighbor (cf. Jn. 10:11), and from receiving the love of God (of. Mt. 16:24). Yet this is a voluntary effort aimed at the restoration of the will. If one "cuts off" one's will, one ceases genuinely and fully to live the present moment. We simply cannot fulfill the will of God without a robust, healthy will. A person's will should not become weaker, but stronger through love, "growing from strength to strength" (Ps. 83:7).

Authentic self-denial in the Christian sense (cf. Mt. 16:24), does not consist of the betrayal or abandonment of our selves, but in a dynamic, internal transfiguration of conscience which is at the center of who we are and of what we do. The will must not be effaced, but spiritually transfigured so that it may be expressed in the best possible way. Through spiritual discipleship, we learn gradually to walk with Christ and to live with the intensity and love for which we were created and destined.

### (viii) The Privilege of Pastoral Care

Pastors and religious leaders frequently find themselves in intimate meetings with other people. In many of these meetings, the other has turned to the minister for spiritual comfort and companionship in a time of heightened vulnerability.[16] The pastor, as "father," has been chosen from among the faithful and ordained as the intercessor through whom the love and grace of God are to be mediated and manifested. The pastor's relationships with people in vulnerable moments ought to be guided by a spirit of love, sensitivity, and personal disinterest that has the well-being of the other as its foundation. Sometimes the desire for one's own personal or spiritual relationship or nourishment will be set aside for the sake of a greater love, the nurture of the other person.

In the case of confession, a person consciously and deliberately humbles oneself and voluntarily exposes weaknesses and failures in the hope of receiving human compassion, divine forgiveness and spiritual healing. It is the pastor's privilege and duty humbly and lovingly to receive people at such vulnerable and potentially transformative moments. In so doing, he bears witness to the oneness of humanity and to the great mercy of God for all creation. Imploring divine forgiveness and mercy for the repentant sinner as if for his own self, he knows that these are the people "for whom Christ died." He knows that he is no less weak, neither less of a sinner nor less prone to evil, than those who kneel in his presence before God. Inwardly, he, too, kneels before the crucified Lord. There is much joy in heaven when a sinner repents, and the confessor is among the first on earth to feel this joy.

### (ix) On Respecting Personal Boundaries

Entrusted with the confidence and confession of others, pastors must be vigilant to avoid hurting or violating others in any way. Any intentional crossing of personal boundaries, any form of mistreatment, exploitation or manipulative use or abuse is intolerable, irrespective of the presence or degree of provocation. Ministers must be held to the highest standard in this regard – whether in word, silence, presence, and touch.

Sexual contact is not part of the pastoral role. Sexual contact by pastors with parishioners undermines the pastoral relationship and violates the trust necessary in that relationship. The crossing of this boundary changes the nature of the relationship. The potential harm this causes is enormous and the consequences can be devastating.

This does not mean that all physical touch is forbidden in the pastoral relationship, although it calls for great sensitivity. Nonsexual touch may well be appropriate and therapeutic in certain circumstances. Of the twenty-five miracles of healing by Christ which are recounted in the New Testament, fourteen occurred through direct physical contact while four others may have involved touch. In many of our icons, Christ is pictured affectionately touching the cheek of His Mother. Touch may facilitate communication, express compassion, convey worth, provide nurture, dissipate anxiety, diminish isolation, and offer strength.

Pastors must recognize, however, that people have different perceptions about the meaning of touch. In general, Western cultures seem more inclined to interpret touch in sexual terms than do Mediterranean, southern European, African and Latin American cultures. Additionally, a person's "prior experience with touch will affect how current touch is perceived," write Mic Hunter and Jim Struve in their book *The Ethical Use of Touch in Psychotherapy*.[17] Touching is more likely to have a positive outcome when it occurs in relationships where the boundaries are clear and when it is not experienced as a demand or need on the part of the pastor. And at the same time, touch may be ambiguous, confusing, even threatening to those who are vulnerable. It can, furthermore, be used as a means of control, harassment, or abuse. The use of touch in pastoral relationships needs to be guided by prudent discernment that has the deepest well-being of the other as its basis.

### (x) Gender Dynamics in the Church

Although we have come to appreciate and recognize a great deal in terms of gender issues and politics, as well as in regard to the inequality of power between men and women, we can only hope to bring about any balance if we confront reality with honesty and boldness. Gender prejudice is evident in every level and ever facet of life, and especially in the very foundation of many organizations, groups or communities. Every day and every where – in the workplace, at home, in the street, in the Church, and even in our consciences – women are found to be exposed to numerous forms of gender-related abuse and violence. The examples publicized are not exceptions, but only the tip of the iceberg. Without a doubt, the abuse of spiritual authority and relationships described above is also the product of a male-centered mindset, in accordance with which male-dominance and female-submission are imposed as models.

Some would argue that instances of oppression, which occur within the Church are attributable to its hierarchical and "patriarchal" structure. If "patriarchy," as the word is frequently used by contemporary feminist theorists, implies *a system* of sexual and economic oppression and exploitation of women, enforced through their sexualization and subordination as well as through violence, and interlocked with the oppression of people of color, the poor, gays and lesbians, and other marginalized and underrepresented groups in society, then, at least in my opinion, the Orthodox Church does not qualify as a "patriarchal" system in that sense.

In fact, the Orthodox Church is both patriarchal and matriarchal. It is known and experienced as the holy mother Church, the body and bride of Christ. Orthodoxy honors, together with Christ, the Theotokos, the Mother of God, who figures prominently in Orthodox prayers and whose icon is prominently placed before the sanctuary on the iconostasis and in the apse behind the holy table of every Orthodox temple. A very high number of churches are dedicated to the Mother of God, as well as to women saints who are also honored and remembered for their holiness and spiritual strength. In Orthodox churches throughout the world and throughout history, the presence and contribution of women has been strongly felt.[18]

In Orthodox theology, God is not interpreted as an oppressive or abusive father who forces himself upon his children and demands from them obedience and love. We confess, not a "male" divinity, but a relational Trinity of divine persons – the Father (which means, literally, "source"), the Son who is Christ, and the Holy Spirit who is "everywhere present and filling all things." Orthodox theology and worship have always emphasized the mercy and love of God. Likewise, the Orthodox spiritual path calls for the co-functioning of the mind and the heart, the purification of the passions, the development of the virtues, and the acquisition of the Holy Spirit.

That is the theory, indeed the theology. The practice, however, differs. The system is not to be confused with the ministers who constitute the institutional structures. Having nominally disputed the charge that the Orthodox Church is a merely "masculine" or "patriarchal" institution in the negative sense of these terms – and, therefore, oppressive and abusive – it must be acknowledged that there are, nevertheless, ample cases of authoritarian abuse of ecclesiastical power throughout the history of the Church up to the present day. Furthermore, the opportunities for women to assume positions of leadership within church structures are unacceptably limited for our times. While it is possible for a woman in the Church in North America to be elected president of a parish council and serve for one or more terms in office, this is but one form of ministry. In what ways may an Orthodox Christian woman who wishes to serve in the ministry of pastoral care do so? Aside from becoming a nun and abbess and spiritual mother, or a youth minister, or a hospital chaplain, or a pastoral counselor who works in private practice or for an agency, the options seem relatively few. When it comes to worship, how visible is the presence of women in roles of leadership? The question then becomes, to what extent do such imbalances convey a devaluation of or disregard for women as equal members of the body of Christ? Furthermore, to what extent do they contribute toward the sexual victimization of some women by some pastors? These are questions that require careful and critical attention.

### (xi) The Work of Purification

What invariably underlies the abuse of spiritual authority and the exploitation of others is a failure on the part of a pastor to confront his own sinfulness, that is, his "shadow" or "dark side." Such people seem to lack a willingness to acknowledge and deal with the sin in their lives. They choose not to face their sinfulness and their unconscious motivations, preferring to live in ignorance of themselves and of God while purporting to serve Him. Thus they become the hypocritical religious leaders of today, for whom the Lord predicted so many "woes" (cf. Mt. 23, Lk. 11). They sacrifice others in order to maintain intact the false image of their own perfection.

Sexuality, religion, business and politics are four realms of our personal and social life wherein we experience the most intense passions. In order to check one's sexual and aggressive impulses and sublimate them in creative, healthy ways, it is necessary to become aware of, acknowledge and monitor these impulses. An ancient practice among monastics which is designed to assist in this regard is the daily confession of thoughts (*logismoi*) to one's spiritual elder. Similarly, all Christians must find ways to hold themselves accountable not only for their actions but also for their thoughts which are the seeds of action. Ultimately, of course, we are accountable to God, to the most holy Mother of God, to the saints, to the angels, to the bishop, to the council of presbyters, to the faithful, to the wider society and, indeed, to the whole of creation.

We are called to share with one another the life-giving well of light which is Christ, not the dark wound which hides us from ourselves. When Christ is the common bond, the pastor, "even naked, will not be ashamed" (cf. Gen. 2:25). Conversely, if he hides his weakness now in order to seem "dressed up" in virtue, the day will come when he hears the voice of God and will be unable to hide (Gen. 3:9-10).

Ultimately, it is impossible to hide our weaknesses and sins. They are manifested and magnified in our relationships with others. St. John Chrysostom pointed this out long ago:

It is neither easy nor possible to conceal the deficiencies of clergymen, because even the slightest become quickly apparent. For it is just like an athlete who can avoid being noticed, even if he is the weakest among his colleagues, so long as he stays home and comes into contact with no one else; but when he participates in any races, he is immediately reproved.[19]

St. Isaac the Syrian, a perceptive observer and healer of the soul who lived in the seventh century, said that for one to travel the road of spiritual healing, one must be prepared to smell the four-day stench (that is, of Lazarus in the tomb) of one's spiritual reality. In other words, to become "pleasing to the Lord" (Eph. 5:10), one must be willing to endure the pain and death of humiliation. Only if one is determined courageously to face the unpleasant reality and truth of one's own life story, whatever this may entail – recalling frightened childhood years, an oppressive adolescence, a joyless marriage, corruption in one's line of work or in one's society, one's mortality, fears, faults and weaknesses – only then can one transcend the various forms of discouragement and the anxiety of failure. On the other hand, to avoid confrontation with one's "dark side" is to remain forever under its influence.

It is not without reason that our ancestors in the faith bothered to describe in detail the way of struggle against temptation, for the purification of the soul's passions. It is Christ's role to be victorious over the evil and the sin of the whole world, but it is our responsibility to uproot the evil from the field we know, and to leave behind a better world for the next generation. This is the whole point of the relationship between spiritual mentor and disciple – to cleanse, even to some small degree, the sin from the hearts *of both*, and thus contribute toward the transformation of the world. Thankfully, the mystery of godliness and goodness is infinitely greater than the reality of darkness and evil. Herein lies the light and hope of the whole world.

### (xii) The Offending Pastor

Sexual misconduct may be a matter of a single incident or a series of incidents of ongoing intimate relationship. With the repetition of a sin, a person's conscience becomes dulled. Instead of converting one's failings into an opportunity for humble repentance and personal redirection, the unrepentant sinner allows his heart to become hardened. Such a person may well continue exploiting and abusing others until he is forcibly stopped. The underlying psychological deficits which lie at the root of such conduct may be many and various: a history of victimization, a psychological illness, a deep sense of childhood neglect, a deep-seated feeling of inferiority, an inability or unwillingness to acknowledge and address one's inner conflicts, and so forth.[20] Often such people do not seem to see the pain in others, because their narcissism literally blinds them to it. The behavior of such people has already been denounced by the Prophets in the Old Testament:

> For from the least to the greatest of them, everyone is greedy for unjust gain; and from prophet to priest, everyone deals falsely. They have treated the wound of my people carelessly saying, 'Peace, peace,' when there is no peace. They acted shamefully, they committed abomination; yet they were not ashamed, they did not know how to blush. Therefore, they shall fall among those who fall; at the time that I punish them, they shall be overthrown, says the Lord. (Jer. 6:13-15)

Extremely narcissistic individuals see others as prey upon which to feed themselves. Again, how precisely the prophetic word describes this phenomenon:

> Prophesy against the shepherds of Israel... Have you been feeding yourselves? Should not shepherds feed the sheep? You drink the milk, you clothe yourselves with the wool, you slaughter the fatlings; but you do not feed the sheep. You have not strengthened the weak, you have not healed the sick, you have not bound up the injured, you have not brought back the strayed, you have not sought the lost, but with force and harshness you have ruled them. (Ez. 34:2-4)

Such "spiritual guides" are truly blind (cf. Mt. 23:16-26). If they were not, they would recognize their limitations and weaknesses and seek help. Instead, they like to dominate and control others. They want authority without responsibility. Their pride and haughtiness may become apparent when they preside over events and people. This kind of authority is eventually brought down by itself and destroyed by its own corruption.

When a clergyman abuses his authority and privileged position, and harms or exploits another, he ceases to be a "father" in the image of the true source of love and life.[21] Instead, he becomes a source of corruption and death, a spiritual child abuser, spreading suffering and pain upon the earth. Such a person must be swiftly confronted and stopped. St. Mark the Ascetic argues that even the use of fear [that is, of a coercive threat, or even collective psychotherapy] may be required when confronting such reckless people:

> The hard-hearted will not benefit by learning from a gentle word, because, except for the sake of fear, he will not endure to feel the pains of repentance.[22]

No matter where or to whom a fallen pastor turns for psychological and spiritual help – and he ought to seek the best psychotherapeutic treatment and spiritual direction he can find – he will ultimately need to seek healing from God who seeks not punishment but repentance and healing for sinners. Then, having finally understood his limitations he may discover "the divine grace [which] heals the weak and fulfills what is lacking."[23]

Indeed, the manner in which the Church reacts in cases of spiritual abuse or sexual misconduct, and especially the openness with which the Church relates to an offending clergyman and his family, reflects the degree of its readiness to handle such issues at all. It also indicates the seriousness which it attributes to the healing ministry in general. For, a Church that is unable to care for its carers is not really a Church. A Church that does not direct its pastoral ministry to its pastors has betrayed its own essence and calling. A Church that is unwilling to act in a healing fashion in the lives of those entrusted with the healing ministry may also be unfit to extend this ministry in any authentic or meaningful way to the rest of the faithful.

### (xiii) The Plight of Victims of Clergy Misconduct

As for those who have suffered on account of the wanton and irresponsible acts of a pastor or spiritual director, the Church must help them through the various stages of healing: shock, denial, bargaining, anger, acceptance of loss.

It is common for victims of pastoral sexual abuse to be scapegoated by some in the Church who find it unbelievable that their pastor could commit such acts. This may occur whether the perpetrator is a respected layperson, monk, nun, priest or bishop. "S/he got what s/he wanted," is a far too typical reaction to many victims.

No support, no one to take one's part or to trust one's word, public scorn and humiliation – these are among the risks a victim of pastoral abuse faces in reporting the truth. Not even within the community of the Church – which should act as a strong, supportive mother, as a refuge and protection for everyone who comes there for aid – can the victim be sure to find the tender concern and empowering advocacy that he or she needs and deserves. Many victims prefer to keep quiet. Too often, such people are left to endure their hell in isolation.

To complicate matters, a victim may not consider herself or himself to be a victim of clergy misconduct if, for example, he or she "cooperated" with the abuser. Nevertheless, the difference in position and authority distinguishes cases of abuse from cases of mutual consent between equals. Unless a person possesses the psychological independence and freedom required to say "yes" or "no," that person cannot be considered to have given full consent, even if he or she does not actively resist.

One of the most painful aspects of sexual abuse is the way in which it is so often silently and passively overlooked and tolerated. "Keep it secret" and "don't ask questions" seem to be the unwritten rules governing people's behavior with regard to this issue. Long habits of silence and avoidance of the topic have led to a widespread but unfortunately false perception that "these things do not happen in the Church." To pass through the curtain of silence and confess the evil requires courage, faith, as well as consciously and righteously channeled anger.

Let the Church hear the survivors of spiritual and sexual abuse. The Church must give survivors of sexual abuse the opportunity to tell their stories and have those stories acknowledged. The Church must be willing to walk with survivors in their suffering, even as Christ does.

Victim-survivors are often prematurely and platitudinously advised to "forgive and forget." Forgiveness, however, more appropriately comes after restitution has been made. It has been said that the less powerful cannot forgive the more powerful. Our Lord upon the cross, for example, does not forgive His crucifiers; He asks His Father to forgive them. Forgiveness of a more powerful person only becomes an option if the more powerful person relinquishes his or her power, such as by payment of restitution, by relinquishing office and status in acknowledgment of the reality of abuse which occurred, and by assuming responsibility for it. These acts of repentance empower the victim-survivor and can make for justice, thus enabling the possibility of forgiveness. Confession and penitence on the part of the offender, therefore, must precede forgiveness and reconciliation.

### (xiv) The Church's Task: Intervention and Prevention

The moral responsibility of pastors and spiritual leaders is certainly no less than that of other leaders in society, particularly since ministry is not simply a profession but also a vocation. Most professions – including medicine, education, law, social work, psychology – have articulated precise codes of ethics which clearly define the duties and boundaries of appropriate behavior. It also seems advisable for the Church to articulate in precise and specific terms the obligations and limitations of its representative ministers and employees. It should be clearly stated, for example, that sexual contact between Church leaders and congregants is unethical and unacceptable.

Certainly, a thorough investigation must be undertaken to

verify or disprove every serious claim of clergy sexual misconduct, some of which may prove invalid. If so, the Church must take action to restore the pastor's credibility. If, however, serious misconduct is proven, permanent removal from pastoral leadership seems the only proper response. The Church must intervene swiftly on behalf of victims, offering protection, restitution, aid and support. Therapy should be offered, as well, to the offending minister, who has devastated his own spiritual health not to mention that of others, as well as possibly destroyed his own family and disturbed that of others.

In order to help prevent clergy misconduct and the abuse of spiritual authority, the following principles are offered for consideration by pastors and spiritual leaders:

- to be involved at all times in a committed relationship of accountability to a spiritual mentor
- to be more sensitive and attentive to the psycho-spiritual and power dynamics which characterize pastor-parishioner and spiritual director-directee relationships
- to avoid situations in which one is likely to feel sexually vulnerable
- to understand one's own sexual identity and vocation
- to seek to open up and expand the horizons of the personal will of others, realizing that the purpose of pastoral ministry is not to control but to collaborate, not to rule but to support and empower
- to learn to experience and express one's own feelings
- to respect and affirm the special dignity and sacred worth of every person
- to decide not to seek love and adoration from those whom one is called to serve and lead along the path of freedom in Christ
- to consider oneself as equal with every other person, and not above them or beneath them
- to take care of oneself physically and emotionally, and take measures to prevent one's level of stress from exceeding a tolerable level
- to nurture and maintain a close, intimate sexual relationship with one's spouse (in the case of married clergy) or a close, healthy, even monastic relationship with one's spiritual father (in the case of celibate clergy)
- to understand the spiritual, psychological, ecclesial, familial, financial and legal consequences of sexual misconduct

- to learn from the social sciences of psychology, sociology, and anthropology, each of which has its limitations but also much that is useful for pastoral ministry.

### (xv) A Mission for the Church

> But you are a chosen race, a royal priesthood, a holy nation, God's own people, in order that you may proclaim the mighty acts of Him who called you out of darkness and into His marvelous light (1 Pet. 2:9).

God calls the Church to a leadership role in the spiritual education and transformation of society. In order to exorcise evil from our world, we must come face to face with the lie, and with the devil, as the "father of lies." If one can expose the lie, first of all in oneself, then the healing sphere of exorcism will naturally expand.

Every relationship – whether in a family, parish, monastic community, organization, institution or nation – remains deficient until each participant assumes full responsibility for one's own actions, as well as for those of the group as a whole. Until this sense of universal responsibility is shared by all, it is unlikely that the evil which is perpetrated collectively by a group will cease. One tragic result of collective evil – in addition to the suffering inflicted directly upon its victims – is a pervasive emotional and spiritual numbing throughout a society.

Priesthood – much like the professions of medicine, law, and psychiatry – has for centuries insisted in the oversight and regulation of its ordained members in matters of morality and ethics. I would not in any way dispute the right of the Church to judge and regulate its internal affairs. I am, however, convinced that there is a need to awaken the conscience of our people on these subjects. While many Christians are involved in positive social action through non-profit and public service agencies, it is a failure of the Church to leave the role of "good Samaritan" to those extra-ecclesial agencies and to follow the example of the "priest" or the "Levite" who "seeing [the injured man], passed by on the other side" (Lk. 10:31-32). The Church must act in cooperation with such agencies to prevent abuse and all forms of injustice, while reaching out to comfort, heal and empower those in need. There is no neutral ground in the universe. As C. S. Lewis wrote, "every millimeter of space and every second of time are claimed by God, and counterclaimed by Satan." By being involved in the work of social justice, the Church can more boldly proclaim that this world is God's world.

Time is yet given for sinners to repent and for saints to be revealed. We must each face the tendency in our selves and in others to use power in an evil way. We must struggle not simply against the evil in others but against the evil impulse within us. The converse is also true. This is the meaning of spiritual warfare – to rebel against temptation and fight for the presence of God within our hearts, in our Church and in our world. In this battle unto death we must be tenacious and unwavering. To be less than fully committed to this struggle is to contribute, however inadvertently, to the wounding and suffering of the world and of God.

Our incarnate God became "obedient even unto death, and death on a cross" (Phil. 2:8), thus rejecting forever every form of authoritarian control. God does not police the world. This is why it is possible for evil to be perpetrated even "in His name" and by those who are positioned to serve "in His image and place."[24] Nevertheless, God vehemently opposes every unjust act. Every act of evil and injustice is an act against the Lord, His creation and His Church. The day of reckoning will come when all such acts will be judged and come to an end. Ultimately injustice will not endure the revealing light of the living God (Heb.10: 31). Meanwhile, the Lord accompanies the powerless and goes with those who "walk through the valley of the shadow of death." The Church must do the same.

Experience informs, indeed painfully reminds us that the Church is not always as prepared as it should be to respond sensitively during times of pain or crisis. This is sometimes apparent even in the lives of its own wounded ministers, whom the Church may choose to isolate further instead of patiently nurturing and healing. I wonder sometimes if it is the very structure of the Church that does not lend itself to caring, but more often than not to hurting. Or perhaps it is the fallen nature of the carers themselves who fall short of their vocation. Whatever the case may be, the Church must relearn the way of caring. In the visionary book of the Revelation of St. John:

> the one who was seated on the throne said: 'See, I am making all things new.' (Rev. 21: 5)

Allowing and assimilating new ways of learning and growing is part and parcel of Christian spiritual life. It is central to caring and community. It is the context within which issues of authority are properly understood. It is the fresh air and refreshing grace of the age to come, the language of the heavenly Kingdom, the reality of a restored image of the world to which we are all called, and which we are called to realize even now.

NOTES

[1] Cf. C. Mango, *Byzantium: The New Roman Empire* (transl. D. Tsoungarakis) Athens 1988, pp. 99-111.

[2] Cf. Hans-Georg Beck, *The Byzantine Millenium* (transl. D. Courtovic) Athens 1992, p. 52.

[3] See Fr. D. Constantelos, *Byzantine Philanthropy and Social Welfare* (New York 1991) 113-139. Also by the same author, *Poverty, Society and Philanthropy in the Late Medieval Greek World* (New York, 1992) 123-128. For a Greek bibliography, see also Fr. D. Constantelos, *Byzantine Heritage* (ed. Damaskos, Athens 1990) 99-111.

[4] See Fr. D. Constantelos, *Byzantine Heritage*, p. 111.

[5] *On the Priesthood*, III, 4-5.

[6] PG 48:651. See also Gregory of Nyssa, *On the Submission of the Son to the Father* (PG 44: 1304-1325), where St. Gregory parallels authentic submission to the freedom of life that characterizes the Holy Trinity, as well as to the relationship of the members of Christ's body with Christ Himself.

[7] For the source and development of this distinction, cf. Dionysius, *Ecclesiastical Hierarchy*. An accessible translation of Dionysius may be found in C. Luibheid and P. Rorem, *Pseudo-Dionysius: The Complete Works*, in *Classics of Western Spirituality* (Paulist Press: New York, 1987). For a study of the theology of Dionysius, see A. Louth, *Denys the Areopagite* (Morehouse-Barlow: Wilton CT, 1989).

[8] Cf. Gregory the Theologian, *Theological Sermon*, 1, 3. See also St. Basil the Great, *On the Holy Spirit* 9 PG 32:108.

[9] Candace R. Benyei, *Understanding Clergy Misconduct in Religious Systems: Scapegoating, Family Secrets and the Abuse of Power* (Binghamton, NY: The Haworth Pastoral Press, 1998) 70-71.

[10] See St. John Chrysostom, *On the Priesthood* PG 48:623-9, and St. Augustine, *Tract. in Evang. Joh.* 123,5.

[11] *Letter* 216 PG 78:900. This letter actually refers to the exercise of authority by the bishop.

[12] *To the Church in Smyrna* vi, 1.

[13] *Homily on Hebrews*, 34, 1 PG 63:231. Cf. also Chrysostom, *Homily on John*, 87, 4 PG 59:472; and *Homily on Titus* 2, 4 PG 62:670.

[14] Cf. J. Welwood, "On Spiritual Authority: Genuine and Counterfeit" in ed. D. Anthony et al., *Spiritual Choices: The Problems of Recognizing Authentic Paths to Inner Transformation* (New York: Paragon House, 1987) 283-303. See also G. Bogart, "Separating from a Spiritual Teacher" in *Journal of Transpersonal Psychology* 24, 1 (1992) 1-21. Also R. Gula, *Ethics in Pastoral Ministry* (New York: Paulist Press, 1996).

[15] *On the Spiritual Law*, 125 PG 65:921. See *Philokalia*, vol. 1, p. 1-3. For the training of the Fathers as healers, see Archim. I. Vlachos, *Orthodox Psychotherapy* (Edessa 1986).

[16] On the sensitivity, reverence, and respect as the "code of ethics" demanded in these situations, see *Integrity of Ministry: a document of principles and standards for catholic clergy and religious in Australia* (June 1999).

[17] Mic Hunter and Jim Struve, *The Ethical Use of Touch in Psychotherapy* (Thousand Oaks, CA: Sage publications, 1998) 99. See also J. Stephen Muse (ed.), *Beside Still Waters* (Macon, GA: Smyth and Helwys, 2000) esp. pp. 1-36 and 109-127.

[18] See ed. K. Karidoyanes Fitzgerald, *Orthodox Women Speak: Discerning the Signs of the Times* (World Council of Churches and Holy Cross Orthodox Press: 1999). For a profound and positive approach to abuse against women, see K. Fischer, *Women at the Well: Feminist Perspectives on Spiritual Direction*, New York: Paulist Press, 1988, esp. chs. 7 "Women and Power" and 8 "Violence against Women: The Spiritual Dimension," pp. 133-174.

[19] *On the Priesthood* PG 48:650. The late Archbishop Michael of America, wrote a book in the 1930's entitled *The Priest* (in Greek: Astir Publications, Athens, 1971) in which he describes "the dangers of priestly ministry," emphasizing characteristically the fact that the general conduct of the clergyman "may scandalize the whole community where he lives and ministers, or else may be the cause of numerous good effects" (p. 20). See also the collective volume, *The Spiritual Father and His Work*, (Apostoliki Diakonia, 1959), especially the articles by Fr. A. Nissiotis.

[20] The reader is directed to a very helpful book by Anne Stirling Hastings *Treating Sexual Shame – A New Map for Overcoming Dysfunction, Abuse and Addiction* (Northvale, NJ: Jason Aronson Inc, 1998). The author's perspective on this important, complex topic seems largely consistent with Orthodox sensibilities.

[21] The word "father" literally means "source."

[22] *On the Spiritual Law* 149 PG 65:924B.

[23] From the Service of Ordination to the clergy of all degrees. Cf. S. Muse and E. Chase, "Healing the Wounded Healers: 'Soul' Food for Clergy," in *Journal of Psychology and Christianity* 12,2 (1993) 141-150. Also N. and T. Ormerod, *When Ministers Sin: Sexual Abuse in the Churches* (Millennium Books: Sydney, 1995).

[24] Cf. Ignatius of Antioch, *Letter to the Magnesians* v-vi; and *Letter to the Smyrnaeans* viii.

# IX

## Sources of a Problem

### the abuse of our children

> But whoever causes one of these little ones who
> believe in me to sin, it would be better for him if a
> millstone were hung around his neck, and were
> drowned in the depth of the sea. (Mt. 18:6)

*(i) Introduction*

In addressing the subject of child abuse, I am called to share
with readers the knowledge of a theologian. Yet in this chapter,
I am writing primarily as a father. I have two sons of my own,
and it is through the eyes of my children, Alexander and Julian,
that I wish to communicate my responsibility for the utmost
care of every child, in every family, in every parish, in every
nation. As an ordained clergyman, I am bound to view the world
from within the Church with a difference: an added third dimension, that of heaven. And in the Church, the very word
"child" is not defined by age, but by vulnerability. We are all
children, for we are all vulnerable. Young children remind us of
the truth that we are all the children of God.

Now another child approaches me, except that he is much
older in age; yet he also is weak and vulnerable. I must take
care of him. You too must take care of him. You may be moved
by the young children. However, you must not move away from
the other child, the offender. For he is God's child, also.

"How can the Church help?" people so often ask. What is the
responsibility of the Church? How does one handle the children? How does one relate to the parents? How is one to deal
with the offender? In brief, what is the role of the Church in the

"helping system"? The facts and consequences are frequently dealt with, but what has actually gone wrong in our way of life? What is the "theology" – or lack of theology – behind child abuse? What does it imply about our misconception of authority or our misunderstanding of obedience?

The social issue of child abuse has been variously and exceedingly analyzed in recent times. Approximately one in three children in contemporary Western society is physically abused. Slightly fewer are sexually abused. Ninety-five percent of offenders are male, seventy percent of their victims are female. Girls and boys of all ages are sexually assaulted. In seventy-five percent of cases, someone trusted (a parent, relative, or friend) or someone known (an acquaintance) is responsible. In physical abuse, in over ninety percent of cases, it is a family member who inflicts the abuse. These statistics have become house-hold knowledge. If anything, they are conservative estimates. In spite of the fact that child abuse has reached almost epidemic levels, the Orthodox Church too often remains silent, especially when the perpetrators are practicing Christians.

### (ii) Child Abuse and the Child

Child abuse is about the silence of lonely nights spent holding in screams, holding back tears, holding in one's very self. When I hear, as I often do, of children abused, I immediately consider Alexander and Julian. The mere thought of a child being hurt emotionally or physically causes in us feelings of discomfort and anger. The suffering that some people endure in this world is unimaginable to me. Yet child abuse is one of the many realities and consequences of the world in which we live.

In some way or another, we have all had our original dignity stolen from us. The "power game" is impressed upon children from a very early age. It is nothing peculiar to see media, school, and parents encouraging self-confidence in children, to the point of their being aggressive. We are, in fact, born into a world where it is inevitable for one to struggle in order to survive, to be cruel in order to be comfortable. After all, child abuse is not only sexual. There are numerous forms of abuse which we often ignore and which we may even at times adopt: humiliation through sarcasm, verbal abuse, mistreatment, neglect, and emotional abuse. Let us not forget, either, the children of the world who are exploited in forced labor and prostitution to satisfy the lust and greed of men.

The ultimate sin in our complacency is our understanding of ownership, possession, and power. Sin is the abuse of freedom, both ours and others'; it is the lack of respect for the freedom of each person. Sinfully, in society today, we tend to treat people as objects, not as persons. Child abuse is but an extreme example of such behavior. Children are the primary victims, then, of our life-style.

The belief fostered by the pedagogy of power and possession, whether directly or indirectly, is that corporal punishment is a useful and beneficial way to teach children to respect and obey their parents. Violence against women and children, and the condoning of that violence, is part of an ancient and widespread, unholy tradition. Scripture and patristic texts have been quoted and misinterpreted in support of this practice. People also use guilt, fear, and intimidation to control their dependents spiritually. The non-Orthodox doctrine of "original sin" has been a major source of justification for many repressive and cruel child-rearing practices. It is sometimes believed that a *child's will* needs to be "broken" in order for the child to behave properly. Any resulting anger on the part of the child is interpreted as a further sign of his or her need for punishment.[1] Such abuse, however, in fact distorts and disables the human will. The result in the child (or in the child-become-adult) may be passivity, anger, and any number of difficulties. The doctrine of ancestral sin is misinterpreted to mean that the child is "born evil." Consider the way in which the words of the 50th Psalm are often interpreted: "I was born in sins, and in sins did my mother conceive me" (v. 5). The message often taken from this is that "I am evil." Whereas, what is meant is that we are born *into* a world where sin and abuse prevail.

One may also be abused in the person of others. A witness to violence is also a victim of violence, learning as a result to be numbed and bonded to violence and to be helpless before violence. Frequently, abuse is intentional, being thought to be "for the good" of the person abused. Sometimes the most abusive people are those who "know" what is good for you and are totally deaf and insensitive to your personal needs.

Within the family, it is commonly assumed that parents *own* their children: "This is my child, and I do as I please in its upbringing" – always "for the good" of the child, of course. Many children are not taught to mature personally, to establish personal boundaries; instead their boundaries are continually violated. They are seldom encouraged to hold an opinion or to disagree. Instead, great pressure is placed on them to agree and obey.

The "poisonous pedagogy" described and defined so revealingly by Alice Miller [2] plays a major role in the tragedy of abuse. It implicitly gives permission for abuse by promoting a kind of ownership of children. If children must obey and honor their parents at any cost, then parents may assume that they have the right over their children's bodies, thoughts, and feelings. Yet this is false. Recall the words of Kahlil Gibran:

> Your children are not your children .... You may strive to be like them but seek not to make them feel like you. For life goes forward not backward.

One should never and in no way take advantage of the age or vulnerability of a child. The parent-child relationship is a reflection of the relationship between God and humanity. God never imposes Himself on us; He does not enforce any code of behavior, even when we reject Him. And although He is the author of all creation, He is not authoritarian. Children, like adults, are images of the living and loving God, and invaluable in His divine sight and providence. "Theirs is the Kingdom of heaven" (Mt. 19:14; Mk. 10:14); they are not possessions of their parents, but themselves possessors of heaven.

The clergyman – whether bishop, presbyter, abbot, or spiritual elder – finds himself in the same predicament in relation to his spiritual children. It is easy to misuse the power of one's office when relating to a vulnerable, wounded person. Yet this will only cause further and deeper wounding. We must critically question and examine what is currently regarded as normative and acceptable if we ever hope to change our attitudes and end child abuse.

Whether parent or presbyter, it is important to listen to the victims of child abuse and to affirm their worth as children of God. For many people, denial, suppression, and repression, are the only defenses available when faced with the intense emotional pain of child abuse. Too often, the abused child inevitably believes that the abuse was his or her own fault. Since the abuse and shame destroy the sense of security and worth, the child may grow up with a needy "inner child."

The love a child has for his or her parents ensures that the parents' conscious and unconscious acts of cruelty go undetected for a long time. This loving dependence also makes it difficult in later years for one to recognize these traumas, which can remain hidden behind the child's early idolization and idealization of the parents. As adults, such survivors often minimize the painful impact of their childhood. They may become caught up in protecting their parents or assuming the burden and blame. The resulting sense of guilt – often placed upon them by others – is another issue that riddles them. A priest who pastors such children must convince them that the responsibility for subsequent actions is not only their own, but is shared by all. The word for confession in Greek (*exomologesis*) not only denotes an opening up to another person, which is the first step in the healing process, but also an identification with the sinner on the part of the priest. It is this solidarity and trust that, in the end, heals.

Abused children feel very much alone, isolated in their suffering and pain. They feel alone in themselves, in their family, and in their world. They may feel they cannot share their pain with anyone. For some, the added element of betrayal by a supposed loved one aggravates this sense of alienation of the victim, who may literally "go away" and close himself or herself off from others.

Abuse of power causes lack of trust. Trust may be violated from a young age, and so the regaining of this ground must be the first aim of the healer or counselor. There is no reason for preaching a sermon when the person preaching is not trusted. Being honest and sensitive with both offender and victim is crucial. This is what ultimately indicates to them that they are not worthless and unloved. Beyond mere concern, there is needed a tangible realization of communication. Then abused and abuser alike are better able to discover and face the pain of the past. Although this past cannot be changed, yet God's love can begin to heal once one has accepted one's weakness. As St. Paul wrote centuries ago: "my strength is perfected in weakness" (2 Cor. 12:9).

Today, a victim of abuse shares her story in a different way:

Please do not tell me it's all in the past, as some have told me. Please don't tell me it can't hurt me now. It is still hurting me! Some "helpers" listen, think they understand how I feel, then put me straight, give me a sermon, tell me to have more faith and try harder, or even, thoughtlessly, ask me if I am really a Christian! They apply their solution, but I am left reeling under another blow.[3]

Sometimes those involved in "helping," "ministering," and "counseling" may be responding more to their own needs than to the needs of the people they claim to help. The same may be said of parenting, which should be about enabling the creativity and maturity of the child to unfold. The essential task of parents is *to be there* for their children. Sadly, however, it is frequently the child who is expected *to be there* for the parent, meeting the needs of a mother or father. One wonders, too, how much teaching or therapy or spiritual direction in fact disguises and conceals the needs of those helping. Even the more refined and subtle forms of manipulation, may, in fact, cause considerable harm.

If we are to love people, then we must first listen to and try to understand what they are experiencing, no matter how painful or traumatic this may happen to be. Pain too is an important way of maturing. We must enter into their world with the grace and sensitivity of the Holy Spirit.

This is the full significance of love as revealed by Christ. Love is not simply emotional, but also responsible. Love, moreover, may sometimes mean *not* "turning the other cheek" or refusing to show affection. It is wrong to teach children only *one* side of love. The child must learn that saying "no" may sometimes be the real way of love. This is certainly a duty of the Church – whether represented by the presbyter, the Sunday school teacher, or the parent. The One who taught the virtue of turning the other cheek (Lk. 6:29), in fact refused to do so on the single occasion when He was struck on the cheek by an abusive authority (Jn. 18:22-3).

We have been created by God and commanded to care for

each other and for the world (Gen. 1:28). At all times, however, one has a choice to make – that of obeying or of disobeying God. We may use the gifts and powers we have received to do either good or evil. The wine consumed by some as a means of disinhibition leading to abusive behavior, may be shared by others as a source of communion with God and the world. It is up to each of us to choose (1 Jn. 4:7-21).

In the same way, the victim of abuse has the choice of adopting similar tactics that caused one's own suffering, or else of transforming the pain into energy, of being re-washed and cleansed in order to be free. The presbyter too has the choice of accepting the victim as a person loved by God just as he is, or else of regarding himself as being in a position of superiority from which he may look down upon the other condescendingly. The role of the pastor, it seems to me, is simply to walk beside others, to accompany them in their every move and at their own pace. What wounded people often need is affirmation, to have their sacred worth detected and affirmed.

Some people may not feel God's healing presence, but God is present in other persons who care. The way, then, that others do or do not respond is crucial to a victim. A slight improvement or step forward in the life of the victim must never be diminished but always recognized as a spark of life, in the same way that Jesus turned and acknowledged the hemorrhaging woman who had simply touched Him (cf. Mk. 5:27-34).

### (iii) The Parent

The bread that the Church breaks each Lord's Day for communion and salvation, "for the life of the world," essentially symbolizes the fragmentation of human nature that must humbly yet responsibly be overcome, healed, and unified.

This same understanding and sensitivity must be applied to the parent. The area of communication is so significant when dealing with parents or parental figures. People are often untrained in any clinical skills – and this surely holds true of clergy – and yet they are left to "mend" souls. We console, we respond to questions, we absolutely love to involve God – by quoting Scripture, or anything that sounds like Scripture – but we neglect, indeed avoid, attempting to help mend the parents' relationship with the child or with the offender. Ultimately, in the case also of the parent, we are again very frequently guilty of isolation, of "band-aid" healing that ultimately brings about no real change in behavior or attitude. Whether the offender is a stranger, a spouse, or a close relative, we often leave the wound unhealed, perhaps even ignored. Thus we not only fail to be sensitive to the rupture in relationships, but we create a further vacuum, yet another empty space in the Church: namely, between ourselves and those who have been hurt.

We have referred above to the "poisonous pedagogy" which teaches that parents *own* their children. Based on this false premise, some parents feel that they have a right over their children's behavior, feelings, thoughts, and bodies. This is false. No parent should ever believe that he or she has unlimited power over a child. Likewise, every child should be taught to have personal boundaries, to guard a sacred space of privacy (cf. Mt. 6:6) where no one else may enter, and where one is assured the security and comfort of the presence of God. This sacred interior should become the firm ground of fullness of life for the child, so that he or she does not look to outward performance or other worldly things for fulfillment. Unhealthy families display *control* (of feelings and behavior), *perfectionism* (how you look matters more than what you are), *blame* (blaming of others or yourself), *unreliability* (lack of trust in relationships) and *unaccountability*. The rule of this last characteristic is that of "no talk" and "no expression" of problems or feelings. We must, however, encourage children toward healthy inter-dependence and empowerment.

Parents who abuse their children have most often been themselves abused in childhood. The trauma of that original abuse has remained unhealed, and so they reenact the behavior in later life on their children. How does this happen? It may be due to the parent's low self-worth from former abuse. Behaving like one's parents may be an attempt to deny the past and to prove that one's parents really were good, really did love, really did act as they did for one's own good. This may help explain why such behavior is carried on from generation to generation. Physical violence is highly addictive, for the parent no less than for the child that learns to bond to violence.

### (iv) The Offender

Separation of the offender from the victim and other potential victims is usually a necessary measure. This may invariably be a *solution*, but we are still very far from *salvation*. Perhaps, in this chapter, it would have been more appropriate to consider the offender before the victim, not simply for logical reasons – because the offender is the cause and the victim the result – but also for moral or personal reasons. It is, however, a mistake forever to isolate the offender, thinking that herein lies a permanent solution to the problem. I refer to *personal* reasons, precisely because I wish to bring the case of the offender much "closer to home" – it is, at any rate, the immediate family that is to blame in so many cases. The offender may be in our home; indeed, it may be you, it may be I. The offender should not be dismissed as a psychopathic pervert. Reports state that the men (and women) involved are "average" people from across occupational, cultural, religious, and socio-economic groups.

The Church, as we have seen, bears witness to the oneness in all of human nature. This means that the existence of but one offender, anywhere, at any time, is the very failure of humanity, of yours and mine. "Let, therefore, the one who has no sin cast the first stone" (cf. Jn 8:7). It is I that must be blamed, and it is I that must be cleansed. This in no way absolves the offender who should be punished. However, we must not feel any sense of complacency or superiority in presuming that the responsibility is all his, in considering ourselves relieved of all burden. Our purpose is not primarily to punish the sinner but to kneel beside each offender in humility, to stand beside him as one who cares, for he, too, is one of us. We must realistically admit that "in the house of our Father in heaven there are many mansions" (cf. Jn 14:2), and *all* of them are made of glass, each of them is so fragile. We are all potential abusers. The offender is so much like us, very much one of us. The line is indeed very fine between abuser and victim. Before God, each of us stands in judgment. Abuse, indeed, sin in general, is almost always a matter of hurt, of people hurting other people. And that hurts God.

The Church exists not simply to heal but to save, and we know that Christ's will is "that the whole world be saved" (Jn 3:17), especially those who are lost (Mt. 18;11, Lk. 19:10), unwanted, exiled, ostracized, unloved. That includes both victim *and* offender. If we separate the offender from the Church, we cut him off from his source of oxygen – which is God's love through other human beings. Then we are committing the same crime as he, namely abuse.

The pain of the Church is the *same* for all its children. The offender is the *other* silent victim in the drama of abuse, often overlooked – perhaps because the offender's actions come "too close for comfort" to our own attitudes and behavior. Ultimately, all are "wounded," all are in need of healing. The Church mourns and cares for the whole of fallen humanity. We are saved in and through one another, and never above or without each other. It is in the eyes of a human person that one beholds the fullness of the glory of God, for God became human (cf. Jn. 1:14). From that moment in history, finding God became as simple as turning to another human person – what the Scriptures refer to as "one's neighbor" – and loving that person "with all one's strength, and with all one's soul, and with all one's heart, and with all one's life" (Mk. 12:30, Lk. 10:27). The Scriptures also command: "Love your neighbor as yourself" (Mk. 12:31) which does not imply self-centeredness or egoism, but that one's neighbor is one's very self. One's neighbor is the genuine reflection of one's self and also of God (cf. Jn 15:9,12). We cannot do without each other. Thus, St. John Climacus writes:

> When we anger God, [a human being] can reconcile us; but when we anger a human being, we no longer have anyone to defend us. [4]

### (v) "Suffer the Little Children" (Mt. 19:14)

As we have already seen, difficulties appear when parents seek to fulfill their own needs in a child. Confusion arises as a result of the fusion between parent and child, in the erosion of the boundaries between the two. People often project their childhood pain onto their children, instead of confronting and healing this pain *within themselves*. Not only, then, are we all easily identified with the offender, but we may all identify with the victim child inasmuch as we have all been abused to a degree. So many people and so many circumstances "are seeking the child's life" (Mt. 2:20) "in order to destroy it" (Mt. 2:13).

We first notice and know the world through the eyes of a little child. That child-like image of the world remains with us throughout our lives, no matter how outwardly "grown up" and mature we later become. If our "inner child" was hurt or abandoned, shamed or neglected, then that vulnerable child – together with all its pain, grief, and anger – lives on within us. [5] Without seriously working on and healing the pain of this inner child, things do not get better; they get worse. We can never know ourselves and relate properly to others, nor can we approach the mystery of God, if we do not realize in our mind and in our life that "the kingdom of heaven is within" (Lk. 17:21):

> Therefore unless we change and become like children, we will never enter the kingdom of heaven. Whoever becomes humble like a child is the greatest in the kingdom of heaven (Mt. 18:3-4).

We are asked to "seek first the kingdom of heaven" (Mt. 6:33), and are assured that "it is to such as these little children that the kingdom of heaven belongs" (Mt. 19:14). We are called "to find the child" (Mt. 2:11) inside us, to heal and comfort this child in the name of Christ (cf. Mt. 18:5). It is important to take the journey inside and discover the kingdom within. For some of us it may appear difficult; or perhaps we do not even remember what it is like to be a child – although we may relate to children, and although we may have our own children.

However, each of us may hold an image of ourselves as a young child and hold tight to this image, like a photo in our hand. For many, finding that child is like finding home for the very first time. In fact, it is the *first* step to discovering who we are and, at the same time, to discovering God.

This child inside us is our source of strength, our life-force. It is like our sixth sense, which can "pick up" vibrations of God, of life and of pain. It has been described as our "wonder child." This wonder child is that part of us that is most *full of God*. It believes, with unwavering faith, in a father ("our father in heaven," Mt. 6:9). It is trusting, surrendering, tender, and loving. This child is never afraid of losing its way and is always open to new impressions and experiences, to alternatives and surprises. It is what enables us, with enthusiasm and spontaneity, to live in the *now* – neither in the guilt of yesterday, nor in the fear of tomorrow. It empowers us to find fulfillment inside, in God.

Secondly, this wonder child is that part of us that is most *full of life.* It is playful, spontaneous, joyous, and creative. This child has a strong will, not easily destroyed or disabled. This child is able to feel happy and sad; it laughs and cries. It is full of fun, full of wonder, full of surprise. It wants, needs, and creates space to thrive, room to grow.

Now, however, this child has been hurt. For this world is *full of suffering*, and evil is a reality. The inner child has survived so much – a death in the family, a disability, a loss, an abandonment, an abuse, an isolation, an injustice. All of us have somehow and at some time borne pain and wounds. Yet in order to survive, the wonder child developed ways to cope and to manage. It created a "false self." Nevertheless, the wonder child always remained a living spark, always allowed a ray of hope. It took us by the hand through our difficulties. It still does. We have the opportunity to refashion our lives at every moment, to find out who we really are. Our wounds may once again become our strength.

It is the wonder of the child within that enables us to see beauty beyond ugliness, light beyond darkness, and life beyond abuse. Honoring and valuing that child is of utmost spiritual importance. The child knows: "I am not my pain, just as I am not my achievements. I am much, much more."

Resurrection is a decision to see the light in the midst of darkness. The kingdom of heaven is a decision each one makes *for* oneself, although not *by* oneself. By the grace of God, through this inner child, we may look and truly see, may listen and actually hear, may speak and mean, may move and be aware, may touch and feel both blessing and pain, in ourselves and in others. This child allows us to feel fully *at home* everywhere, with everyone, and with every circumstance. For the child knows that our real home is in heaven:

> here we have no lasting city, but we are looking for the city that is to come (Heb. 13:14).

That will be our true homecoming at last. Yet we arrive there step by step. And through God's grace acting through our wonder child within, we know that at each step of the way we are not alone. We are at all moments being welcomed. Such is the power and grace of baptism, the integrity and authority of our creation "in the image of God" (Gen. 1:26).

## (vi) Conclusion

In abuse, the innermost part of a person, one's sacred space, has been invaded. In the case of sexual abuse, the most intimate part of the person, the sacred temple of the body, has been violated. Our body is perhaps our most fundamental and foundational boundary. When this boundary is violated and the body is assaulted, the core of the self is injured.

The question, however, always remains whether we are prepared to be aware of the extent of child abuse and of its proximity to us? Are we ready to admit our own individual contribution to and corporate responsibility for this grave social ill? Are we willing to be more flexible in our understanding of the offender, more silent and prayerful in our relationship with the victim? Are we able to be more alert to what is happening to those around us, especially to the children, to the vulnerable parents in our midst? Are we ready to seek those who hurt, and comfort them with the love of God? Are we daring to intervene in the lives of hurt and lonely people so that they do not turn to hurt other people? Are we truly prepared to recognize the problem within our own parishes and in the homes of those whom we like to consider "good Christians?" Can we challenge all forms of violence and abuse in our society, within our families, among our friends, and in ourselves? Are we prepared to see the wounds that we, ourselves, carry? Do we genuinely wish to be healed? Just how eager are we to be saved? How honest are we to open up the discussion, by raising issues of authority and abuse in theological and ecclesiastical circles?

Notes

[1] We have already examined in chapter 1 the proper connection between baptism and sin.

[2] *For Your Own Good* (Virago: 1987). See also her more recent work, such as *Banished Knowledge* (Virago: 1990).

[3] Cathy-Ann Matthew, *Southern Cross* (Melbourne, Nov., 1986) 13.

[4] *Step 4*, 126.

[5] Here I am indebted to the work of John Bradshaw. See his books: *Bradshaw on the Family* (1988), *Healing the Shame that Binds You* (1988), and *Homecoming* (1990). See also M. McCullough and E. Worthington, "Encouraging clients to forgive people who have hurt them" in *Journal of Psychology and Theology* 22, 1 (1994) 3-20.

# Sources

## On Spiritual Direction

The following Patristic sources comprise fundamental, formative, and practical resources on the subject of spiritual direction.

The texts – covering spiritual classics from the Christian tradition and influential authors ranging from the fourth to the eleventh centuries – are presented here in a fresh translation.

The final passage reflects the contemporary voice of Mount Athos, a striking example of the living continuity of the practice and priority of spiritual direction.

## BASIL THE GREAT (C.330-379)*

Bishop of Cappadocia in Caesaria, Basil the Great
was significantly influenced by the basic principles
of early monasticism, having visited Egypt as a
young man. In his *Longer* and *Shorter Rules,* he presents a series of responses to questions on the
monastic life, where he emphasizes the notions of
community and social service. The uniqueness of
Basil's spiritual vision and teaching lies in its ecumenical breadth, that transcends any individual
or regional restrictions.

### Longer Rules:

*Question 24.* Now ... it is natural for us to learn how to live
with one another.

*Response.* When the Apostle says: "all things should be done
properly and in order" (1 Cor. 14:40), I think that he is referring
to the proper and orderly behavior in the community of the
faithful, where the order of the members of the body is preserved. Thus one person is entrusted with the general
supervision [of the community], and that person evaluates what
has been accomplished, while also foreseeing and providing
for what is to happen, exercising in this fashion the function of
the eye. Another does the work of the ear or of the hand, hearing or practicing what is commanded. And all the others have
the role of the remaining members. It is critical, then, to recog-

---

* Basil the Great, *Longer Rules and Shorter Rules.* Earlier English trans-
lations may also be found in W. K. L. Clarke, *The Ascetic Works of Saint
Basil* (London, 1925), and M. Monica Wagner, *St. Basil: Ascetical Works*
(Catholic University of America Press: Washington DC, 1962) 223-337.
The Greek original appears in J.-P. Migne, *Patrologia Graeca,* vol. 31:
889-1320.

nize that it is dangerous for any member of our body to ignore its duties or else to overlook the other members. This is not the reason why each member of the body was created by God – whether it is the hand or the foot that does not obey the orders of the eye. For the hand will inevitably touch dangerous objects that destroy the whole body; the foot will falter or be led over cliffs; and even if the eye is closed, so that it cannot see, it too will be destroyed together with the other members which will suffer similar things. Therefore, just as happens with the members of the body, it is likewise dangerous for a superior to overlook his responsibility, because he is judged on behalf of all the others. At the same time, for the other members it is also dangerous and harmful not to be obedient, especially so if there are some among them who are scandalized. Thus each person who shows a tireless zeal from his own position, and fulfills the apostolic command: "do not lag in zeal" (Rom. 12:11), is rewarded accordingly; but for negligence, one receives the opposite, namely misery and woefulness. For it is said: "Cursed is the one who is slack in doing the work of the Lord" (Jer. 48:10).

*Question 25.* Judgment is terrible for the superior who does not rebuke those who sin.

*Response.* One who is entrusted with general supervision should behave as if he will have to give account for everyone. He should know that, if one of the brothers falls into sin, without having been foretold of God's judgment; or if the same brother falls and persists, not having been taught the way of correction, then the blood of the sinner will be sought from the hands of the person responsible, as it is written (cf. Ezek. 3:20). This is especially so, if the one responsible knowingly overlooks some commandment of God and relaxes the discipline of the community. For it is said: "your leaders mislead you, and confuse the course of your paths" (Is. 3:12). "But whoever it is that is confusing you will pay the penalty" (Gal. 5:10). In order, then, to avoid suffering this, let us follow the apostolic rule in our conversations with the brothers:

As you know and as God is our witness, we never came with words of flattery or with a pretext for greed; nor did we seek praise from mortals, whether from you or from others (1 Thess. 2:5-6).

So whoever is pure of these passions will be able to follow these directions without error, for one's own reward and for the salvation of those who follow. For one who practices love without either looking to human honor or avoiding the offense of sinners, in order to appear sweet and pleasant to them, will also speak boldly and sincerely. Such a person will not choose to adulterate the truth in any way, so that even the following words will apply to that person:

> But we were gentle among you, like a nurse tenderly caring for her own children. So deeply do we care for you that we are determined to share with you not only the gospel of God but also our own selves (1 Thess. 2:7-8).

Whoever does not behave in this manner is a blind guide, hurling himself over the cliff and drawing his followers after him.

How evil, then, it is for you to be the cause of a brother's error may easily be ascertained from all that has been mentioned above. And this is a sign that the commandment of love has not been fulfilled. For no father is indifferent when his own child is about to fall into a pit, or leaves it there after it has fallen. Surely it is necessary to say how much more terrible it is for a soul to be left to destruction, once it has fallen into the pit of evil. So the superior is responsible before the community to be vigilant over the soul and to care for each brother's salvation, as if he were to give account. In fact, he should care so much as to show his zeal for them even unto death, firstly in accordance with the Lord's general command that we love everyone: "laying down our life for our friends" (John 15:13), and secondly in the particular way revealed by the one who said:

> So deeply do we care for you that we are determined to share with you not only the gospel of God but our own selves (1 Thess. 2:8).

*Question 26.* Everything, including the secrets of the heart, should be placed before the superior.

*Response.* If any of the brothers intend to make any worthwhile progress and to lead a life that follows the commandments of our Lord Jesus Christ, they should not conceal any movement of the heart, or utter any thoughtless word. Rather, they should reveal the secrets of the heart to those of the brothers entrusted to care for the sick with mercy and compassion. For in this way, what is commendable will be ratified, while what is unacceptable will receive the healing it deserves. Through such cooperative practice, we shall gradually attain to perfection.

*Question 27.* Even if the superior too errs, he should be admonished by the eminent brothers of the community.

*Response.* Just as the superior is responsible for directing the community in everything, so also it is necessary for the other brothers to admonish him if the superior is suspected of any offense. And in order not to relax the proper order, such admonition should be assigned to those more eminent in both age and wisdom. So if there is something that deserves correction, we will benefit our brother (as well as ourselves through him) by bringing him to the straight path. For he is, as it were, the very rule of our own life and he is obliged to correct our own wrong ways through his uprightness. In this way, if some are disturbed in vain by him, their doubts will be dispelled after they are informed by the clarification of these groundless suspicions.

*Question 28.* How everyone should behave toward the disobedient.

*Response.* All should certainly be compassionate at first toward the person that is negligent in obeying the Lord's commandments, as if toward a sick member; and the superior should try to heal the sickness with his advice. However, if he persists in disobedience and does not accept to be corrected, he should be rebuked more strictly before the entire community and be offered treatment with every kind of exhortation. And if after much advice, he is neither ashamed of nor cured in his behavior, since according to the proverb he is the cause of his own destruction, then he must be cut off with many tears and lamentations from the common body of the community, just as doctors would do for a corrupt and entirely useless member of the physical body. For doctors are accustomed to removing by surgery and cauterization a member that they find infected with an incurable disease, in order that the infection does not spread and destroy the adjoining members. This is what we too should do in the case of those who oppose or hinder the commandments of the Lord, according to the Lord's own precept: "If your right eye causes you to sin, tear it out and throw it away" (Mt. 5:29). Kindness toward such people resembles the immature goodness of Eli, who was punished for his revelation to his sons against God's will (cf. 1 Sam. 3:13). False niceness toward wicked people is therefore a betrayal of truth, an act of treachery to the community, and a means of becoming accustomed to indifference toward evil. In that case, the saying is not fulfilled: "Should you not rather have mourned, so that he who has done this would have been removed from among you?" (1 Cor. 5:2). Instead the following saying is inevitably applicable: "a little yeast leavens the whole batch of dough" (1 Cor. 5:6). The apostle says: "As for those who persist in sin, rebuke them in the presence of all," and he immediately adds the reason for this, "so that the rest also may stand in fear" (1 Tim. 5:20).

In general, then, whoever refuses the treatment offered by the superior is also inconsistent with himself. For if he refuses to obey and instead imposes his own will, then why remain with the superior at all? Why accept the superior as the protector of his life? However, once he has accepted to become a member of the community, having judged the superior to be a suitable vessel for this ministry, then even if a certain command appears to be beyond his strength, he should leave the judgment of this to the one who commanded him to do something beyond his strength. And he should show submission and obedience unto death, remembering that the Lord became "obedient to the point of death – even death on a cross" (Phil. 2:8). However rebellion and contradiction reveal many evils: weak faith, doubtful hope, vain and arrogant character. For none is disobedient unless he first ignores the one who gave the order. Nor does one who believes in God's promises and firmly fixes his hopes on these, ever avoid these commandments, however difficult they may be, knowing that "the sufferings of this present time are not worth comparing with the glory about to be revealed to us" (Rom. 8:18). And one who is convinced that "all who humble themselves will be exalted" (Mt. 23:12) shows greater willingness than the expectation of the one who gave the order, knowing that the slight momentary affliction is preparing us for an eternal weight of glory beyond all measure" (2 Cor. 4:17).

*Question 29.* On the person who behaves with arrogance or murmuring.

*Response.* The work of a person given to murmuring or arrogance must not be confused with work done by those who are humble of heart and contrite of spirit. Such work must never be practiced by the pious, "or else what is prized by human beings will be an abomination in the sight of God" (Lk. 16:15). As other apostolic precepts say, "Do not complain as some of them did, and they were destroyed by the destroyer" (1 Cor. 10:10); and, "[act] not reluctantly or under compulsion" (2 Cor. 9:7). The work, then, of such people is unacceptable, as being a blemished sacrifice; and it is not good to confound it with the work of others. For, if those who bring strange fire to the altar have experienced such wrath (cf. Lev. 10:1-2), how can it not be dangerous to accept a work that fulfills the commandments but comes from a hateful attitude to God? "For," it says, "what partnership is there between righteousness and lawlessness? ... Or what does a believer share with an unbeliever?" (2 Cor. 6:14-15). This is why it is said: "Whoever sacrifices a lamb is wicked, like one who breaks a dog's neck; and whoever presents a grain offering, like one who offers swine's blood" (Is. 66:3). Consequently, the community should reject the actions of a lazy person or dissenter. The superiors should take great care on this matter, that they may not themselves violate the command of the one who said: "Whoever walks in the way that is blameless shall minister to me; no one who practices deceit shall remain in my house" (Ps. 101:6-7). Nor again should the superiors accept anyone who confuses sin with the fulfillment of the commandments, or who spoils work with an unwillingness to toil or else with an arrogance in regard to achievement, so as not to encourage that person to persist in corruption by not allowing the awareness of wrongdoing. Thus the superior must himself be convinced that, if he fails to offer proper guidance to a brother, he brings upon himself a heavy and inevitable wrath; for his brother's blood will be asked from his hands, as it is written (cf. Ezek. 3:18). However the brother too must be thus prepared in order not to hesitate before any command, even the most difficult one, being convinced that his reward is great in heaven. Let, then, the hope of glory give joy to the obedient brother, so that the work of the Lord may be done in all joy and patience.

*Question 30.* With what attitude should the superiors care for the brothers?

*Response.* The superior should not feel arrogant about his rank, so that he too may not fall from the blessing of humility (cf. Mt. 5:3) or be puffed up and fall into the judgment of the devil (cf. 1 Tim. 3:6). However, let him be assured that greater responsibility means greater service. One who serves many wounded people, wiping away the unclean matter of each wound and offering treatment appropriate to the particular injury, does not consider this service a cause for arrogance but rather for humility, concern, and effort. Likewise, then, and much more so, one who is entrusted with healing the wounds of the community must be thoughtful and anxious, as the servant of all and as liable to an account on behalf of all. For in this way he will achieve the purpose about which the Lord said: "Whoever wants to be first must be last of all and servant of all" (Mk. 9:35).

*Question 43.* Clarification of the characteristics required of superiors in a community and of how they should direct the brothers.

*Response.* This matter has already been discussed summarily. However, since you rightly wish to expand on it further (for those under a spiritual rule often like to imitate their leader and elder), it is necessary for me not to pass over it without proper attention. The superior must remember the apostolic command: "set the believers an example" (1 Tim. 4:12), making his own life a shining example for the fulfillment of every commandment of the Lord, so as to leave no cause for his disciples to believe that the Lord's commandment is unattainable or contemptible. First, then – that which is indeed of primary importance – the superior should be so confirmed in humility through the love of Christ, that, even when he is silent, the example of his actions may be more effective instruction than any words. For, if indeed the definition of Christianity is the imitation of Christ according to the measure of His Incarnation and in proportion to each person's vocation, then those entrusted with the direction of others are obliged to inspire those still weaker than themselves, by assisting them to imitate Christ, as the blessed Paul says: "Be imitators of me, as I am of Christ" (1 Cor. 11:1).

The superiors, then, should first become perfect examples by achieving the measure of humility passed down by our Lord Jesus Christ. And He says: "learn from me, for I am gentle and humble in heart" (Mt. 11:29). Thus gentleness of manner and humility of heart must characterize the superior. For if the Lord was not ashamed to minister to His own servants, but accepted to be a minister of the earth and clay which He Himself had formed and shaped into us (for He said: "I am among you as one who serves" [Lk. 22:27]), what should we do to our equals in order to believe that we have reached an imitation of Him? So this is one quality that must be found in the superior.

Next, he should be merciful and long-suffering, patient with those who omit one of their duties out of inexperience; he should not fail to reprove their sins, but also gently tolerate those who stray and offer them treatment with all mercy and moderation. He should, furthermore, be competent in discerning the proper treatment for a particular passion, not punishing with crudeness, but advising and educating with gentleness, as it is written (2 Tim. 2:25). In addition, he should show vigilance in matters of the present, foresight in matters of the future, ability to contend with the strong as well as to bear the infirmities of the weak, and the skill to do and say all things for the edification of his brethren. He should not assume alone the role of superior, but should be chosen by the superiors of other communities, as well as having sufficient proof of his character from his own past. For it is said: "And let them first be tested; then, if they prove themselves blameless, let them serve" (1 Tim. 3:10). Therefore, this is how such a person should be allowed to become a superior; and let this person establish order in the community, allocating tasks according to the ability of each brother.

*Question 45.* There should be another person who, in the absence or preoccupation of the superior, is able to serve the community.

*Response.* The superior frequently happens to be away from the community by reason of physical illness, or necessity of travel, or some other circumstance. So there should also be some other person, approved by him as well as by other competent brothers, who is selected precisely to continue the care of the community in the absence of the superior, so that all the brothers may heed the advice of one person. The community should not assume a democratic form of government in the absence of the superior, thereby dissolving the rule and traditional order; for the approved customs should be preserved unto the glory of God. There should be someone who will also give prudent answers to visiting guests, so that those who seek a word may be properly edified, while the community may not be embarrassed. For when everyone together hastens to speak, it is a cause of distraction and a sign of disorder. Even the Apostle does not allow several people to speak at once, even if they be endowed with the gift of teaching: "If a revelation is made to someone else sitting nearby, let the first person be silent" (1 Cor. 14:30). And elsewhere he disapproves of improper disorder: "If, therefore, the whole church comes together and all speak in tongues, and outsiders or unbelievers enter, will they not say that you are out of your mind?" (1 Cor. 14:23).

Should the guest ask questions of another brother out of ignorance, then even if the brother who is mistakenly asked happens to be capable of responding correctly, he should be silent for the sake of order. Instead, he should direct the guest to the person responsible for answering, just as the apostles did when the Lord was present (cf. Jn. 12:21-2). In this way, speech is employed in an orderly and proper manner. For, as in the case of physical healing, not everyone is able to use a knife to cure an illness, but only the one who has learned the art after much time, practical experience and theoretical study from specialists. What is the point of an ordinary person assuming the role of healing through counseling? For even the slightest oversight brings about the greatest harm. And if not even the distribution of bread is allowed indiscriminately, but is the duty of the one to whom this ministry has been entrusted after approval, how much greater need is there that a carefully chosen and competent person should offer spiritual nourishment to those who ask for it? Therefore, it is no small arrogance for one who is asked about God's judgment to dare carelessly and casually to respond. Instead he should refer this to the person whose responsibility it is to speak, as a very faithful and wise minister, chosen to distribute spiritual nourishment in season (cf. Lk. 12:42) and to watch his words with discernment (cf. Ps. 111:5), as it is written. Even if something escapes the one who ought to respond, and someone else realizes this, the latter should not hasten at once to correct the former but only offer a suggestion privately. For the opposite gives rise to insolence against one's superiors; so that even if one's response is helpful, when it is outside one's obligation, one is liable to penalties for such disorderly conduct.

*Question 50.* How the superior should reprove the brothers.

*Response.* The superior should not administer rebukes to wrongdoers in a passionate manner. For by reproving a brother with anger and indignation, he does not free the brother from sin but in fact involves himself in sinfulness. This is why it is said: "correct your opponents with gentleness" (2 Tim. 2:25). Nor should he be harsh when he is personally wronged, and then be kind to the sinner when someone else is wronged; in fact he should be harder against the wrong committed in the latter case. For in this way he will avoid the suspicion of self-love and prove that he does not hate the sinner but only the sin – by the difference of behavior in his own case from the other's. However, if he is frustrated in the opposite case, then it is clear that he is angered neither for God's sake nor for the sinner's danger, but only for his own ambition and authority. It is necessary to show zeal for the glory of God who is dishonored by the transgression of His commandment. And it is right to show the mercy of brotherly love for the salvation of a brother who is endangered by sin (because "the person who sins shall die" [Ezek. 18:4]). The superior should, in every case of sin, be stirred against the sin and reveal such burning disposition in the severity of the penalty.

*Question 54.* The superiors should consult with one another.

*Response.* It is also a good thing for superiors to meet occasionally, at certain appointed times and places, in order to consult with one another about irregular situations that arise, about difficult moral questions, and about each one's administrative matters. In this way, if one of them happens to err, this may be exposed confidentially and corrected by the others, while what is done rightly may be confirmed by their collective testimony.

### Shorter Rules:

*Question 82.* Since it is written: "[treat] older women as mothers" (1 Tim. 5:2), if an older woman happens to fall into the same sin as a younger woman, should she be disciplined in the same way?

*Response.* The Apostle taught us to honor older women as mothers, provided they not do anything that deserves discipline. However, if it ever happens that an older woman falls into the same sin as a younger woman, we must first take into consideration the so-called physical weakness of age, and afterward determine the proper measure of severity for each age. For example, fatigue is almost natural for an older person, but not for a younger person; just as daydreaming, disturbance, audacity and the like are natural for a younger person, but not an older person. It appears that the latter weaknesses are even assisted by the physical vigor of youth. Thus the same sin – for instance, fatigue – deserves a heavier penalty for a younger person, because young age does not permit this. Or the same sin – such as daydreaming or audacity, or disturbance – renders the older person worthy of a heavier penalty, because age inclines rather towards gentleness and calmness. Furthermore, it is necessary to examine the manner of sin in each case, and only then to offer the appropriate manner of treatment by means of the proper penalty.

*Question 98.* What should be the attitude of the superior when he gives commands or orders?

*Response.* Before God, the superior should be as a minister of Christ and as a steward of divine mysteries, fearing that he may say or do anything against the will of God revealed in Scripture. He should also be careful not to be found a false witness of God or sacrilegious in either introducing something foreign to the Lord's teaching or else omitting something pleasing to God. Before his brothers, he should be "like a nurse tenderly caring for her own children" (1 Thess. 2:7). His desire should be to transmit to each of them that which is pleasing to God, and to the general community not only the Gospel of God, but his own life. And all this should be done in accordance with the commandment of our Lord and God Jesus Christ who said: "I give you a new commandment, that you love one another, just as I have loved you" (Jn. 13:34). For, "no one has greater love than this, to lay down one's life for one's friends" (Jn. 15:13).

*Question 99.* What should be the attitude of the superior when he gives out punishment?

*Response.* Before God, he should be like David who said, "I looked at the transgressor and was disturbed, because he did not keep your commandments" (Ps. 118:158). Before those reprimanded, his attitude should be like that of a father and a doctor who is treating his own son with compassion and mercy according to the medical science, especially when he is sad and when the manner of treatment is painful.

*Question 103.* We have already been taught that we must submit to our superiors unto death. However, since it happens that sometimes even the superior falls into sin, we wish to learn if he should be reproved and how and by whom; and what should happen if he does not accept reproof?

*Response.* We have already given a clear response to this in the *Longer Rules* (No. 27). [see above]

*Question 104.* How should the duties be assigned to the brothers? Is it only the responsibility of the superior, or should the brothers also have a say? The same question applies to the sisters.

*Response.* If each person has been taught to consult another about his thoughts, how much more should such decisions be taken following approval from the appropriate people? For the management of God's affairs should, according to God, be assigned to those who have proved that they are able to manage whatever has been assigned to them in a manner pleasing to the Lord. And in general, the superior must remember in every circumstance the words of Scripture: "Do nothing without deliberation" (Sir. 32:19).

*Question 113.* Is the one entrusted with the care of souls able to keep the commandment: "unless you change and become like children" (Mt. 18:33), when he is occupied with many and various persons?

*Response.* Since the most wise Solomon said: "for everything there is a season" (Eccl. 3:1), we must know that there is a proper season for humility, authority, reproof, consolation, care, courage, goodness, abruptness, and generally everything. Therefore, sometimes we must show humility and imitate children in the virtue of humility (cf. Mt. 18:3), especially when it is time to honor one another or oblige one another, or else to serve and treat the bodily needs, as the Lord taught. At other times we must show authority, which was in fact given by the Lord for edification and not for destruction, especially when the need calls for severity. When it is time for consolation, we must show goodness. When it is time for abruptness, we must show zeal. And in other circumstances, we should again act accordingly.

*Question 114.* The Lord commanded: "if anyone forces you to go one mile, go also the second mile" (Mt. 5:41); and the Apostle taught: "be subject to one another out of reverence for Christ" (Eph. 5:21). Should we then obey everyone who orders anything?

*Response.* A person who gives an order is not necessarily an obstacle for the one who receives this order, because even Moses did not disobey Jethro's good advice (cf. Ex. 18:19). However, there is some distinction in the commands themselves: for some of them contradict the Lord's commandments, either corrupting or defiling them in many ways by confusing them with what is disallowed; others, even if they are not apparently in agreement, nevertheless contribute and almost assist in their fulfillment. It is necessary to recall the apostolic sayings: "do not despise the words of the prophets; but test everything and hold fast to what is good; abstain from every form of evil" (1 Thess. 5:20-22). And: "we destroy arguments and every proud obstacle raised up against the knowledge of God, taking every thought captive to obey Christ" (2 Cor. 10:4-5). Thus if we are ordered to do something that coincides with or contributes to the Lord's commandments, we must accept it with greater attention and zeal, as the will of God, fulfilling the saying: "bearing with one another in the love of Christ" (Eph. 4:2). However, when someone orders us to do something opposed to, deviating from, or corrupting the Lord's commandments, then it is time to say: "We must obey God rather than any human authority" (Acts 5:29). We must remember the words of the Lord: "They will not follow a stranger, but they will run from him because they do not know the voice of strangers" (Jn. 10:5), as well as the words of the Apostle who dared for the sake of our security to confront the angels themselves: "Even if we or an angel from heaven should proclaim to you a gospel contrary to what we have proclaimed to you, let that person be accursed" (Gal. 1:8).

From all this, we are taught that every person who loves the Lord must avoid, even detest anyone who hinders the Lord's commandments or who encourages us to do that which is forbidden, even if the latter is very noble or extremely renowned.

# MACARIUS "OF EGYPT" (4-5TH CENTURY) *

A late fourth-early fifth century collection of sermons and homilies is attributed to Macarius the Great of Egypt, although it appears to be the work of a monk living in Syria. The *Macarian Homilies* underline themes that are prominent as well as popular in Eastern Christian spirituality, such as deification, personal experience, and the intimate encounter of Christ through repentance and the sacraments. These writings have long proved formative reading for the young spiritual directee in the monastic and spiritual tradition.

1. There are three virtues, with numerous manifestations, which precede purity: these are truth in its entirety, abstinence, and the endurance of things that come our way. These virtues cannot be acquired by any other means but through fasting and prayer, where we do not despise the tribulations of long-suffering, but only seek patience. When we cannot bear the pain, we offer words of prayer. For good is lasting only when it is accompanied by pain of heart. Whereas those things which come to us without pain, are also easily taken away from us.

Therefore, without voluntary tribulation it is impossible to follow Christ and actively to understand about heaven and hell. This is why He says: "I am the door; anyone who enters through me can come in and go out" (Jn. 10:9). And again: "Learn from me, for I am meek and humble in heart" (Mt. 11:29). So the person who is humbled with meekness of heart also enters this door, where the truth is preferred above all else and the conscience is condemning, where the deeds of the hypocrites are confessed and the fear of God revealed.

---

* Macarius/Symeon, *Logos* I, 39. See ed. H. Dörries, *Wort und Stunde*, in *Die Griechischen Christlichen Schriftsteller* (Göttingen, 1966) 248-250. Also in ed. G. Berthold, in *GCS*: Berlin, 1973.

Then the soul which is illumined through fear also sees within itself its own rational nature standing in good order: peaceful, calm, undisturbed, undistracted, pleasing to God, devout, hopeful, pure in faith, single-headed, strong-willed, with peculiar turns, prepared for worship.

Then too does it see its own darkness, learning just how far it is from its proper nature; and so it proceeds toward genuine repentance, and desires to obtain this. For the light shines only in order for us to see. Therefore, the soul prays with pain to the Master, confessing that it has sinned greatly and combining pain and shame for the sake of receiving the truth. And all this for the sole purpose that it may attain to all that it has seen through the grace of Christ, who has also granted us from here the first-fruits and manifested the gifts of the kingdom darkly, according to the Apostle (1 Cor. 11:12), in order that having believed with certainty we may not grow faint-hearted as we die each day for the sake of life.

However, how can anyone be comforted who does not wish to reprove oneself according to conscience, or to learn from another? Such a person does not gladly welcome the medicine of righteousness, but only knows and pursues fleshly thoughts of human glory and praise. Yet each of us can know through our own heart which preparations are properly deserved. So let every person look at oneself to see which spirit rather embraces one. For we must contend with both spirits up until death.

Therefore, let no one rejoice at being introduced to good, but only at overcoming evil, at conquering the enemy, at transcending one's measure through tribulation, at obtaining a spiritual perception through meekness, at progressing each day, at not yet losing one's patience. And so one must seek the aforementioned fear of God for the illumination of knowledge. One should search whether evil has concealed the wrongs of the soul, wishing to manifest good in a partial way, in order that it may thereby bring about conceit and in order that, having assured the intellect through conceit, it may rob us of everything. For conceit happens to destroy every good thing. This is why each of us must do good, and reprove ourselves according to our conscience on a daily basis about wrongs done, and even to love reproof; we should not attribute evil falsely to ourselves pretending to be humble, because the enemy also finds opportunities in this. Learn from the art of evil: for it conceals the terrible things as if they were nothing; and those things which are nothing it attributes to us, setting us up in order later to say: "you are blessed, that you are not such a person." And so it hides arrogance within humility, and causes spiritual death to the person who does not guard the truth.

Let us therefore begin with the truth; let us learn to love tribulations for the sake of truth, which lead us to the purity of soul; let us not accept a false thought; let us acquire experience of the good things to come; let us obtain faith with assurance. For faith with assurance comes to us through experience; and experience comes through purity of heart; and purity comes through long-suffering; and long-suffering comes through fasting and prayer.

2. *Question*: But how can we, never actually having entered the heart, begin to do so?

*Response*: We have already said that through fasting and prayer, we stand outside and knock, just as He commanded us saying: "Knock and it shall be opened to you" (Mt. 7:7). Therefore, blessed are they who enter and remain to the end, and who have acquired a pure heart. By clean heart we mean not so much a heart that does not receive evil; for the free will is never destroyed. Instead we mean a heart purified by grace, having its proper inclination by nature, as the Lord said: "Look, you have been purified; go and sin no more" (Jn. 5:14), showing us that even after receiving grace, each of us retains our proper will. For when His disciples said: "Increase our faith" (Lk. 17:5), He told them: "If you had faith the size of a mustard seed, you would say to this mountain, 'Move over there, and enter the sea,' and it would obey" (Lk. 17:6). By this Christ signified the active faith, which is difficult to attain. For it is not clear to the person who has not seen reality through the heart how it is that we are cast out by our disobedience, and again allowed inside by our obedience – each person according to the inclination of the will.

3. *Question*: You said that it is necessary for us to reprove ourselves before God according to conscience. Nevertheless, how is this possible, when I am unaware of most things? For sin has enveloped me.

. *Response*: As human beings, we are unaware. Yet we must believe that grace is infallible. And when grace finds the soul's inner wounds concealed, then it appropriately concedes you to the outward tribulations. If you should bear these patiently, grace heals that which is concealed and with the same impact also reveals to you the hidden sin. However, when we do not endure the things that come upon us, neither do we see our hidden passions nor do we acquire healing. Therefore, do not be troubled against your neighbor when something happens, but remain balanced before every occurrence, and your wounds will not be concealed or unhealed. For just as it is harmful to anoint with oil a person who has a fever, so is it dangerous for an injured sinner to seek justice; just as the former is harmed through untimely anointment, so the latter is condemned through unrestrained vindication.

# DOROTHEUS OF GAZA (D.C. 560)*

Dorotheus was one of the most attractive figures among the representatives of the ascetic tradition in the sixth century, which transferred much of the spiritual teaching from the desert of Egypt and transmitted it to the monastic settlements in the regions of Gaza and Palestine. Marvelously delicate as a person, profoundly sensitive as a writer, and paternally caring as an abbot, Dorotheus is part of a long heritage that emphasized the role of discernment in spiritual direction.

*To superiors and disciples in monasteries: on how to supervise the brothers, and how the latter should submit to their supervisors.*

1. If you are a superior to certain brothers, take care of them with strict heart and compassionate mercy, teaching them by your word and deed what they must do – and especially by your deeds because examples are always more effective. If your body is strong, be their example in ascetic works; and if your body is weak, be their example through the good state of your soul. Become a model of the fruits of the Spirit listed by the Apostle Paul: love, joy, peace, patience, goodness, kindness, faith, meekness and self-control in all passions (cf. Gal. 5:22-23). Do not be too frustrated about any mistakes that may happen, but calmly point out the harm that results from them. And if it is necessary to rebuke someone, take into account who

---

* Abba Dorotheus of Gaza, *Letter 2*, in *Sources Chrétiennes* 92 (Paris, 1963) 498-504. For earlier English translations, cf. Eric P. Wheeler, *Dorotheos of Gaza: Discourses and Sayings*, in *Cistercian Publications* 33 (Kalamazoo, 1977) 237-40; and also Keith Schram, in G.I. Mantzarides, *Orthodox Spiritual Life* (Holy Cross Orthodox Press: Brookline, 1994) 86-9.

the person is and what the appropriate time for the rebuke might be. Do not be too demanding in regard to small mistakes, as though you were so scrupulous yourself, nor criticize others continually; for this is burdensome, and continual criticism only leads to insensitivity and contempt. Do not issue orders in an arrogant manner, but counsel your brother with humility; for this way is more encouraging, convincing, and comforting.

2. When a brother resists you and causes trouble, guard your tongue so that you do not say anything at all in anger. Do not let your heart rise up against him. Remember that he is your brother, a member in Christ, an image of God, influenced by our common enemy. So be compassionate toward him, lest the devil entangle him on account of the wound resulting from your anger, killing him with the sin of resentment, and through your carelessness destroying his soul for which Christ died (cf. 1 Cor. 8-1 1). Remember that you yourself are subject to the same sin of anger. And show compassion on your brother from your own weakness, rendering thanks that you have found an opportunity to forgive, so that you may also be forgiven more and for greater things by God. For it is said: "forgive, and you shall be forgiven" (Lk. 6:37). Perhaps you think that your brother will be harmed by your patience. Yet St. Paul commands us to overcome evil with good, and not with evil (cf. Rom. 12:11). And the Fathers say: "If you are moved to anger in rebuking another person, you have fulfilled your own passion."[1] And no prudent person would tear down his own house in order to build one for his neighbor.

3. If the trouble persists, restrain your heart and say the following prayer: "O God who loves people and their soul; who in your ineffable goodness brought us from non-being into being in order to share your blessings; who, when we rebelled against your commandments, recalled us through the blood of your only Son our Savior; be now also present in our weakness, and command the turmoil in our hearts to be calmed, just as you once calmed the troubled sea (cf. Mt. 8:26). Do not leave the two of us alone at this time, for we are dying through sin. And do not say, 'What benefit has come from my blood, and from my descent into corruption?' (cf. Ps. 29:10); or, 'Amen I say to you, I do not know you' (Mt. 25:12), because our lamps have gone out from a lack of oil" (cf. Mt. 25:8).

4. After this prayer, when your heart has been calmed, you are then able to reprove with wisdom and humility according to the Apostolic exhortation (cf. 2 Tim. 4:2), as well as to discipline and comfort with compassion in order to heal and correct your brother as a weaker member. For then that brother too will accept your correction with confidence, accusing himself of hardness. So through your own peace you will pacify his heart. Therefore, let nothing separate you from the holy tradition of Christ who says: "Learn from me, for I am gentle and humble in heart" (Mt. 11:29). It is necessary first to be careful to acquire a peaceful state, so as not to confuse the heart either with fair excuses or supposedly with commands, being convinced that we fulfill all the commandments for the sake of love and purity of heart. If you treat your brother in this way, you will hear a voice saying: "If you utter what is precious, and not what is worthless, you shall serve as my mouth" (Jer. 15:19).

5. If you are under obedience, never trust your own heart; for it is blinded by old inclinations. Neither follow your own judgment in anything, nor decide anything by yourself without inquiring first or receiving counsel. Do not consider or believe yourself to be more reasonable or fair in your thoughts than your superior. Do not become an examiner of his deeds and, often, a deceived tester. For this is an illusion from the evil one who endeavors to hinder you from obedience with faith in all things and from the salvation that is assured through this. Submit with contentment, and you will advance without danger or error in the way of the Fathers. Constrain yourself in all things by cutting off your will, and by the grace of Christ you will become accustomed to cutting it off habitually, so that in the future you will do this without any effort or trouble, because it will always happen to be as you want. "For you do not want things to be as you desire, but rather as they in fact are."[2] In this way you are at peace with everything, at least with those things which do not transgress the commandments of God or the Fathers.

Strive to discover in all things something for which to blame yourself, and maintain disinterestedness with knowledge. Believe that everything that concerns us, even the most trivial detail, lies within God's providence, and you will calmly endure all circumstances. Believe that dishonor and insult are medicines that heal the pride of your soul; and pray for those who ridicule you, as being true doctors, convinced that one who hates dishonor also hates humility, and one who flees those who are irritating also flees gentleness. Do not desire to know your neighbor's evil or accept rumors about that person; and if such rumors are spread on account of human wickedness, strive to transform these into good thoughts, giving thanks for all things, while preserving goodness and holy love.

6. Above all let us all guard our conscience in everything, in regard to godly concerns, our neighbor's affairs, and material things. Before saying or doing anything, let us examine whether it is according to God's will. And only after so praying, let us speak or act. Let us cast our weakness before God, and His goodness will accompany us in all.

NOTES

[1] *Sayings of the Desert Fathers*, Macarius 17 PG 65:269.
[2] Epictetus, *Manual* 8-9. Cf. also Basil, *Letter* 151 PG 32: 608.

## JOHN OF THE LADDER (c.579-c.649)*

An ascetic and abbot on Mount Sinai, John Climacus became known, even identified, by his *Ladder* [or *Klimax] of Divine Ascent,* a classic work of Orthodox spirituality that has formed alike lay persons and monastics through the centuries, being required reading in monasteries every Great Lent since the seventh century. Attached as an appendix to the *Ladder is* a small treatise entitled "To the Shepherd," which provides extraordinarily penetrating insights into the notion of spiritual fatherhood and the practice of spiritual direction.

### *Letter to the Shepherd:*
1. In this earthly book, wondrous Father, I have left you last, but I am convinced that you are inscribed in the heavenly book before all of us. For truly He is trustworthy who said: "The last in thought will be first in dignity" (cf. Mt. 20:16).

2. A shepherd is above all one that is able to seek and heal the lost, rational sheep through guilelessness, zeal, and prayer.

3. A pilot is one who has received spiritual strength from God and from personal toils, and who is thus able to raise the ship not only from the storm but from the abyss itself.

4. A physician is one who is healed from every illness of body and soul, and has no need of medicine from others.

5. A genuine teacher is one who has received the tablet of spiritual knowledge from God, written by God's divine finger, namely through the experience of divine illumination, and there-

---

* St. John Climacus, *The Ladder of Divine Ascent: To the Shepherd.* An earlier English translation may be found in Holy Transfiguration Monastery (Boston, 1979) 231-50. The Greek text appears in Migne, *Patrologia Graeca,* vol. 88: 1165-1208. The entire text of *The Ladder* is in cols. 632-1161.

fore has no need of other books. It is inappropriate for teachers to offer instruction from notes and copies, just as it is inappropriate for painters to copy others' creations.

6. In instructing those on earth, offer teachings from on high; and train them in spiritual matters with the use of material images and methods. Do not forget him who said: "I did not receive my teaching from any human source, nor was I taught it" (Gal. 1:12). For lowly teachings can never heal lowly people.

7. An able pilot saves the ship, and a good shepherd inspires and heals the ill sheep. So long as the sheep follow their shepherd and progress continually, the shepherd will be able to give account for them to the master of the house. Let the shepherd cast stones of reprimand at those sheep which fall behind as a result of their laziness or gluttony. For this too is the sign of a good shepherd.

8. When the sheep begin to drowse spiritually from the burning heat, or rather the bodily heat, then the shepherd should raise his eyes toward heaven and be even more watchful over them. For often, during this burning time, many sheep fall prey to wolves. However, if the rational sheep show humility, like the animal sheep which lower their heads during the heat, then we may recall the words of the one who said: "a broken and contrite heart, God will not despise" (Ps. 50:14).

9. When darkness and the night of passions fall upon the flock, render your guard-dog immovable before God in night-watch. It is not at all improper to describe the intellect as a guard-dog, for it drives away the wild beasts.

10. The good Lord also gave us this natural characteristic: when a sick person sees the physician, that person rejoices, even if perhaps there is nothing to benefit from the physician.

11. You too, wondrous Father, should acquire plasters, medical potions, razors, eye-washers, sponges, blood-letting instruments, cauterizing instruments, ointments, sleeping pills, a knife, bandages, and sickness-tablets. If we do not have access to anyone of these, how can we practice our medical profession? There is no way, for indeed physicians are rewarded not for their words but for their actions.

12. A plaster is a cure for the visible, namely the bodily passions. A medical potion is a cure for the inner passions, and the draining of inner impurity that is unseen. A razor is any acute

dishonor that purifies the rot of arrogance. An eye-washer is a cleansing of the spiritual eye which has been dimmed and disturbed by anger. An eye-washer is also a caustic reproach which very soon brings about healing. A blood-letting instrument is a quick draining of hidden impurity and rot. A blood-letting instrument is an especially intensive and sudden incision for the salvation of the sick. A sponge is the caring and refreshing water applied by the physician to the patient with his gentle, kind, and tender words after the blood-letting and surgery. Cauterization is the penalty and penance given in a compassionate way for a particular time to the sinner for the purpose of repentance. Ointment is the comfort after the cauterization, offered to the patient by word or some other form of consolation. A sleeping pill is the bearing of the disciple's burden, giving rest through obedience, as well as vigilant sleep and holy blindness, so that one does not see one's own virtues. A bandage is for strengthening until death and for binding firmly with patience those paralyzed and weakened by vainglory. And finally, a knife is the measure and decision to amputate a limb that has spiritually died or a member that has rotted, so that its harm does not spread elsewhere.

13. Blessed and noteworthy is painlessness for physicians and passionlessness for superiors. For the former will effortlessly strive to heal every cause of stench, because they feel neither nausea nor repulsion; the latter will again be able to resurrect every dead soul.

14. Let this also be one of the superior's prayers: that he may come to participate in the pain and disposition of each brother according to each brother's order and merit. Then he will avoid what happened to Jacob (cf. Gen. 37), greatly harming both his beloved disciple and the rest of the monastic community. This often happens to superiors who have not yet entirely trained their spiritual senses (cf. Heb. 5:14) in order to discern what is good and what is evil, and the difference between the two.

15. It is a great shame for the superior to pray for his disciple to receive a gift which he himself has not yet acquired. Those who have beheld the countenance of a king, and known him as a friend, are able to introduce any of his servants and helpers, even to reconcile strangers and enemies, if they so wish, in order to share in his glory. The same may also be thought in regard to the saints.

16. People respect and listen to their closest and sincerest friends; they are even pressed and pressured by them. It is good to acquire spiritual friends in the angels, for no one else can help us so much toward virtue.

17. A certain God-pleasing soul related to me that God always, and especially on annual festivals and major feasts, rewards His servants with gifts.

18. The physician should be entirely rid of passions, so as to feign them at the appropriate time, especially the passion of anger. For if he has not entirely expelled the passions, then he will not be able to feign them dispassionately.

19. I noticed a horse that was still somewhat untrained, and it was calmly trotting while being restrained by the reins. Then suddenly, when the reins were relaxed, it threatened the life of its own master. This case, which resembles a riddle, generally occurs as a result of two demons. Those who wish to look into this, should do so with diligence. For physicians will only understand what knowledge they have been granted by God, when they are able to cure passions which for the majority of people appear incurable.

20. It is not the teacher who has rendered good and apt pupils learned that is praiseworthy, but the one who has educated the illiterate and slow in learning. For the skill of horse-riders is manifested and praised when they triumph with inappropriate and untrained horses, while causing the latter no harm.

21. If you have received the eyes to foresee the swelling of the waves, then give good and clear warnings to those in the ship. Otherwise, you too will be blamed for the shipwreck, since you have assumed the role of pilot of the ship over all the others who have no responsibility.

22. I have seen physicians who did not early enough reveal to their patients the source of their illness, thereby causing great pain and anguish to the patients as well as to themselves.

23. The more the superior sees the great confidence of the disciples and of others toward himself, the greater attention he should give to all that he does and says. For he understands that everyone is looking to him as to an archetypal image, considering his words and deeds as a rule and law for their life.

24. A true shepherd is revealed in love. For it is out of love that the Great Shepherd was crucified.

25. Consider, in your words, the deeds of others as if they were your own, and you will not always have to feel ashamed of others.

26. Allow the sinner to hurt for a while, so that the illness becomes neither prolonged nor the cause of death as a result of your accursed silence. For because of the pilot's silence, many have presumed to be sailing smoothly, until they struck a reef.

27. Let us listen to the great Paul who writes to Timothy: "be prepared both in season and out of season" (2 Tim. 4:2). I think that "in season" signifies the occasions when people gladly accept rebuke; and "out of season" implies the times when people are embittered by rebuke. This is what happens with water springs which often continue to flow even when there is no one thirsty at hand.

28. Some superiors have, so to speak, a shy character, and as a result often refrain from saying what they should to their disciples. These too should not refrain from teaching their disciples, but could undertake to give the necessary instructions in writing.

29. Let us hear what the Holy Scripture says in certain passages: "Cut down the fig tree. Why should it use up the soil?" (Lk. 13:7). "Expel the wicked person from among you" (1 Cor. 5:13). "Do not pray for this people" (Jer. 7:16). The same was told to Samuel about Saul (1 Kings 16:1). The shepherd must know all of this, as well as to whom, how, and when each of these passages is to be applied. For none is more trustworthy than God.

30. If one does not feel shame when rebuked in private, then even a public reproach will be an opportunity for greater shamelessness; for this person has voluntarily shunned and disdained salvation.

31. I am also thinking of something I have seen in many well-intentioned patients. Knowing their cowardice and weakness, they begged their physicians to bind them and to heal them against their will, forcibly. For "the spirit is willing," hoping as they do in the future life, "but the flesh is weak" (Mt. 26:41), accustomed as it is to former sins. Upon noticing this, I asked their physicians to comply and obey.

32. The guide should not tell all those who approach, that "the way is straight and narrow" (Mt. 7:14), or that "the yoke is easy

and the burden light" (Mt. 11:30). Instead, the guide should examine each case, and accordingly prescribe the appropriate medicine. To those who are burdened with grave sins and easily inclined toward despair, he should offer the latter remedy; while to those inclined toward pride and conceit, he should give the former passage.

33. Some people who were about to set out on a long journey made inquiries to those who knew the way, and were told that it is smooth and safe. Yet hearing this, they traveled carefree and mid-way either faced danger or else turned back, for they were unprepared for trials. You should also think about the reverse situation.

34. Wherever divine love burned within the heart, fear of words had no power. Wherever fear of punishment was present, patience in every ascetic toil was observed. And wherever hope for the kingdom appeared, disdain for all earthly things was encountered.

35. A good general must be well acquainted with the place and order of each soldier. For among his many troops, there may be some distinguished in battle or in single-combat. These must be set apart in silence, in order to assist him on behalf of their comrades.

36. A pilot cannot save a ship on his own, without the assistance of his sailors. Nor can a physician cure a patient unless he is first entreated and encouraged by the sick person who in complete confidence reveals the wound. Those who were ashamed of consulting a physician, have left their wounds to fester; often, many of them have even died as a result of this.

37. When the sheep are grazing, and especially when they are sleeping, the shepherd should not cease playing the pipe of exhortation. For there is nothing more frightening to the wolf than the sound of the shepherd's pipe.

38. The elder should neither always humble himself unreasonably, nor always exalt himself carelessly, imitating St. Paul who behaved according to the circumstance at hand (cf. 2 Cor. 10:10 and 12:10).

39. Often the Lord conceals certain weaknesses of the elder from the eyes of his disciples. And if the elder himself reveals these, he may shatter their trust.

40. I have seen an elder who, out of extreme humility, sought

the advice of his disciples on certain matters. However, I have seen another who, out of pride, wished to demonstrate his foolish wisdom and behaved strangely with his disciples.

41. On certain occasions, 'though infrequently, I have seen passionate elders directing dispassionate disciples; and gradually, feeling shame before their disciples, they too began to control their passions. I think that this is the result within them of the saved, namely the dispassionate disciples. And so a passionate service became for them a cause for dispassion.

42. We should be careful not to scatter in the open sea what we have gathered in the harbor. This will be clear to those who are still unaccustomed to and unskilled in the turmoil of this world.

43. It is truly a great thing to endure courageously the burning heat of stillness, as well as the suffering and struggle of ignorance and indifference. Likewise, it is a great thing not to seek after distractions, motions, and comforts outside the ship of one's cell, in the manner of careless and indifferent sailors who long to swim around in the water during a period of calm. However, it is incomparably greater to fear no turmoil and to remain steadfast in heart from any assault, keeping calm while living outwardly with people but inwardly with God.

44. Let what happens in law-courts of this world remind you, wondrous Father, to think about your own life. Observe how one person comes guilty to our terrible and real court of judgment, while another comes innocent and with a great desire to work and to serve God. Each person surely approaches in different manner, and each one requires different treatment.

45. First of all, let us ask the guilty one – privately, of course – what sort of sins were committed. I say this for two reasons: first, so that he does not acquire audacity, being always pricked and humbled by this confession; and second, so that he will be moved to love us, conscious of the wounds which we have assumed on our shoulders.

46. Nor should the following escape your notice, venerable friend – as if, God forbid, you did not know it! I mean that, in judging the guilty, we should take into consideration their place of birth, their upbringing, and their habits. For these comprise the source of many and various differences. Often a person who is weaker in body will be more humble in heart. So that person

ought to be punished more lightly by the spiritual judges. It is naturally obvious what should happen in the opposite case.

47. It is not right for a lion to pasture sheep; likewise, it is not safe for a person who is still subject to passions to direct passionate people.

48. A fox among hens is an ugly sight; but nothing is uglier than a shepherd in rage. For, the first disturbs and destroys hens, while the second does this to rational souls.

49. Be careful not to become an exacting investigator of the slightest sins, because then you will no longer be an imitator of God.

50. Have God Himself as your own steward and superior in all your inward and outward affairs, like an excellent pilot. By cutting off your will through His intervention, you too will become carefree and learn to guide through His will alone.

51. Both you and all other shepherds should also examine the following possibility: whether grace has mostly deigned to work through us, not on account of our purity, but on account of the faith of those subject to us. For even many passionate people have worked miracles in this way.

52. If, as the Lord says, "on that day many will say to me: Lord, Lord, did we not prophesy in your name?" (Mt. 7:22) and so on, then the aforementioned is not incredible.

53. A person who has truly obtained mercy from God is able, in an invisible and secret manner, to benefit those who are suffering. Hence, this person accomplishes two very significant things: not only does he preserve himself from human glory, as if from rust, but he also enables those who have preserved God's mercy to offer thanks to God alone.

54. Prepare the best and select meals for those who run well, with youthful eagerness, and courage. But offer milk, as if to young babies, to those who lag behind, whether in their actions or in their attitude. For every consolation has its proper time.

55. Often the same food makes some people eager and others despondent. We must be careful in sowing seed, paying attention to the time, the person, the quality, and the quantity.

56. Some people have thoughtlessly undertaken to shepherd souls, without in the least considering the responsibility involved in taking charge of others. And it so happened that, while they possessed great riches beforehand, they departed this life

empty-handed, because they dispersed their riches among others by assuming the responsibility of their spiritual direction.

57. Just as there are genuine and legitimate children, children from second marriages, children from mistresses, and children deserted on the streets, so also do we discern a parallel distinction in the matter of spiritual direction. There is spiritual responsibility that is literally a complete laying down of one's life for the sake of one's neighbor. There is responsibility only for sins of the past, or else only for sins of the future. There is also responsibility that assumes the burden only of one's own commands, because of a lack of spiritual strength and dispassion. However, the primary and perfect kind of responsibility lies in bearing the burden according to the degree that we impose the cutting off of another person's will.

58. A genuine child is recognized in the absence of the father. The same appears true to me with respect to spiritual direction. Let the superior observe and note well those who contradict and resist him, and in the presence of high guests of honor let him rebuke them with very severe reproofs, even if they are deeply hurt by such a disgrace; for this way also instills fear in the others. It is surely worthwhile punishing one person in order to teach others.

59. There are some who have assumed, beyond their strength, the burden of others out of spiritual love, recalling Him who said: "No one has greater love than this" (Jn. 15:13) and so on. And there are others who perhaps have received from God the strength for spiritual direction, and yet who still do not gladly assume the burden of others for the sake of their brothers' salvation. The latter I pitied as being people without love; while for the former I have found a fitting passage from Scripture: "Whoever makes something precious from something worthless shall serve as my mouth" (Jer. 15:19); and again: "as you have done, so it shall be done to you" (Obad. 1:15).

60. Please also pay attention to the following: a sin committed in thought by the superior is often considered greater than a sin committed in act by one in obedience; just as an error on the part of a soldier is less significant than a general's bad or wrong counsel.

61. Teach those who are in obedience to you not to confess in detail sins related to the flesh or to lust. However, in regard to all other sins, teach them to bring them to mind, day and night, in detail.

62. Train those in obedience to you to be completely sincere and guileless toward each other, but very cautious toward the demons.

63. The aims and motives in the relationships of those in your spiritual flock should not escape your notice. For the wolves try to destroy the zealous ones by means of the despondent.

64. Do not be lazy in intercession and prayer, even on behalf of those who are completely negligent. And pray not so much that they may find mercy – for this is impossible while they do not do their own part – but that God may arouse them to zeal.

65. As defined in the holy canons, let the weak not sit at the same table with heretics. However, if those who are strong in the Lord are invited in good faith and disposition by heretics, then they should go, if they so wish, for the glory of the Lord.

66. Do not plead ignorance, for "the one who did not know and did what deserved a beating, will receive a ... beating" (Lk. 12:48), because he did not try to learn a lesson.

67. It is a disgrace for a shepherd to be afraid of death; for the definition of obedience is fearlessness before death.

68. Find out, blessed one, which virtue it is "without which no one will see the Lord" (Heb. 12:14), and make sure that your children acquire this before all else. Furthermore, rid them entirely from every soft and feminine countenance.

69. There should be, depending on age, different conditions and dwelling-places for all those entrusted to our supervision by the Lord. For no one should have to be sent away who comes to our harbor.

70. Let us not lay our hands hurriedly on anyone, before they have reached legal maturity, as this is defined in the world, lest some sheep be led to the monastic habit out of ignorance. For when they later come to know the monastic life, they cannot bear the weight and the heat, deserting us and returning to the world. This matter is not without consequences for those who tonsure others prematurely.

71. Who is it that has become such a spiritual steward of God that he no longer requires the flow of tears, sighs, and ascetic toils, but can offer these generously to God for the purification of others?

72. Never cease to sponge and cleanse defiled souls, and especially defiled bodies, so that you may boldly ask from the good Judge not only for the wreaths that belong to your own

soul, but also for those that belong to other souls.

73. I have known an infirm person who has, through faith, healed another person's infirmity. This was achieved by beseeching God with praiseworthy shamelessness and by humbly sacrificing one's life for the sake of another. And as a result of the other's healing, the former person's soul was also healed. However, I have also seen someone doing the same thing, but with pride. And he heard the words of rebuke: "Physician, cure yourself" (Lk. 4:23).

74. A person may refuse some good for the sake of a greater good; like the person [i.e., St. Gregory of Neocaesarea, the Wonderworker] who escaped martyrdom, not out of cowardice but for the sake of those benefiting and being saved through him.

75. Another person may surrender to dishonor in order to honor one's neighbor. While this person seems to many people like a sinful and sensual person, in fact he is "as an impostor, and yet true" (2 Cor. 6:8).

76. If a person who has beneficial words but does not share these generously will not be left unpunished, how much more, my friend, are they in danger who are able to help those in distress by the very zeal of their works, and are not eager to work with them?

77. If you have been redeemed by God, then redeem others. If you have been saved, then save those who are led to death; and do not be selfish about redeeming those who are murdered by demons. This is a great accomplishment before God, exceeding every human and angelic activity or vision.

78. One who wipes away and cleans the impurity of others through the purity received by God, thereby offering to God blameless gifts from blemished things, becomes like a coworker of the bodiless and spiritual powers. For this is the unique and continual work of the divine ministers, "all of whom around Him bring gifts" (Ps. 75:12).

79. Nothing else manifests more clearly our Creator's love and goodness toward us than the fact that He left the ninety-nine sheep in search of the one that went astray (cf. Mt. 18:12). Take care, then, wondrous one; and show all your zeal, love, warmth, care, and prayer toward the one who is most astray and broken. For great illness and wounds are undoubtedly paralleled by great rewards.

80. Let us observe, attend, and act appropriately. The superior should not always judge according to what is just, on account of the weakness of some. I happened to see a very wise judge deciding the case of two brothers: he pronounced the guilty man as innocent, since he was weaker; and he condemned the innocent man as guilty, since he was courageous and strong. He did this so as not to widen the gap between them for the sake of justice. Privately, however, and individually he told each one what was appropriate, and especially to the one with the illness of soul.

81. A green valley is suitable for sheep; and instruction and remembrance of death is most appropriate for the rational sheep, having the power to cure every infectious disease (lit., *lice*).

82. When you inspect and test the courageous, dishonor them without reason before the weak, so that with the medicine of the one you may heal the wound of another, thus training the infirm to be firm.

83. Nowhere does God appear to reveal the sins of a confession heard, lest by revealing them He should hinder those who confess and render them incurably sick.

84. If we have the gift of clairvoyance, we should not reveal the errors of the sinful, but rather indirectly encourage them to confession of their own accord. For they receive generous forgiveness by confessing their sins to us of their own accord. And after confession, let us offer them the possibility of greater courage and confidence than before. For in this way they advance greatly in trust and love toward us. Furthermore, we should be for them a model of extreme humility, while also training them to have fear before us. In all things you must be patient, except in the case of disobedience.

85. Take care, lest your excessive humility bring burning coals on the heads of your children.

86. Look carefully, and see whether there are trees in your field which "are wasting the soil" (Lk. 13:7) and which may perhaps bear fruit elsewhere. Do not hesitate, through loving advice, to uproot them from your field and transplant them.

87. There are occasions when the superior may, unendangered, cultivate virtue in inappropriate places, namely in more secular and sensual places.

88. If the physician possesses inner stillness, then he will not

have as great a need of outward silence in order to care for the sick. However, if he lacks the former, then he should resort to the latter.

89. Let the superior carefully check every sheep that comes into his flock. For God in no way forbids us to refuse and remove that which we judge as unsuitable.

90. There is no gift more acceptable to God than for us to bring Him rational souls through repentance. The whole world is not worth as much as the soul; for the world is fleeting, while the soul is and remains incorruptible. Therefore, blessed one, do not praise those who offer money, but rather those who dedicate rational sheep to Christ.

91. Render your whole-burnt offering blameless and clean. Otherwise you will gain no profit from it.

92. Just as we should understand the words of Scripture, that "the Son of Man goes as it is written of Him, but woe to that one by whom the Son of Man is betrayed" (Mk. 14:21), so also it seems to me that we should understand the opposite: namely, that many needed to be saved – those, of course, who desired this – but the reward will be received by those through whom, after the Lord, salvation was worked.

93. Above all else, venerable friend, we need spiritual strength, so that those whom we endeavor to lead into the Holy of Holies, striving to show to them Christ reclining on the mystical and secret altar, we may take by the hand, as though they were baby children; thus when we see them afflicted and distressed, especially at the threshold of the entrance, by a throng of temptations that hinder them, we may free them from this throng of thoughts.

If some are very immature and weak, then we must lift them and carry them on our shoulders until they have passed through the door of this truly narrow entrance. For it is here that all the stifling pressure and distress frequently occurs. This is why someone once said about this: "This seemed to me a wearisome task, until I went into the sanctuary of God" (Ps. 72:16).

94. We have mentioned above, great Father, about that father of fathers and teacher of teachers, how he was entirely clothed in heavenly wisdom, straightforward, critical, exacting, sober, condescending, and radiant of soul. And what was most marvelous, was that he trained with greater strictness those that he

saw as having a desire for salvation; and again, if he saw others having their own will or attachment, he would deprive them of what they desired, so that all would be careful not to show their own individual will or particular attachment.

That renowned man also used to say the following: "It is better to remove a man from the monastery than to allow him to do his own will. For often, by removing him, the superior renders that man more humble and even teaches him henceforth to cut off his own will. However, one who out of apparent loving-kindness and condescension is gracious to those who persist in their own will, will cause them to curse him piteously at the time of their death, as one who deceived rather than benefited them."

After the evening service, therefore, we could see that great man sitting on a throne – outwardly made of wood but inwardly made of spiritual gifts – like a king surrounded by all the brothers of the community resembling wise bees, listening to his words and commands as if from God. He would order one person to recite fifty psalms, another thirty, and another one hundred. He would order one person to make so many prostrations, and another to sleep in a sitting position. He would order one person to read for a period of time, and another to pray during that time.

Furthermore, he appointed two brothers as supervisors during the day to observe those who opened conversations or who became lazy in order to correct them, and during the night to observe those who stayed awake in vain or did things too inappropriate for me to record. Moreover, that great man had even set a rule for each person in the matter of food. Not everyone had the same or even similar diet, but this was regulated for each person according to his condition. For some that good steward ordered a stricter diet with less food, while for others a more substantial diet. And the wonderful thing was that everyone obeyed his command without complaint, as if it came from God's mouth. There was also a "lavra" under this famous man's spiritual authority, and there this superior – who was perfect in all things – sent those of his monks who were able to lead a life of silence.

95. Do not, I ask you, render the simple and direct monks into wicked and complex people. On the contrary, if it is possible,

try to change the wicked monks into simple ones. This is indeed a marvelous and difficult task.

96. A person who is completely purified of passions by perfect dispassion is able to make a precise judgment, like some divine judge. For the lack of dispassion bothers the judge's heart, not allowing him to punish or purge as he should.

97. Leave your spiritual children with a blameless faith and pious dogmas as their most valuable inheritance, so that you may guide not only your children but also your grandchildren to the Lord through your path of orthodoxy.

98. Do not feel sorry about wearing out and taming those full of youthful vigor, so that they may praise you at the time of their death.

99. Let the great Moses also be your model in this, most wise one. For he was unable to free his dependents from Pharaoh, although they followed him eagerly, until they ate unleavened bread and bitter herbs (cf. Ex. 20:12). The unleavened bread is the soul without the additional element of willfulness. For this is what creates puffing and pride, whereas unleavened bread always remains lowly. And the bitter herbs should at times be interpreted as the piercing pain of obedience, while at other times as the sorrow caused by the bitterness of fasting.

100. As I am writing these things to you, great Father, imagine me hearing him who says: "You then that teach others, will you not teach yourself?" (Rom. 2:21). So now I will say only one more thing and close this letter. A soul that has been united to God through purity needs no further word of instruction, because that blessed soul bears within itself the eternal Word as its initiator, guide, and illuminator. This is precisely how I have perceived your soul to be, as a most holy and illumined superior. And I know well your most pure thought and disposition – not simply by words, but by actions and personal experience – that it shines with a meekness and humility that destroy beasts, just like the virtues of that great law-giver Moses. You are following in his footsteps, most patient one; and continually advancing to new heights, you have even almost surpassed him – I mean in regard to the honor of purity and the reward of chastity, by means of which we may especially and exclusively approach God who is all-pure, and who grants and encourages all dispassion through which those still living on earth are trans-

ferred to heaven. Like Elijah, the friend of purity, you have ascended to the height of these virtues, as if with a chariot of fire, with untiring feet. Not only have you slain the Egyptian and hidden your achievement in the sand of humility, but you have even ascended the mountain. There, by means of a thorny, wild, and rugged journey, you beheld God and were made worthy of enjoying His voice and light. You loosened your sandals, namely every garment and cover of the mortal, sinful passions. You seized from the tail, namely the end, the angel who was turned into a serpent, and cast him into his hole, into the deepest pit of darkness. You conquered the supreme and mighty Pharaoh, frightened the Egyptians whom you struck down, and – the greatest feat of all – put their first-born to death.

Therefore the Lord entrusted to you, as to one immovable and unshakable, the guidance of the brothers. And you, guide of guides, have fearlessly separated and liberated them from Pharaoh and from the impure clay of brick-making. Through your experience you transmitted – enabling them to taste and know – the divine fire and the cloud of purity that quenches and dispels every flame of desire. Furthermore, you divided before them the red and fiery sea – in which most of us are normally endangered – and, with your staff and pastoral wisdom, you made them victors and champions, completely drowning all the enemy that pursued them.

Even after this, by raising your hands on behalf of your divinely-illumined people, and by standing between practice and theory, you overcame the Amalek of pride, whom most victors usually encounter after conquering the sea. You conquered the nations. You raised those who are with you to the mountain of dispassion. You ordained them priests. You gave the law of purifying circumcision, without which it is impossible to see God. You ascended to the heights, dispelling every dark cloud, gloominess and tempest, namely the thrice-gloomy darkness of ignorance.

You approached the light which appeared far more venerable, brighter, and superior than the burning bush. You were deemed worthy of the divine voice, vision, and prophesy. In a way, while still in this life, you saw "the back parts of God," namely the future grandeur, the full illumination of knowledge that awaits us in the age to come. Then you heard the voice that said: "no

one shall see me" (Ex. 33:20). And so you descended from the
vision of God in Horeb to the deepest valley of humility, bearing with you the tablets of divine ascent and glorified in the
countenance of both your soul and body. Alas, however, for the
vision of the golden calf made by my company! Alas for the
smashing of the tablets! And then? You took your people by the
hand. You crossed them through the desert. And when they
were burnt by their inner flame, you opened a spring of water
from tears by means of your wooden rod, namely the "crucifixion of the flesh with its passions and desires" (Gal. 5:24). Then
you proclaim war against the nations that you encounter, destroying them with the fire of the Lord. Arriving at the Jordan –
for nothing prevents me from continuing the thread of this story
– like Joshua you divide your people into groups by your word.
Then you divide the waters: the lower waters (namely the introductory tears) you allow to flow into the salty Dead Sea, the
sea of the mortification of passions; while the waters from on
high (namely the tears of love) you allow to rise up before the
eyes of your spiritual Israelites.

Then you command them to take twelve stones, either in order to show them the way of the Apostles, or else to symbolize
the conquest of the eight nations and passions, as well as the
acquisition of the four principle virtues.

Leaving far behind the barren Dead Sea, you come upon the
enemy's city, and sounding the trumpet with prayer during this
seventh cycle of human life, you tear down its walls and destroy the city. Therefore you too may chant to your immaterial
and invisible Ally: "The swords of the enemy have vanished;
their cities you have destroyed" (Ps. 9:6).

And should I say what is foremost and greatest of all? You
ascend to Jerusalem, the vision of the perfect peace of souls.
You see Christ, the God of peace. You have "shared in His suffering like a good soldier" (2 Tim. 2:3). You have "crucified with
Him the flesh with its passions and desires" (Gal. 5:24). And so,
rightly, you have become like "God against Pharaoh" (Ex. 7:1)
and all his hostile power. Then you have been buried with Christ
and descended with Him into Hades, namely into the abyss of
theology and of ineffable mystery. You have been anointed with
myrrh and fragrance by kindred and loving women, namely
the virtues. And you have been resurrected – for what prevents

me from saying this too – and are now in heaven, seated at the right hand of God. Oh, what rich spoils, that you arose on the third day, namely after defeating the three tyrants, or, to put it more clearly, the body, the soul, and the spirit; or again, after the purification of the three faculties of the soul: the appetitive, the sensual, and the intellectual.

Finally, you have come to the Mount of Olives – and I must cut my words short so as not to speak unnecessarily, especially to you who are full of wisdom and superior to us all in the knowledge of things that are beyond us – about which a good climber wrote in song: "The high mountains are for the harts" (Ps. 103:20), namely for souls that destroy wild beasts. Running, therefore, alongside this person, you have come to the foot of the mountain. And lifting your eyes toward heaven – again I return to the symbolism of the Word – you blessed us, your disciples. And you saw the heavenly ladder of virtues standing before us.

"According to the grace of God given to you, like a skilled master builder you laid the foundation" (1 Cor. 3:10) for this ladder; or, rather, you built it entirely, although in your great humility you forcibly persuaded us simpletons to offer our impure lips to teach your people. But this is not strange, for according to the sacred history Moses too often described himself as stammering and slow of speech. Yet Moses was deemed worthy of having an excellent assistant and speaker in Aaron; while I do not know why you, initiated in the ineffable mysteries of God, have come to me, namely to a dry spring filled with all the frogs, or rather warts, of Egypt.

However, since I should not leave this endless narration about you incomplete, dear Father who run the course to heaven, I continue again weaving the manifold praise of your beauty. You have approached the holy mountain, and raised your eyes to heaven. You have set your feet on its base, and are running, ascending, being exalted, "riding on the Cherubim," namely the angelic virtues, "and flying" (Ps. 17:11), "going up with a shout" (Ps. 46:6), having destroyed the enemy. You have opened the way for us, going on ahead before us; and you are even now leading and guiding all of us, ascending with a light step to the summit of the holy ladder, and uniting yourself to love. That love is God (cf. 1 Jn. 4:8), to whom be glory to the ages. Amen.

# THEODORE THE STUDITE (759-826)*

The abbot of the Monastery of St. John in Constantinople, Theodore's strength of character, organizational ability, and spiritual leadership led to a revival of the monastic way and to a renewal of ascetic formation in the ninth century. Like the *Monastic Testament*, his *Greater* and *Lesser Catecheses* were addressed to his monks, and reveal a depth of theological understanding and paternal concern.

## (i) Monastic vocation and testament

I hear the divine David saying: "I am ready, and I am not afraid" (Ps. 119:60); and again: "My heart is ready" (Ps. 57:7). Having surrendered to the continual weakness of this wretched body, I will be unprepared to farewell each of you personally at the time of my death, my children, brothers and fathers. For, the monasteries are scattered and far away, while some of you are absent on account of some business. However, since the hour of my passing from this life has already arrived, I have the time at least to leave you with this testament, considering and believing that this is both appropriate and safe for those who desire to hear my final words, as well as for the person who will succeed me as abbot. In this way, you will henceforth enjoy harmony and peace in Christ, the peace which the Lord left to His holy disciples and Apostles as He was about to depart to the heavens (Jn. 14:27).

Therefore, I believe in the Father, Son, and Holy Spirit, the holy, consubstantial and pre-eternal Trinity, in whose name I

---

* Theodore the Studite, *The Testament*. The Greek original appears in J. P. Migne, *Patrologia Graeca*, vol. 99: 1813-1824. Cf. an earlier English translation by N. Constas, *Saint Theodore the Studite: The Testament* (The Monastery of the Holy Cross: Washington, 1991) 7-13.

have been baptized, regenerated, and perfected. I confess God the Father, God the Son, and God the Holy Spirit; the three are one in divinity, and the one again is three in hypostases. The Trinity is one God, on account of being one in essence, although it is distinct in regard to their being different in hypostases. I also confess our Lord Jesus Christ, one of the Trinity, who out of boundless love for humanity came into flesh for the salvation of our race, assuming flesh from the holy and all-pure Theotokos, without human seed, and was born from her womb by natural law, according to the holy Scriptures. The same Lord is two in natures, fully perfect in divinity, in which He underwent no change from what He was, and fully perfect in humanity, inasmuch as He lacked nothing in what He assumed. I confess the same Lord to be one in hypostasis, just as He is known in two natures, and thus in two wills and energies through which He appropriately worked things both divine and human.

In addition to this, I reject every deceit of heretical belief. Following the six holy and Ecumenical Councils, as well as the second Synod recently convened in Nicaea [i.e., the seventh Ecumenical Council] against those who condemn the Christians, I bow down before and accept the holy and sacred icons of our Lord Jesus Christ, the Theotokos, the Apostles, Prophets, Martyrs, and of all the righteous and just persons. Further, I also seek their pure intercessions which are able to realize divine propitiation. In fear and in faith, I embrace their all-holy relics which are filled with divine grace.

Moreover, I accept every book of both the Old and New Testaments as divinely-inspired. And I accept all the lives and sacred writings of the holy Fathers, teachers, and ascetics. This I say in reference to the mad Pamphilus, who came from the East and who criticized the ascetic fathers, namely Mark [the Monk], [Abba] Isaiah, Barsanuphius [the Great], Dorotheus [of Gaza], and Hesychius [the Presbyter]. These are not the Barsanuphius, Isaiah, and Dorotheus who were of one mind with the "Akephaloi" and the so-called "Dekakeratoi", and who were anathematized in the encyclical of St. Sophronius of Jerusalem. These men have nothing to do with the aforementioned, whom I accept according to the tradition of our Fathers, as I have myself learned by asking the holy Patriarch Tarasius and other trustworthy persons both here [in Constantinople] and farther east. Besides, the icon of Barsanuphius may be found over the altar of the Great Church, alongside those of Anthony [the Great], Ephrem [the Syrian], and other holy Fathers; and so in their writings there is not even the slightest suggestion of impiety. On the contrary, there is much to be found in their writings which can benefit the soul, at least until some distortion of the truth is found in these writings by some synodical inquiry....

I further confess that the monastic habit is supreme, sublime, and angelic, cleansing every sin by its perfect conduct. This is clearly and comprehensively stated in the rules for ascetics formulated by St. Basil the Great, although some people adhere only to certain rules while ignoring the rest. No one should deviate from the three states set forth in the *Ladder of Divine Ascent* [Step 1], for there is no other way that one may be said to live in accordance with the monastic rules. And you should not have any servant, or any female livestock, for this is both improper for the monastic vocation and dangerous for the soul. I have gone through these things very briefly, for this is not the time to write at length. Nonetheless, I have done so in order that none will attribute to me a worse opinion, apart from what I correctly think and believe.

## (ii) The role of the spiritual elder

Having said this, it is now time to say something also concerning the abbot. First, I pay my respects to my lord and my father, and your father, the most holy recluse who is a father, a luminary, and a teacher. He has personally directed both me and you in the Lord and has been set up as a head, even though he has placed himself below all others, living in silence through Christ-like humility. Through his guidance and prayers I believe that you will be saved, so long as in return you render to him the proper discipline and obedience. Afterward, you will submit to the person elected in godly manner by a common vote, following the paternal wish. My own choice will naturally be the one with whom the entire community is pleased.

Come, then, my father and brother, whoever you may be. Behold, in the sight of God and of His elect angels, I place in your charge the entire community in Christ, so that you might receive it. How will you assume this responsibility? In what manner will you guide the brothers? Just how will you guard them? As the flock of Christ, and as your beloved members, comforting them and caring for them, dearly yearning after each one according to the equal measure of love. For the desire to care for the members of the body is innate to every human being. Open up to them your embrace in all compassion; be friendly with all of them in a spirit of mercy; nurture them; refashion them; perfect them in the Lord; sharpen your mind in wisdom; arouse your zeal with confidence; establish your heart in faith and hope; go ahead before them in every good work; be first to do battle against the spiritual enemies; defend them; direct them; lead them into the place of virtue; bequeath to them the land of dispassion. For this reason, I offer you the following commandments, which you are definitely obliged to fulfill.

### (iii) Rules for the spiritual elder

1. You shall not in any way change the form and rule which you have received from my humility without urgent cause.

2. You shall not acquire anything of this world, neither shall you store up your own personal treasure, even if only a silver coin.

3. You shall not disperse your soul and your heart in worldly relations and cares, contradicting what was trusted to you by God and transmitted to you by me, as well as by those who have become your spiritual sons and brothers. Neither shall you appropriate things that belong to the monastery for those who in the flesh were once your family members, relatives, friends, or acquaintances. Neither while you are alive should you provide the above with charity, nor after your death are you to leave them any inheritance. For you are not of the world in order to share in the things of the world. However, if some of them should withdraw from society into our monastic order, you are to care for them according to the example of the holy Fathers.

4. You shall not have a slave, whether for your personal needs or for the needs of the monastery and its fields; for everyone is created according to the image of God. This is allowed only for those living in the world, just as marriage also is. Instead, you must offer yourself as a servant to those who have willingly become your spiritual brothers, 'though externally you may

appear and even be considered as both their master and teacher.

5. You shall not have any animal of the female sex in order to assist you in your needs, whether in the monastery or on its lands; for you have totally renounced everything feminine. None of our holy ascetic Fathers made use of such, nor is it permitted by nature.

6. You shall not ride about on a horse or a mule, unless it is necessary. Instead, you should imitate Christ and go about on foot. Otherwise, a foal should be your beast of burden.

7. See to it in every way that everything in the community is held in common and without division, and that nothing is individually possessed by any person, not even a single sewing-needle. Let your body and soul, and nothing else, be divided equally in love among all your spiritual children and brothers.

8. You shall not adopt or raise children like people who live in the world, for you have renounced the world and marriage. Such behavior is not to be found among the Fathers, and if so only rarely and not as a general rule.

9. You shall not eat with women, whether monastic or lay, except with your mother and sister in the flesh. I do not know any obligation or necessity that calls you to break this rule of the holy Fathers.

10. You shall not frequently leave the monastery nor travel around, abandoning your proper flock without need. Your love and your silence will enable you to protect your ever-changing and wandering spiritual flock.

11. See that catechism is offered without fail three evenings during the week, whether by yourself or by one of your spiritual children. For this too is a tradition of the Fathers and leads to salvation.

12. You shall not grant the so-called small habit [or, "schema"], followed later by the great habit, for the monastic habit is one, just as baptism is one. This was how it was practiced by the holy Fathers.

13. You shall not disobey the rules and canons of the holy Fathers, especially those of St. Basil the Great. And let everything you do or say be in accordance with the commandments of God, having its witness in the Scriptures or in the custom of the Fathers.

14. You shall not abandon your flock and go to another, or revert to some higher office, without the consent of your own community.

15. You shall not behave casually with consecrated virgins, neither shall you enter convents. Nor again shall you hold private conversations with any nun or laywoman, unless necessity dictates, in which case each should be accompanied by two others; for the witness of one person alone is, as they say, easily influenced.

16. You shall not open the doors of the monastery to all sorts of women without some urgent need. If it is possible to receive such women without looking at them, then this is even better.

17. You shall not build for yourself a private home, nor a worldly dwelling-place for your spiritual children, where women may frequent. Instead, you shall delegate such worldly affairs and duties to pious laymen.

18. You shall not allow in your cell an adolescent disciple, to whom you are attached. Instead, you are to serve your needs through an unsuspected person [of the community], and that by rotation.

19. You shall not possess elaborate or expensive clothing, beyond your liturgical vestments. Instead, in the tradition of the Fathers, you should wear clothes and shoes in humble fashion.

20. You shall not eat sumptuously, whether in private or in hospitality, for you have stripped yourself of these luxuries which belong to the voluptuous life.

21. You shall not treasure up gold in your monastery. Whatever you have in excess, you should give to those in need, by opening up your courtyard, in the manner of the holy Fathers.

22. You shall not keep things locked away, nor be concerned with matters of finance. Instead, let your key be the great care of souls, for the sake of loosing and binding, according to the Scriptures (Jn. 20:23). Money and finances should be delegated to the stewards, and to those supervising the cells, or to whoever else may be especially responsible for particular services, so that each of these is personally accountable to you in everything.

23. You shall not show preference to any person with eminence and authority in the present age, over the interests of the community. Neither shall you refrain from keeping the divine

laws and commandments, laying down your life to the point of even shedding your blood.

24. You shall not do or make something according to your own proper will, whether it be a matter of anything spiritual or material. First, nothing should be done without the counsel and blessing of your Lord and Father, followed by the advice of those advanced in knowledge and piety with respect to the matter at hand; for we need the advice of at least one or two, or even three or more persons, as we have been commanded by our Fathers, and as we have so kept.

Follow and keep all these things and whatever else you have received, so that you may fare well. And thus you will rightly walk in the Lord; but the opposite will produce a result which it is forbidden to describe or even imagine.

### (iv) Rules for the brothers

Draw near, you also, my children and brothers, and hear my wretched words. Accept your master and abbot, inasmuch as he has been chosen by all of you; for our way of life permits no other alternative; and such is the bond of the Lord. Embrace him as my successor, looking to him with respect and honor; be obedient to him, even as you are to me, obeying his commands and not despising his youthful age in the Lord (cf. 1 Tim. 4:12); and do not expect from him more than those gifts which he has received from the Holy Spirit. For it is sufficient for him to hold onto whatever he has been commanded by my humility. If you love me, my children, you will keep my commandments (cf. Jn. 14:15). Have peace among yourselves, preserve your angelic calling undefiled, and move in a heavenly direction.

Having despised the world, do not turn back to the works of the world. Having loosed the bonds of worldly attachment, do not bind yourselves again to fleshly relations.

Having denied all the ephemeral pleasures of the present life, do not through faint-heartedness slip away from your athletic [i.e., ascetic] obedience, thereby becoming the object of demonic ridicule.

Persist in the way of obedience to the very end, so that you may gain the diamond crown of righteousness.

By leading a life of humility, you will be able to deny your proper will; conform yourselves only to those things which are approved by the abbot. Knowing these things, you will be blessed, if you keep them to the end. For the choir of martyrs will welcome you. And, wearing crowns in the kingdom of heaven, you will rejoice in the eternal blessings.

### (v) Conclusion

So now, my children, seek after your salvation. For, I am leaving on a journey that has no return; a journey which from all time everyone has traveled. After a short while, having completed your earthly life, you too will embark on it. Brothers, I do not know where I am going, or what sort of judgment awaits me, nor what type of place will receive me. I have not performed even a single good deed before God, and I am responsible for every sin. Nonetheless, I rejoice and am glad that I am going from earth to heaven, from darkness to light, from slavery to freedom, from wandering to true rest. I am going from things foreign and alien to that which is properly mine: "For I am an alien, and a sojourner, like all my fathers" (Ps. 39:12). I will speak more boldly: for I am departing to my Master, to my Lord and my God, whom my soul has loved. I have known Him as a Father, although I have not served Him as a son; I have preferred Him above everything else, although I have not served Him as a true servant. I have said these things as one who is beside himself; I have said them for you, so that you will desire your salvation and pray for mine. And if I attain this salvation, I shall give account before the truth, and shall not be silent but boldly beseech my Lord and Master for all of you, so that you may fare well, be saved, and increase in number. I shall be awaiting each and every one of you as you depart from this life, watching out for you, welcoming you, and embracing you. For such is my confidence, that His goodness is in this community, and will preserve all of you, both here and in the age to come, since you have adhered to His commandments, for the glory of His all-holy power. Little children, remember my humble words; keep the deposit [of the faith]; in Jesus Christ our Lord, to whom be glory and power to the ages of ages. Amen.

# SYMEON THE NEW THEOLOGIAN (949-1022)*

Symeon was the abbot of St. Mamas monastery in Constantinople and a remarkable mystical writer who underlined the conscious experience of the Holy Spirit in the form of light. In his life, Symeon was blessed with an intimate and influential relationship with a charismatic elder, called Symeon the Pious, while in his writings Symeon never ceased to extol - in a characteristically spontaneous and warm manner - the benefits of spiritual consultation and direction.

## Letter on Confession

### (i) The importance of confession

1. Dear father and brother, you have ordered my unworthiness to respond to your question: "Is it truly permissible to confess one's sins to monks who are not ordained priests?" and then you also add, "since we hear that (the authority) to bind and loose was given exclusively to the priests." This is an edifying question of your godly soul, and your fiery longing and fear. While we have accepted your good intention, since you are seeking to learn about matters which are divine and sacred, we are not personally in a position to make such distinctions or write about them. We would therefore have preferred to keep silent. For to interpret spiritual things by the spiritual (cf. 1 Cor. 2:13) belongs to people who are dispassionate and holy; and in

---

* For the Greek original, cf. Karl Holl, *Enthusiasmus und Bussgewalt beim griechischen Mönchtum: eine Studie zum Symeon dem neuen Theologen* (Leipzig, 1898) 110-127. A recent English translation appeared in ed. Alexander Golitzin, *Symeon the New Theologian, On the Mystical Life*, vol. 3 (St. Vladimir's Seminary Press: New York, 1997) 185-203, which I have consulted.

our way of life, in word and in virtues, we are very far from such holiness.

2. However, since it is written that "the Lord is near to all who call upon Him in truth" (Ps. 145:18), I too, 'though unworthy, have called upon Him, and so I shall speak to you about these matters not with my own words, but with the holy and divinely-inspired Scripture itself. I shall not teach you, but shall present you with the witness of Scripture in regard to the question you ask. By God's grace, I shall thus preserve both myself and my listeners from a two-fold precipice: that of the person who hid the talent, and that other of the person who with unworthiness and vainglory, or rather with a darkened mind expounds on doctrines.

Where then can our discourse begin other than with the beginning of all things, from Him who is without beginning? This is surely the better way, for it also guarantees our words. We were not created by the angels, nor have we learned from human beings. Rather, we have been mystically taught by the wisdom that is from above, indeed by the grace which comes through the Spirit. And we are always and at every hour being taught. Calling now also upon that wisdom, let us proceed by describing first of all the manner of confession and its power.

3. Now confession is nothing other than the necessary admission or recognition of one's own failings and foolishness, namely a realization of one's poverty. As the Lord says in the Gospel parable: "A certain creditor," He says, "had two debtors: one owed him fifty denarii and the other five hundred. When they could not pay, he forgave them both" (Lk 7:41-42). Every believer therefore is in debt to his true master and God, and will be held accountable for what he has received at the throne of God's awesome and fearful judgment where each of us, emperors and poor alike, shall stand naked and bowed down before Him. Consider everything that He has given to us. While these gifts are so numerous that no one could count them all, nevertheless the greater and more perfect include our liberation from condemnation, our sanctification from pollution, our progression from darkness toward His ineffable light, our becoming His children and sons and heirs through divine baptism, our being clothed with God Himself, our becoming His members, and our reception of the Holy Spirit dwelling in us; such is the

royal seal with which the Lord brands His own sheep. But why am I saying so much? They especially include His making us like Himself and rendering us His brothers and co-heirs. All these, and others still greater gifts than these, holy baptism grants immediately to everyone who is baptized; and these are what the divine Apostle called God's wealth and inheritance (cf. Col. 1:12; Eph.3:8; 2 Cor.4:7).

4. The Lord's commandments are like guardians of these mystical gifts and benefits. They surround both the believer and the treasure stored up inside his soul like a kind of wall, keeping them safe and preventing any thief or enemy from laying hands on them. We, however, feel that we are ourselves the guardians of our loving God's commandments, and as a result assume their burden. We ignore the fact that it is we rather who are guarded by them. For the person who keeps God's commandments does not preserve them so much as himself, protecting himself from the visible and invisible enemies which Paul declared to be innumerable and terrible, saying: "We are not contending with flesh and blood, but against the principalities, against the powers, against the world rulers of the darkness of this age, against the spiritual beings of wickedness in the heavenly places..." (Eph 6:12). These are clearly the spirits of the air which are always invisibly arrayed against us.

Therefore, whoever keeps the commandments is guarded by them and does not lose the wealth which God has entrusted to him. Whoever despises them, however, finds himself naked and easily overcome by his enemies and, having lost all the wealth, becomes accountable to the King and Master for everything that we mentioned above, which it is not possible for anyone to return in any way or to achieve alone. They are heavenly, and belong to Him who came down from heaven, and comes down daily, bearing and distributing them to the faithful. Where then could those who received and then lost them be able to find them again? Surely nowhere at all. Just as neither Adam nor any of his sons was able to effect his own restoration or that of any of his descendants, until the God beyond our nature had become his (Adam's) son according to the flesh, our Lord Jesus Christ, who came and raised both Adam and ourselves from the Fall by His divine power.

The person who thinks he does not need to keep all of the

commandments, but can keep some while neglecting others, should understand that even if he neglects only one of them he will lose the entire wealth. Suppose, for example, that the commandments are twelve men who are armed and who are arranged in a circle. You stand in the middle, naked, but protected by these soldiers. Then imagine that there are still other soldiers advancing against these twelve from all sides, opposing warriors who are attacking and trying to seize you in order to slaughter you immediately. Now if one of the twelve were voluntarily to fall out of line and neglect his defense, and so leave his spot like an open door to the enemy, what would be the advantage of having the other eleven there when one of the enemy had slipped in among them and cut you to pieces because the guards were unable to come to your assistance? For even if they did wish to turn around and help you, they too would be destroyed by their assailants. The same thing will certainly happen to you if you do not keep the commandments. For once you have been wounded by just one enemy and fall down, all the commandments will abandon you, and then gradually all your strength will be taken from you as well.

Or let me use another example: imagine a jar filled with wine or oil. Even if the jar is not punctured on every side, and only a small hole appears on one side, all its contents will slowly spill out. In the same way, if you fall away through negligence even a little from one of the commandments, you also fall away from all the rest. As Christ says: "To the one who has more will be given, and he will have abundance; but from him who has not, even what he thinks he has will be taken away" (Mt. 25:29); and again: "Whoever relaxes one of these commandments" – that is to say, through transgressing the law – "and teaches others so, shall be called least in the kingdom of heaven" (Mt. 5:19). And as Paul says: "Whatever overcomes a person, to that he is enslaved" (2 Pet. 2:19, and Rom. 6:16); and again: "The sting of death is sin" (1 Cor. 15:56). He does not mean "this sin" or "that sin," but whatever sin it might be is the sting of death. He calls sin death's sting because those who are wounded by it die. So every sin leads to death. As the same Apostle says: "Once one has sinned, one has already died" (cf. Rom. 6:10). Such a person has become subject to debt and sin, and the thieves have left him lying dead on the roadside (cf. Lk. 10:30).

*(ii) The role of the spiritual father*

5. What else does a person who is dying want except to be raised up again; or, what else does a debtor without the means to repay want except to receive remission of his debt and not be thrown into prison until he repays his debt? Indeed, he will never escape from the eternal prison of his darkness. So also will the person who has been broken by the spiritual thieves seek a sympathetic and compassionate physician to come (and minister) to him. For he no longer has the fear of God burning inside him so that he can go out and search for the doctor himself. Instead, having entirely lost the strength of his soul through his contempt, he proves a terrible and pitiable spectacle for those who can see clearly, or rather spiritually, into the failures of the soul. Such a person has become a slave to the devil because of his sin. For, as Paul says, "Do you not know ... you are slaves of the one whom you obey, whether of righteousness which leads to righteousness, or of lawlessness which leads to lawlessness?" (Rom. 6:16). This person has become a thing of mockery to God the Father, and is trampled down by the enemies who have fallen away from God, stripped of the robe of royal purple, and blackened, rendered a child of the devil rather than of God. What can that person do in order once again to possess those things from which he has fallen away? Clearly he will look for an intercessor and a friend of God, for someone capable of restoring him to his former state and of reconciling him to God the Father. For a person who has been joined to Christ by grace and has become His member and been adopted by Him, should this person then abandon Christ and return like a dog to his vomit (cf. 2 Pet. 2:22) by either being joined to a sinful woman or to somebody else, then he shall be condemned with the unbelievers as having dishonored and insulted Christ. For according to the Apostle: "We are Christ's body, and individually members of it" (1 Cor. 12:27). So whoever is joined with a harlot makes the members of Christ's body members of a harlot (cf. 1 Cor. 6:15). And whoever has practiced such things, thereby outraging his Master and God, cannot be reconciled with God except by means of someone else who is an intercessor and holy person, a friend and servant of Christ, and by avoiding evil.

6. Let us therefore flee first of all from sin. And even if we are wounded by its arrows, let us not delay, letting the sin's poison

grow sweet in us like honey. Nor like a wounded bear, should we irritate the wound by repeating the same sin. Let us run instead directly to the spiritual physician and vomit the poison of sin through confession, spitting out its venom. Let us receive the penances that are assigned to us as an antidote, and always strive to fulfill them with a warm faith and the fear of God. For all who have emptied themselves completely of the wealth entrusted to them, who have wasted their father's inheritance with harlots and publicans (cf. Lk. 15:13, 30), whose conscience is so inclined downward by their sense of great shame that they are unable to look upwards because they have lost their boldness before God, naturally seek out a man of God to stand as sponsor for their debt in order that, through him, they may approach God. I think that it is impossible for anyone to be, or to want to be, reconciled with God without a sincere and labored repentance. Never has anyone heard, nor has it been written in the divinely-inspired Scriptures, that someone could accept the sins of another or give an account of them without the sinner having first proved worthy of fruits of repentance, proportionate to the form of his sin, and depositing his own toil. Thus says the voice of the Word's forerunner: "Bear fruit that are worthy of repentance, and do not presume to say to yourselves, 'We have Abraham as our father'" (Mt. 3:8-9). For our Lord Himself spoke as follows about those who behave senselessly: "Amen I say to you, even if Moses and Daniel should arise in order to choose out their sons and daughters, they shall in no way be chosen" (Jer. 14:14-16). So what should we do, what should we who wish to repent contrive for the remission of our debt and our recall from the fall? Listen, and with God's help I will settle the question for each of you.

7. Seek out one who is, if you will, an intercessor, a physician, and a good counselor; a good counsellor, that he may offer ways of repentance which agree with his good advice; a physician, that he may prescribe the appropriate medicine for each of your wounds; and an intercessor, that he may propitiate God, standing before Him face to face, and offering Him prayer and intercession on your behalf. Do not try to find some flatterer or slave to his belly and make him your counselor and ally lest, by accommodating himself to your will and not to what God desires, he teach you what you would like to hear and leave you in reality an irreconciled enemy. Nor should you choose an in-

experienced physician lest, by his over-aggressiveness and untimely incisions and cauterizations, he plunge you into the depth
of despair or, worse, allow you by his extreme sympathy to think
you are getting better when in fact you are still unwell, and so
deliver you to the eternal hell which you had not expected. For
this does no more than cause in us the very illness that is already killing the soul. As for an intercessor between God and
people, I do not think that it is quite so easily found. "For not
all who are descended from Israel are Israelites" (Rom. 9:6), but
rather those who both hold the name and have clearly understood the force of the name, namely the intellect that looks upon
God (cf. Gen. 32). Neither are all who call upon the name of
Christ truly Christians: "For not everyone who says to me 'Lord,
Lord,'" says Christ, "shall enter the kingdom of heaven, but he
who does the will of my Father" (Mt. 7:21); and likewise He
says: "Many will on that day say to me, 'Lord, Lord, did we not
cast out demons in your name?'; and I will say to them: 'Amen
I say to you, I do not know you. Depart from me, you workers
of iniquity'" (Mt. 7:22-23 and 25:13).

8. Therefore, brothers, we must be careful in this matter, both
those of us who intercede as well as those who have sinned and
wish to be reconciled to God, in order that neither those who
intercede may draw down wrath rather than reward, nor those
who have offended and are striving to be reconciled may happen to encounter a hostile, murderous and evil counselor instead
of an intercessor. Such counselors will hear the terrible warning: "Who set you up as rulers and judges of my people?" and
again: "Hypocrite, first take the log out of your own eye, and
then you will see clearly to take the speck out of your brother's
eye" (Mt. 7:51). The log signifies some passion or desire which
darkens the eye of the soul. And again: "Physician, heal yourself" (Lk. 4:23); and also: "But to the sinner God says: 'What
right have you to recite my statutes, or take up my covenant
with your mouth? For you have hated discipline, and you have
cast my words behind you'" (Ps. 50:16-17). Paul too, says: "Who
are you to pass judgment on the servant of another? It is before
his own master that he stands or falls. God is capable, by means
of His faithful servant, of making him stand" (Rom. 14:41).

9. Brothers and fathers, it is precisely for these reasons that I
shudder and tremble as I beseech all of you, securing also my-

self by means of this request, that you not behave contemptuously with regard to these mysteries, which are holy and terrible for everyone. Do not play with things that are not toys, nor let any of this be held against our souls for reasons such as vainglory, ambition, commerce, or indifference. For it so happens that strange thoughts tempt people when they are called "Rabbi" or "Father." Let us not, I repeat, let us not shamelessly reach for the dignity of the Apostles, being rather instructed by the following example from the world. If someone had the audacity to dare to pretend that he is the representative of the earthly king, and was convicted of secretly holding and doing those things entrusted to the office of king, or was subsequently to announce that he practices them, both he and his co-conspirators and subordinates would be subject to the worst penalties as an example to others, becoming the laughing-stock of everyone for his foolishness and insensitivity. What, then, will surely happen in future to those who unworthily snatch the office of the Apostles?

10. Nevertheles, you should not want to become intercessors for others before you have been filled with the Holy Spirit, or before you know, through the perception of your soul, that you are loved as a friend by the King of all. For not everyone who knows the earthly king is able to intercede with him for others. There are very few who are able to do this: those who of their own virtue, sweat, and labors have acquired boldness before him. Such people have no need of any intercessor themselves, but speak with the king person to person. Fathers and brothers, shall we not then preserve this rank for God's sake? Shall we not honor the heavenly King at least as much as the earthly king? Or shall we instead snatch and grant ourselves the thrones at His right hand and at His left before we have asked for and received it? Oh, the audacity! How great a shame would lay hold of us! Because unless we were condemned for some other reason, for this cause alone we would be dishonorably deprived of enthronement as convicted of contempt and would then be thrown out into the unquenchable fire. But, let this suffice as advice for those who wish to pay attention to themselves. For indeed, it is for this reason that we have made this lengthy digression. Now then, my child, let us return to the question you asked at the beginning.

### (iii) The binding and loosing of sins

11. It is permissible for an unordained monk to hear our confession. You will find this to be the case everywhere. This is
because of the [monastic] habit and the likeness given by God
as the monk's inheritance, by which also monks are so named,
as it is written in the divinely-inspired writings of the Fathers;
you will find this to be true, should you examine them. Prior to
the monks, only the bishops had the authority to bind and loose,
as they had received this in succession to the holy Apostles.
But, as time passed and the bishops became useless, this awesome authority passed on to priests with blameless life and
worthy of divine grace. Then, when the latter had also become
polluted – both priests and bishops becoming alike, indeed confused with the rest of the people, with many, to this day, being
caused to fall and to perish by spirits of deceit and by vain and
empty titles – it was transferred, as we said, to God's elect
people, I mean to the monks. It was not that it had been taken
away from the priests and the bishops, but rather that they had
become estranged from it. "For every priest is appointed a mediator between God and people by God," as Paul says, "and is
bound to offer sacrifice as much for the people as for himself"
(cf. Heb. 5:1-3).

12. But let us take up our discussion at an earlier point and
see whence, how, and to whom this power of celebrating the
sacraments, and of binding and loosing, was given from the
beginning, and thus proceed in proper order just as you asked
the question so that the solution may become clear, not just for
you but for everyone else. When our Lord God and Savior said
to the man who had a withered hand, "Your sins are forgiven
you," the Jews in attendance all said: "This man is blasphem-
ing. Who can forgive sins except God alone?" (cf. Mt. 9:3; Mk.
2:7; Lk. 5:21). Up to that time remission of sins had never been
granted, whether by the prophets, or by the priests, or even by
any of the patriarchs. It was therefore difficult for the scribes to
accept this because it was a kind of strange new teaching and
reality that was being proclaimed. And for this reason, the Lord
did not blame them, but instead He taught them what they were
ignorant of by proving that it was as God and not as man that
He granted remission of sins. For He says to them: "But that
you may know that the Son of Man has authority to forgive

sins" (Mt. 9:6), He says to the man with the withered hand, 'Stretch out your hand,' and he stretched it out and it was restored healthy like the other" (Mt. 12:13). By means of the visible wonder, He provided evidence of the greater and invisible one. The same applies to Zacchaeus (Lk. 19:1f.), to the harlot (Lk. 7:36f.), to Matthew from his tax collector's post (Mt. 9:9f.), to Peter who denied the Lord three times (Jn. 18:17f.), to the paralytic (Jn. 5:5f.) to whom, after healing him, the Lord said: "See, you are well. Sin no more, that nothing worse happens to you" (Jn. 5:14). By saying this He showed that the man had been taken by illness because of his sins and that, when freed from the former, he also received forgiveness of sins, not because he had been praying for it for a long time, nor as a result of fasting or sleeping on the ground, but instead and only because of his conversion and unwavering faith, his breaking-off with evil, true repentance, and many tears, just as the harlot (Lk. 7:38 and 44) and Peter who wept bitterly (Mt. 26:75).

Here is the source of that great gift which is proper uniquely to God and which He alone possessed. Then, just as He was about to ascend to heaven, He bequeathed this great gift to His disciples. How did He grant them this dignity and authority? Let us learn what, and how much, and when it was granted. The chosen eleven disciples were gathered inside together behind closed doors. He entered and stood in their midst, and breathed on them, saying: "Receive the Holy Spirit; whosesoever sins you forgive, they are forgiven them; if you retain the sins of any, they are retained" (Jn. 20:22-23). At that time He did not order them at all about penances, since they were going to be taught by the Holy Spirit.

13. As we have said, therefore, the holy Apostles transmitted this authority in succession those who were also to hold their thrones, and noone ever dared to presume otherwise. In this way, the Lord's disciples preserved with precision the correctness of this authority. But, as we said, as time passed, the worthy grew mixed and mingled with the unworthy, being overtaken by the multitudes, with one contending to have precedence over another and feigning virtue for the sake of priority. Since those who were holding the Apostles' thrones were shown to be fleshly minded, lovers of pleasure and seekers of glory, and since they inclined toward heresies, divine grace abandoned them

and this authority was removed from them. Therefore having also abandoned everything else required of those who celebrate the sacraments, what alone is demanded of them is that they be orthodox. But I do not think that they are even this. Someone is not orthodox just because one does not introduce some new doctrine into the Church of God, but because one possesses a life which is in harmony with this true teaching. Such a life and such a person contemporary patriarchs and metropolitans have at different times either looked for and not found, or, if they did find, they preferred the unworthy candidate instead. They ask only this of the candidate for priesthood, that he put in writing the symbol of faith. They find this alone acceptable, not that the man is a zealot for the sake of good, nor that he do battle with anyone because of evil. In this way they pretend that they keep peace here in the Church, but this is worse than any hostility, and it is the cause of great unrest. So this is why the priests have also become worthless and no better than the people. None of them are that salt of which the Lord spoke (Mt. 5:13), able to constrain and reprove and keep the life of another from wasting away. Instead, they are aware of and cover each other's passions, and have themselves become inferior to the people, and the people in turn still worse than before. Some of the people, however, have been revealed as superior to the priests, illuminating the world as burning coals in the lightless gloom of the clergy. For if the latter were, according to the Lord's word (Mt. 5:16), to shine in their lives as the sun, then these coals would seem radiant but would be dark in comparison to the greater light. However, since only the likeness and the dress of the priesthood is left among them, the gift of the Spirit has passed to the monks, and it has been revealed through signs that these have entered by their actions into the life of the Apostles. Yet here too the devil has been carrying out his proper work. For when he saw that they had been revealed as some new disciples of Christ in the world, and that they had shone forth in their lives and performed miracles, he introduced false brethren, his disciples, to mingle with them, and when, after a little while, these had multiplied – as you can see for yourself – the monks too were rendered useless and became altogether unmonastic.

14. Therefore, it is neither to those in the monastic habit, nor

to those ordained and enrolled in the priestly order, nor even to those who have been honored with the dignity of the episcopate – I mean the patriarchs, metropolitans, and bishops – that God has given the grace of forgiving sins simply by virtue of their having been ordained. Certainly not! For these are allowed only to celebrate the sacraments; and I think myself that even this does not apply to many of them, lest they be burned up entirely as straw by this. Rather, this grace is given alone to those, as many as there are among priests and bishops and monks, who have been numbered with Christ's disciples on account of their purity.

15. How do these people know that they are numbered among those whom I have described, and how exactly will others who are seeking them recognize them? The Lord Himself has taught us this when He said: "And these signs will accompany those who believe: in my name they will cast out demons; they will speak in new tongues" – which signifies the divinely-inspired and edifying teaching of the Word – "they will pick up serpents, and if they drink any deadly thing, it will not hurt them" (Mk. 16:17-18). Again he says: "My sheep hear my voice" (Jn. 10:27); and also: "You will know them by their fruits" (Mt. 7:16). What are these fruits? The ones which Paul lists in detail saying: "But the fruit of the Spirit is love, joy, peace, patience, kindness, faith, gentleness, self-control" (Gal. 5:22); and to these we add compassion, kindness, almsgiving and everything which follows from these. In addition there are: "A word of wisdom, a word of knowledge, gifts of healing, and a multitude of other things, all of which are worked by one and the same Spirit that assigns to each one individually as it wills" (cf. 1 Cor. 12:8-11).

Those who have shared in these virtues – whether in whole or in part, according to what is profitable to each – have been enlisted in the choir of the Apostles, and as many as accomplish them even today are also enrolled there. These people are therefore the "light of the world," as Christ Himself says: "No one lights a lamp and puts it under a bushel or beneath his bed, but on a stand so that it gives light to all in the house" (Mt 5:14-15). Such people are recognized not just by these gifts, but also by their manner of life. It is precisely in this way that those who seek them will recognize them, each one of them more clearly than himself. For they, as it were in the likeness of our Lord

Jesus Christ, not only think it not shameful, but rather consider humility and wretchedness the highest honor; and, just as Christ, they give proof of unfeigned obedience to their own fathers and guides while still subject to them; they are recognized in the way they have loved dishonors and insults, curses and mockeries with all their soul, and have welcomed those who have brought upon them these things as providers of great blessings, and have prayed for them with all their soul and with tears; they are recognized in that they have spat upon all the world's glory and have considered everything in it as worthless. But why prolong the discourse by stating so much that is obvious? If, on the one hand, someone finds that he has attained every virtue set out in the holy scriptures, and if, on the other hand, that person has also pursued every practice of good, and at every stage has experienced progress, transformation, and attainment, and if he has been lifted to the height of divine glory, then indeed that person will recognize himself as a participant of God and of His gifts, and so will be known by those who can see clearly, or even by those whose vision is less acute. In this way, such people can say to everyone with confidence: "we are ambassadors for Christ; God makes His appeal through us; so be reconciled to God" (2 Cor. 5:20).

All such people have kept God's commandments to the end of their lives. They have sold their belongings and distributed them among the poor. They have followed Christ by enduring temptations. They have lost their own lives in the world for the sake of their love for God, and have found them again unto eternal life. And, when they discovered again their own souls, they found within themselves a spiritual light, and in this light they saw the inaccessible light, God Himself, according to what is written: "In Your light we shall see light" (Ps. 36:9). Pay attention now to learn how it is possible to see anything which is proper to the soul. The soul of each person is like that drachma which – not God, but each of us – lost (Lk 15:8ff) when we sank into the darkness of sin. But Christ, the true light, came and met with those who seek Him, and in a way that He alone knows, gave them the grace to see Himself. This is what it means to find one's soul: to see God, and in His light to be raised higher than all the visible creation, and to have God as one's shepherd and teacher. From Him as well, this person will also know how, if you like, to bind and loose; for, knowing truly, he will worship the One who gave him this grace, and will provide it in turn to those who need it.

### (iv) Symeon's own spiritual father

16. I know my child, that (the authority) to bind and loose is given to such people by God the Father and our Lord Jesus Christ through the Holy Spirit, to those who are His sons by adoption and to His holy servants. I was myself a disciple to such a father, one who did not have ordination from men, but who brought me by the hand – or better, by the spirit – of God into discipleship, who commanded me, encouraging me for a long time to receive the proper ordination from men according to the traditional order, since I was formerly moved by the Holy Spirit to a sincere longing for this.

17. Therefore, brothers and fathers, let us pray first of all to become such people, and only then let us talk to others about deliverance from passions and endurance of evil thoughts. Let us then seek out such a spiritual elder. Indeed, let us put every effort into finding such persons and true disciples of Christ; and let us beseech God with pain of heart and many tears, literally for days on end, that He may unveil the eyes of our hearts in order for us to recognize them – if indeed such a person is to be found anywhere in this evil generation – so that, on finding one, we may receive forgiveness of our sins through him, obeying his ordinances and commandments with all our soul, just as he, having heard those of Christ, became a participant of His grace and gifts, and received from Christ the authority to bind and to loose, burning entirely with the Holy Spirit, to whom is due all glory, honor and worship, together with the Father and the Only-Begotten Son, to the ages. Amen.

SYMEON THE NEW THEOLOGIAN*

*Catechetical Discourse on the Conduct of the Spiritual Elder*
On renunciation and the elimination of the will, for those who had asked him to write to them about how one should lead an ascetic life. And that for this purpose, it is good and beneficial to have an experienced guide or spiritual father in order to learn about virtue and the difficult practice of the ascetic art. Also on trusting the spiritual elders, and on the vision of light through which every enlightened soul progresses in the love of God.

*(i) Christ as the beginning and end of all*
My beloved and desired brothers. You have often wished to hear a beneficial word from my modesty, but because you would leave so soon I did not wish to tell you by word of mouth the things necessary for your edification, as if they were secondary. Therefore, since you have asked me to write these things down for your love, I was naturally eager to do so. This I do not in order to teach you, for I am unworthy to do so, but rather out of great love for you in order to advise you and remind you of those things which I know are beneficial and helpful to the soul for the purpose of flight from the world, estrangement to the passions, love of God and perfect dispassion.

Now, in addressing a person who thirsts for the salvation of the soul, I thought it proper to begin from no other place but the very eternal source, our Saviour Christ and God Himself. It is for His sake that I write this discourse and undertake every task; and it is to Him that we address every effort and every desire with good hope. For He is the unshakeable foundation of those who are beginners, the unashamed hope of those in

* *Catechetical Discourse* 20. For the original Greek, see *Sources Chrétiennes* 104 (Paris, 1964) 330-348. For an earlier translation of Symeon's *Discourses,* see C.J. deCatanzaro (*The Classics of Western Spirituality:* Paulist Press, New York, 1980).

the middle, and the insatiable love and endless life of those at the end. It is His holy voice that I heard saying to all in common: "He who does not leave father and mother and brothers and all his possessions and take up his cross and follow me, is not worthy of me" (cf. Mt. 10:37, 19:29, 16:24; Lk. 14:26; Mk. 8:34, 10:29). So I have learned from Scripture also, as well as from experience itself, that the cross comes at the end for no other reason than the endurance of sorrows and temptations, and finally voluntary death itself. Formerly, when heresies prevailed, many people chose death through martyrdom and various tortures. But now, when through the grace of Christ we live in a time of profound and perfect peace, we learn that the cross and death constitute nothing else than the complete mortification of our individual will. For one who fulfills the individual will, no matter to what degree, will never be able to keep the commandments of Christ the Savior.

### (ii) The guidance of a spiritual elder

Therefore in order to begin my discourse to each of you, I say to you the following: brother, entreat God with persistence, that He may show you a person who is able to direct you well, one whom you ought to obey as though obeying God Himself, whose words you will carry out without hesitation even if what is commanded appears to you to be contradictory or harmful. And if your heart is assured even more by grace in regard to the spiritual father you already have, then do as he says and you will be saved. For it is better to be called a disciple of a disciple, than to live at your own whim and gather the worthless fruits of your own will. If the Holy Spirit sends you to another person, do not hesitate at all. For we hear that Paul planted, Apollos watered, and Christ gives growth (cf. 1 Cor. 3:6). So do as I have said brother, and go to a person whom God will reveal to you either mystically within or externally through His servant. Look to him and speak to him as if to Christ Himself; respect him and learn from him that which is beneficial. For if you hear from him: "Depart from the land of your will and from the family of your way" (cf. Gen. 12:1), do not argue nor be ashamed, being overcome by vainglory. If he tells you: "Go to the land of obedience, which I will show you" (*ibid.*), then run as fast as you can, my brother; do not give sleep to you eyes (cf. Prov. 6:4), nor bend your knees (cf. Judg. 7:5), overcome by weakness or laziness. For perhaps it is there that God will appear to you, and show you that you must become a father of many spiritual children (cf. Gen. 17:4) and grant to you the promised land (Heb. 11:9) which the righteous alone will inherit (cf. Mt. 5:5). If he leads you to the mountain (cf. Mt. 17, Mk. 9, Lk. 9), then climb it with eagerness; for I know well that you will see Christ transfigured and shining with the divine light more brightly than the sun. Perhaps you will fall down, being unable to bear seeing that which you have never contemplated, and you will hear the voice of the Father from above, and see the cloud overshadowing, and the prophets present and testifying that He is God and Lord of the living and the dead (cf. Mt. 17:1, Mk. 9:2, Lk. 9:28).

### (iii) On following Christ

If he urges you to follow him, then travel the cities confidently with him (cf. Mt. 9:35), for you will receive the greatest benefit if you look to him, and to him alone. If you see him eating with harlots and publicans and sinners (cf. Mt. 9:11, Mk. 2:16, Lk. 15:2), do not think of anything passionate or human, but only consider everything dispassionate and holy, as well as the saying: "I have become all things to all people, that I might gain all" (1 Cor. 9:22). This is what you should think, when you see him condescending to human passions. And you should not believe at all even what you see with your eyes, for the eyes too are deceived, as I have learned by experience. In following him and obeying his words, do not look to those who are with you (cf. Jn. 21:19-20), nor say about anyone: "Lord what will happen to this person?" (Jn. 21:21), but always pay attention to yourself and hold death before your eyes, considering with what virtue you will glorify God (cf. Jn. 21:19). When you are honored by your seniors, do not become proud because of your teacher, or because many people obey you on account of his name. Instead, rejoice if your name is written in the heaven of humility (cf. Lk. 10:20). Even when you see the demons trembling at your shadow *(ibid.)*, ascribe this not to yourself but entirely to the intercession of your father, and they will fear you all the more.

*(iv) At the supper*

If he urges you to sit at the table, beside him, accept this gratefully. Respond to him with both silent respect and honor, and do not touch anything that is set before you without his blessing. Nor give anything to anyone else, or dare to give preference to another without his opinion and command. However, if he calls you last of all, do not say: "Shall I sit at the right or the left," knowing that this place has been prepared for others (cf. Mk. 10:37 and 40) and hearing that: "If anyone wishes to be first of all, he must be last" (Mk. 9:35). Accept the lowly place as the means of obtaining the higher place, and love your teacher who by means of the lowly obtains for you the greater things. And do not audaciously reach out your hand with him to the platter (cf. Mt. 26:23), for you do remember whose daring this was (cf. Mt. 26:25). If he wants to wash your feet, show modesty towards him as if to the Lord and teacher (Jn. 13:13), but refuse the act. If you hear: "If I do not wash your feet, you have no part with me" (Jn. 13:8), then eagerly offer your entire body for washing (cf. Jn. 13:9), in order to learn the great height of deifying humility from what happens to you. You will benefit all the more in this way, if you have a conscience, rather than if you were washing the feet of your father. If he says, after sitting at table: "One of you will betray me or will cause offense to me" (Mt. 26:21 and 16:23), do not hide your treachery, but confess it if you are conscious of it. Otherwise, fall on your face at his feet, and ask him with tears: "Is it I master?" (Mt. 26:25). For we make numerous mistakes out of ignorance. But it is not in your interest to fall on the breast of your father. For even if John was bold enough to do so out of great love for Christ as if to a human being (cf. Jn. 13:23), yet he too did this after everything else, and after he was ordered to call himself an unprofitable servant along with all the others (cf. Lk. 17:10).

*(v) At the passion*

If you see the one who guides you performing miracles and receiving glory, believe and rejoice and give thanks to God that you have such a teacher. Do not be scandalized when you see him dishonored by those who are envious, or even when perhaps you see him struck and dragged, but like the fervent Peter take the sword and stretch out your hand in order to cut off not only the ear (cf. Mt. 26:51) but also the hand and the tongue of anyone who tries to speak against or touch your father. And if you too, like Peter are rebuked, you will surely be praised all the more because of your great love and faith. And if you succumb to fear, since you too are human, and say: "I do not know the man" (Mt. 26:73), then again weep bitterly (cf. Mt. 26:75) about him and do not be overwhelmed with despair. I am sure that he first will receive you back to himself. And if you see him being crucified like a criminal, and suffering at the hands of criminals, die with him if this is possible; otherwise do not join the evil ones as an evil person and a traitor, nor have any part with them in innocent blood (cf. Lk. 23:32 and Mt. 27:4), but like a cowardly and small-hearted person who has briefly forsaken his shepherd, remain faithful to him. If he is released from his bonds, return to him again and venerate him still more as a martyr. If he dies from the trials, boldly ask for his body (cf. Mk. 15:43), and honor him still more than when you were in his living presence, and bury him with costly ointments and perfumes (cf. Mk. 16:1). For although he will not rise in three days, yet he will rise again at the last day with everyone else. Believe that he will stand before God with boldness, even though you have placed his body in the grave, and invoke his intercession without hesitation. He will help you here and will preserve you from every adversity, receiving you also when you depart from the body, and preparing for you an eternal dwelling (cf. Jn. 14:1-2).

### (vi) In the luminous glory

If after all the aforesaid he calls you aside and encourages you to live in silence, telling you: "Stay here without moving on, until you are clothed with power from above" (cf. Acts 1:8), listen to him with sure hope and boundless joy. My brother, such a teacher is truthful and genuine. For the same power of the all-Holy Spirit will come upon you even now (cf. Acts 2:2), not in the form of fire which is visibly apparent, nor with a great noise and a violent wind; for these things occurred for those who did not believe at that time. But it will appear to you spiritually in the form of a spiritual light with great calm and joy. This is the prelude of the eternal and primeval light, which is a reflection of the brightness of eternal blessedness (cf. Heb. 1:3).

When this appears, every passionate thought disappears, every passion of the soul is dispelled, and every bodily illness is healed. Then the eyes of the heart are purified, in order to see that which is described in the beatitudes (cf. Mt. 5:8). Then the soul sees, as if in a mirror, even its slightest failures and is brought down to the abyss of humility, perceiving the greatness of glory and being filled with every joy and gladness. The soul is struck with a wonder that transcends hope and gives rise to fountains of tears. In this way one is entirely changed and knows God, or rather is known first by God. For this alone of all things earthly and heavenly, present as well as future, sorrowful and joyful alike, makes a person despise everything, rendering the same person both a friend of God and a son of the Most High and – so far as this is possible for human beings – a god.

### (vii) Humility and love

Therefore, I have written these things to your love, so that you may have in writing those things which you once asked to hear from my wretched person, and so that you may read these whenever you wish. However if you believe that the all-Holy Spirit commands these things through me out of providence and for your benefit, everything will occurr in the order I have said, and anything I have omitted – for there are many such things – Christ Himself will teach you personally. Now, if these things appear to you incredible or disagreeable, forgive me for advising you what I have learned, and follow all the things that you know are better. My brother, make sure that you do not unwillingly also follow the worse things. For truly rare are those who know how to direct properly and heal rational souls, especially today. For many people may perhaps pretend to fast and keep vigil and a form of piety, or even to have achieved these in practice. And most people can easily learn much by heart and teach with words. But very few may be found who have managed to eliminate the passions through mourning or who have acquired and secured the capital virtues. By capital virtues, I mean humility which eliminates the passions and attracts the heavenly and angelic dispassion; and love, which never ceases or falters (cf. 1 Cor. 13:8), but continually presses on to those things which lie ahead (cf. Phil. 3:13), adding desire to desire and eros to eros. Through this, perfect discernment is obtained, which of itself is a good guide to those who follow it, infallibly crossing the spiritual sea (cf. Wis. 10:18). I pray that you may be granted this by God even now, so that you may discern your affairs in a manner that is pleasing to God, and that you may so act and strive to find Christ who is both cooperating with you in the present, and who will grant you abundantly the enjoyment of His illumination in the future.

Do not follow the wolf instead of the shepherd (cf. Mt. 7:15); and do not enter a flock that is diseased (cf. Ezek. 34:4). Do not be found alone, lest you be seen to be the prey of the soul-killing wolf, or as succumbing to one illness after the other, thereby dying spiritually and alone attaining that "woe" after your fall. For one who gives oneself to a good teacher will have no such concerns, but will live without anxiety and be saved in Christ Jesus our Lord, to whom be the glory to the ages. Amen.

# Fr. Vasileios of Iveron (b. 1936)*

Archimandrite Vasileios is abbot of Iveron monastery on Mount Athos and the author of several essays on the spiritual life from the ascetic and liturgical perspective. A leader in the recent revival of monasticism on the Holy Mountain, Fr. Vasileios was formerly abbot of Stavroniketa and wrote *Hymn of Entry: Liturgy and life in the Orthodox Church.* His work and thought are characterized by an air of liberty and breadth that is reminiscent of the Patristic tradition.

## We as Spiritual Fathers

There is a certain balance throughout the entire story of the Prodigal Son (cf. Lk. 15) because the Father deals with everything in such a divine manner; he endures everything. He calmly takes up the cross of his home's calamities. Both of his sons had problems: they suffered and caused him to suffer. The Father, however, conducts himself faultlessly and divinely. He neither stigmatizes his younger son by calling him a prodigal nor upbraids the elder who had spoken to him so improperly. The Father's actions reveal a boundless love; they bring consolation and solace.

As long as we have such a Father, we may have hope. We will be able to find the road home and find ourselves. In our life as human beings we are always the children of God. Our example for returning home to the heavenly Father is the younger son. We may also find ourselves in the position of being a father or, perhaps, a spiritual father. If this be the case, then the "man"

* From Archimandrite Vasileios of Iveron, *The Parable of the Prodigal Son* (Alexander Press: Montreal, 1997) 43-48. Reprinted with permission.

(verse 11) in this parable has shown us the way we must act towards our children or spiritual children.

If we, like the younger son, have returned home, or are in the process of returning, then we will be able to behave with tolerance and forbearance towards others, towards our children. Only then do we realize – and confess – that we are powerless and very weak – "without Him we can do nothing" (Jn. 15:5). But we must not despair because we have a Father who is "capable of sharing our weaknesses" (Heb. 4:15).

But what if we should find ourselves like the younger son, living as prodigals in distant lands, or behaving like the elder son, seeking to justify ourselves and condemn others? Then without a doubt, we will have adulterated the conduct of a true father. Despite our intentions, which in all likelihood are good, we will suffer; what's more, we will cause others to suffer.

Consequently, we can distinguish between two types of improper behavior on the part of fathers or spiritual fathers:

(i) *The first type of fathers* corresponds to the younger son before his return. These present themselves as very liberal, acquiescent, and tolerant. They refrain from making discerning comments; they try to justify and make excuses for the young. They do not heal their "illnesses," for they lack this ability. No matter what their children do, they think them to be perfect and their behaviour natural. Such a position does not result from love but is the consequence of indifference and superficiality; it is an attempt to gain the temporary friendship of their children. These teachers-fathers hide their incompetence and ignorance behind what purports to be love and understanding. In actuality, it is a disdain and abandonment of mankind that needs whatever best and most precious we have.

Young people will follow such guides for only a short time, while they are deceived by the external appearance of their boldness and misleading liberalism. But when they realize the dangerous emptiness of such teachers, they will soon abandon them, if their demands and expectations are sincere and their spiritual constitutions strong. Teachers such as these are strangers to the life, to the nature and deep thirst of mankind. "Yet they will never follow a stranger but will flee from him, because they do not know the voice of strangers" (Jn. 10:5).

(ii) *The second type of fathers* appears to dwell in the Father's house – they are an example of the elder son – but actually live far from His spirit and the greatness of His love.

These spiritual fathers are self-ordained, having reckoned they have laboured "these many years" (verse 29). They act as crude and vulgar critics of others. In their own words, they have completed their personal struggle with repentance and humility and, having appointed themselves, they are now concerned with the problems of others. Their conduct is not determined by a paternal love which is guileless – such a love is foreign to them – but by malignant hearts and an envy which cannot be justified for someone their age. Their internal disorder and obsession for vengeance quickly become obvious. Their expression and conduct are foreign to the voice of the true shepherd who sacrifices himself for his sheep and calls each of them personally by name as he leads them out.

For this reason, people abandon them. And the more people continue to distance themselves from them – and justifiably so – the more they behave as if they were demon-possessed, hurling threats and curses at those who do not seek their advice.

We cannot show – indeed, we are not permitted to show – either more or less leniency or strictness than that shown by the heavenly Father. To put it differently, both our leniency and our strictness are insufficient and unnecessary for others. It is necessary, if we are able, to stop living our lives as we imagine them to be, and live instead for Him who dies and was resurrected for us. In this way we will live for everyone. And through us, people will see Him, the leader of life, and not our own accomplishments and opinions which at best have only a relative value, but more likely are worthless.

(iii) There is *a third group of spiritual fathers*, those who have made the return or are in the process of returning; a father in this group can only see his own unworthiness – "I am no longer worthy to be called your son" (verse 21). By virtue of this, he is able to discern God's love which amazes him. He sees himself as chief among sinners and everyone else as clean and holy. Such a person loves "in the likeness of God" (Genesis 1:26); he loves with the love with which God loves and judges and saves. Only through such people does God love and reveal Himself.

They become gods by grace and not theologians in their own imaginations. The former is very difficult and hard to find, while the latter is cheap and commonplace.

Those who are being sanctified, the saints, comfort us and save us. They are able to undertake the Father's work because they speak the truth with both their words and their lives. They show us that the struggle will continue until the end. It may change form but it never ends until we enter the grave. The work of repentance must go on for as long as we live. Only the day of our burial is the day on which we may take our Sabbath's rest.

And those of us who are weak and have problems want to listen to the saints and trust them with our very being. We want to approach them and remain close to them as much as possible. For we can sense that they feel for us; they are beneficial for us and they heal us, no matter how tough they might be – when they choose to be tough. Their love for mankind *(philanthropia)* is efficacious; it brings salvation; their strictness is motivated by *philanthropia*.

Without the love of God the Father, and without the presence of the Saints who make His tender love and light real and palpable, life on earth would grow dark and cold like that in hell. The citizens of that "distant country" (verse 13) would destroy us by sending us to herd swine, which represents the passions of the flesh. And the "righteous" – in the style of the elder son – would condemn us; they would not accept even our repentance.

But the Father who bore us lives forever; He shares our pain, and saves us. As long as we have God as our Father, and our fellow man as our brother, then the entire universe is habitable and hospitable; there will be no more "distant lands."

Made in the USA